Spotlight on Advanced

Teacher's Book

Second Edition

Francesca Mansfield
Carol Nuttall
and Language Testing 123

Australia • Brazil • Japan • Korea • Mexico • Singapore • Spain • United Kingdom • United States

Spotlight on Advanced Teacher's Book (2nd Edition)
Francesca Mansfield and Carol Nuttall
Revised by a team from Language Testing 123, led by
Michael Black

Publisher: Gavin McLean

Publishing Consultant: Karen Spiller

Freelance Editor: Clare Shaw

Strategic Marketing Manager: Charlotte Ellis

Content Project Manager: Tom Relf

Manufacturing Buyer: Eyvett Davis

Head of Production: Alissa McWhinnie

Cover design: Oliver Hutton

Original page design: Echelon Design/MPS Limited

Compositor: Q2A Media Services Pvt. Ltd.

National Geographic Liaison: Wesley Della Volla

ISBN: 978-1-285-84937-9

National Geographic Learning
Cheriton House, North Way, Andover, Hampshire, SP10 5BE
United Kingdom

Cengage Learning is a leading provider of customised learning solutions with office locations around the globe, including Singapore, the United Kingdom, Australia, Mexico, Brazil and Japan. Locate our local office at **international.cengage.com/region**

Cengage Learning products are represented in Canada by Nelson Education Ltd.

Visit National Geographic Learning online at **ngl.cengage.com**
Visit our corporate website at **www.cengage.com**

Photo credits

Although every effort has been made to contact copyright holders before publication, this has not always been possible. If contacted, the publisher will undertake to rectify errors or omissions at the earliest opportunity.

The publisher would like to thank the following sources for permission to reproduce their copyright protected images:

Cover photo: Raul Touzon/National Geographic

Inside photos: 4 a (STACY GOLD /National Geographic Image Collection), 4 b (GIANLUCA COLLA /National Geographic Image Collection), 4 c (Christophe Launay/Getty Images), 4 d (LOOK Die Bildagentur der Fotografen GmbH/Alamy), 4 e (Jochen Tack/Alamy), 4 f (THOMAS J. ABERCROMBIE /National Geographic Image Collection), 4 g (KEENPRESS/National Geographic Image Collection), 4 h (Heeb Christian/Prisma/Superstock Ltd.), 6 a (GIPSTEIN, TODD/ National Geograp/National Geographic Image Collection), 6 b (MIKE THEISS/National Geographic Creative/National Geographic Image Collection), 6 c (Erik T Witsoe/ Getty Images), 6 d (VOLKMAR WENTZEL /National Geographic Image Collection), 6 e (B. Wylezich/Fotolia), 6 f (O. LOUIS MAZZATENTA /National Geographic Image Collection), 6 g (XPACIFICA /National Geographic Image Collection), 6 h (Image Source Plus/Alamy).

Printed in China by RR Donnelley
Print number 02 Print Year 2014

CONTENTS

Unit		Vocabulary	Grammar	Use of English	Reading
1	Beginnings	Starting again Key word *make*	Review of tenses (past and present)	Part 4: key word transformation	Reading for specific information
2	A child's world	Parts of the body idioms Phrasal verb: *pick up* Key word *run*	Passive forms Passive form with *have* and *get*	Part 1: multiple-choice cloze	*Pioneer nursery stays outdoors* Part 7: gapped text
3	Are you game?	Phrases with *up* and *down* Phrasal verbs with *take* Phrases with *take* Key word *game*	Modal auxiliaries (1)	Part 4: key word transformation Part 2: open cloze	*A close encounter* Part 5: multiple choice
4	Eureka!	Colourful language Key word *tell* Prefixes	The future	Part 3: word formation	*Dinosaur books* Part 8: multiple matching
5	Safe and sound?	Crimes Phrasal verbs with *turn* Key word *law*	Verbs followed by infinitive or *-ing*	Part 4: key word transformation Part 2: open cloze	*Of worms and woodpeckers* Part 7: gapped text
6	Hale and hearty	Expressions with food Key word *life*	Conditionals	Part 4: key word transformation Identifying collocations Part 1: multiple-choice cloze	*Superfoods: are they really so super?* Part 6: cross-text multiple matching
7	Wish you were there …	Describing places Phrasal verbs and phrases with *look* Key word *road*	Inversion	Part 3: word formation Part 2: open cloze	*City reviews* Part 8: multiple matching
8	Making our mark	Phrases with *bring* Key word *that*	Relative pronouns Defining and non-defining relative clauses Reduced relative clauses	Part 3: word formation	*Straw bale futures* Part 5: multiple choice

Listening	Speaking	Writing	Video / Review
Short extracts; interpreting context from vocabulary	Talking about new experiences	Part 2: a letter	Video: Profiles in exploration Ideas generator: structuring spontaneous answers
Language development in children Part 2: sentence completion	Part 3: using visual prompts	Part 2: a review	
An interview with an explorer Part 3: multiple choice	Part 3: interacting	Part 2: a formal letter	Video: Frozen search and rescue Ideas generator: brainstorming and selecting
Inventions Part 4: multiple matching	Part 4: three-way task	Part 1: an essay – using the notes provided	Review 1 Reading and Use of English, Part 4: key word transformation Reading and Use of English, Part 2: open cloze
DNA analysis Part 2: Sentence completion	Part 1: giving personal information	Part 2: a report	Video: The world in a station Ideas generator: interpreting pictures
The benefits of eating raw food Part 3: multiple choice	Part 2: comparing pictures	Part 1: an essay – developing an argument	
Commercial space travel Part 4: multiple matching	Part 4: discussing	Part 2: a proposal	Video: Our ATM is a goat Ideas generator: focusing your ideas to talk about abstract topics
Working life Part 1: multiple choice	Part 3: reaching a decision through negotiation	Part 2: a review	Review 2 Reading and Use of English, Part 3: word formation Reading and Use of English, Part 4: key word transformation

Listening	Speaking	Writing	Video / Review
Interview with an artist Part 3: multiple choice	Part 3: suggesting solutions, justifying ideas	Part 1: an essay – supporting your ideas	Video: Aboriginal rock art Ideas generator: making a decision
(1) Identifying feelings Part 4: multiple matching (2) *Freecycling* Note-taking	Part 2: organising a larger unit of discourse	Part 2: a proposal	
The history of credit Part 2: sentence completion	Parts 3 and 4: disagreeing with someone else's opinion	Part 2: a report	Video: Rainy day flea market Ideas generator: alternative viewpoints
Film makers Part 1: multiple choice	Parts 3 and 4: exchanging ideas	Part 2: a review	Review 3 Reading and Use of English, Part 3: word formation Reading and Use of English, Part 4: key word transformation
Communication skills Part 4: multiple matching	Part 3: sustaining interaction	Part 2: a proposal	Video: The Braille Hubble Ideas generator: making your responses relevant to the discussion
Atmospheric conditions in the Earth's past Part 2: sentence completion	Part 3: evaluating	Part 1: an essay – discussing issues that surround a topic	
The origin of kissing Part 3: multiple choice *Living abroad* Part 4: multiple matching	Part 1: talking about your country, culture and background	Part 2: a report	Video: The Hadzabe tribe Ideas generator: explaining familiar topics
Three short extracts Part 1: multiple choice	Part 2: individual long turn	Part 2: a letter	Review 4 Reading and Use of English, Part 4: key word transformation Reading and Use of English, Part 2: open cloze

What are the differences between the old exam and the revised exam for 2015?

You're probably wondering what the differences between the old and revised exam are. The most important change is that there are now four instead of five papers. The Reading paper has been merged with a reduced version of the Use of English paper. The number of questions has been cut in both sections.

Revised Exam	Changes
1 Reading and Use of English **1 hour 30 minutes** 1 Multiple-choice cloze (8 questions) 2 Open cloze (8 questions) 3 Word formation (8 questions) 4 Key word transformation (6 questions) 5 Multiple choice (6 questions) 6 Cross-text multiple matching (4 questions) NEW 7 Gapped text (6 questions) 8 Multiple matching (10 questions)	**Old exam: 2 hours 15 minutes** • The Reading Paper and Use of English paper have now been merged into one paper with fewer parts. • The gapped sentences have been cut from the Use of English paper and the short texts from the Reading Paper. • There is a new cross-text multiple-matching task. • The paper has a more academic bias.
2 Writing **1 hour 30 minutes** 1 An essay based on two points given in the input text (220–260 words) 2 One task from a choice of four: a letter, a proposal, a report, a review (220–260 words)	**Old exam: 1 hour 30 minutes** The compulsory question in Part 1 is now an essay based on input material. Candidate's response is increased to 220–260 words. In Part 2 several task types have been cut, including the set text option. There is a choice of four tasks, not five.
3 Listening **Approximately 40 minutes** 1 Short extracts, multiple choice (6 questions) 2 Sentence completion (8 questions) 3 Long dialogue, multiple choice (6 questions) 4 Multiple matching (10 questions)	**Old exam: approximately 40 minutes** In Part 3 there are now four options to choose from for each question, compared to three in the old exam. There are now three distractors instead of two.
4 Speaking **15 minutes** 1 Spoken questions between the interlocutor and each candidate (3 minutes) 2 Individual 'long turn' for each candidate and a brief response from the other candidate (1 minute + 30 seconds) 3 A two-way conversation between candidates with written stimuli used in a decision-making task (4 minutes) 4 A discussion on topics related to the collaborative task (4 minutes)	**Old exam: 15 minutes** Only written prompts (no visual prompts) now used in Part 3.

What will I find in this Teacher's Book?

In this introduction, you'll find an overview of the new *Cambridge English: Advanced* exam, key differences between the old and new version, and some remarks about the differences between general English teaching and teaching exam classes.

In the main body of this Teacher's Book, you'll find notes and guidance for each unit. Answer keys and audioscripts accompany the notes to the activities. The notes often contain suggestions for alternative approaches and ideas. Teaching tips feature throughout, as well as suggestions for extension activities. Each unit has photocopiable material. This may contain activities and games to practise vocabulary and grammar learnt in the unit, or freer activities to practise speaking skills.

Why do students do the exam?

The *Cambridge English: Advanced* Examination is an internationally recognised qualification, which follows on from *Cambridge English: First*. The new version is more closely related to *First* and develops skills taught at that level. Students are attracted to it because it proves to prospective employers and educational institutions around the world that the holder's knowledge of English grammar and vocabulary is of a high level. It also shows that they can display a corresponding level of ability across the skills. It acts as a significant bridge between *Cambridge English: First* and *Cambridge English: Proficiency*, helping students adjust to what is otherwise a very big jump! It is considered to be at C1 level in the Common European Framework of Reference (CEFR).

What does *Cambridge English: Advanced* show?

Students who successfully complete a *Cambridge English: Advanced* preparation course will finish with a useful and very solid knowledge of grammar, vocabulary and skills. In particular, they will be confident speakers of the language in most situations, and many businesses and institutions of further education view this certificate as a valuable asset when considering a candidate for a position. Students themselves may also use this course as a solid foundation on which to base their studies for the *Cambridge English: Proficiency* examination.

What do students need to pass the *Advanced* examination?

To pass, students need:
- a sufficient level of language
- a clear understanding of how the exam works and how they will be tested
- practice in all skills
- exam skills
- regular and extensive practice of all question types.

What's in a name?

Spotlight on Advanced (CAE) is the second book in the Spotlight series, and follows on from the highly successful *Spotlight on First (FCE)* book. It works with the same principles in mind, emphasising the importance of focusing and shedding light on the language and skills students need for success.

WHAT ARE THE SPOTLIGHTS?

The Exam spotlights throughout the course focus on developing key areas of exam skills. They draw the student's attention to what is being tested and illuminate problem areas such as understanding a writer's tone in a reading passage, or a speaker's opinion in a listening task. They teach students about the nature of the exam and examination technique. They may help learners avoid common pitfalls and traps.

How does *Spotlight* help?

Spotlight on Advanced helps by being both challenging and cohesive in its development. It contains a lot of language and information, presented in an engaging thematic framework. While offering fully comprehensive preparation for the *Advanced* examination, the course also provides consolidation and development of all the main grammatical structures and language areas needed to develop the learner's general English. It does this by providing the following features:

- a Grammar reference section at the back of the Student's Book

- a Language development section in each unit, where vocabulary items are prioritised and developed

- a Key word feature within this section, which aims to encourage students to examine the different ways a single word can be used

- an 'In other words' feature appears either in the writing or the speaking section of each unit, and focuses on useful ways students can vary their vocabulary when using the English language actively

- a Vocabulary organiser page for each unit, which helps students organise, develop and consolidate vocabulary as it is learnt in the unit. Ideally, each exercise should be completed alongside the relevant tasks in the unit, so that students can transfer useful information to their notebooks.

How is teaching an exam class different from general English?

If you haven't taught an examination class before, here is some advice on how to adapt your teaching style and approach effectively. You need to consider the following points:

- the emphasis of a *Cambridge English: Advanced* class
- the content and balance of what you teach
- the way you teach and the demands you place on your students.

Quite rightly, general English classes often focus on developing students' fluency and confidence and developing their overall communicative competence; that is, maximising successful communicative outcomes from what they know. In general English classes, teachers may prize fluency and spontaneity over accuracy and reflection. In a general English class there is always the temptation to allow speaking and discussion activities to run on as long as they need. In an examination class, you need to be more vigilant about optimising your use of time.

Who are our students?

Advanced learners in language schools vary widely. You may find yourself with a class of students who have been studying together for several years, and have just successfully completed a *Cambridge English: First* course. In this case, they will be familiar with most of the task types that appear in *Cambridge English: Advanced*. However, it is quite likely that you will have students who are new to the school, or some who are returning to their English studies after a break of several years. The latter group may have studied English in a traditional manner, with emphasis on grammar, reading and writing, and so their speaking skills may be relatively weak.

Conversely, students who have acquired English from living in an English-speaking community, or who have studied in institutions where fluency and communicative competence are favoured over accuracy, may often be weaker at writing and formal grammar. Should you have a class of students with such mixed experiences in their language learning, you will need to take some time for everyone to become 'acclimatised' to the current learning environment.

What do students need?

Cambridge English: Advanced students will have already achieved a B2 level standard of English, and so should have sound knowledge of grammatical structures and vocabulary to this level. If, however, they are returning to English after a break, this knowledge may need refreshing. It will also need developing in order for them to attain the necessary standard to sit the Advanced examination. This development should be balanced across the four skills of listening, speaking, reading and writing. Be warned: even students who have just passed a B2 level examination have a surprising habit of forgetting how to use basic grammatical structures! For this reason, the Grammar reference section in the Student's Book is particularly useful. Finally, successful candidates will need total familiarity with all the aspects of the examination coupled with good exam technique.

TEACHING IN PRACTICE

A few tips:

- Be strict about time-keeping and disciplined about how classroom time is spent. Don't allow speaking activities or discussion to drag on.
- Set homework after every lesson. Contact parents if it is not done.
- Encourage students to be aware of their problem areas, and to correct their mistakes, while also praising their achievements.
- Once students are about two thirds through the course, organise a full mock examination. Make sure this is carried out under exam conditions. Then, give students individual tutorials telling them what they need to focus on.
- Use a lot of simulations of the Speaking test, as students often find this the most stressful part of the exam.
- Also give plenty of practice in exam-style listening tasks, as this is another stressful area for language students.

As the exam approaches, be more and more strict about respecting time limits and doing more work under exam conditions. Check students' writing by getting them to produce a piece of writing in the classroom without preparation. Students are often appallingly lax about checking their work. Stress the importance of doing this.

'CAN DO' SUMMARY

Typical abilities	Listening and Speaking	Reading and Writing
General ability	Can contribute effectively to meetings and seminars within own area of work or keep up a casual conversation with a good degree of fluency, coping with abstract expressions.	Can read quickly enough to cope with an academic course, and can take reasonably accurate notes in meetings or write a piece of work which shows an ability to communicate.
Social/Tourist	Can pick up nuances of meaning / opinion. Can keep up conversations of a casual nature for an extended period of time and discuss abstract / cultural topics with a good degree of fluency and range of expression.	Can understand complex opinions / arguments as expressed in serious newspapers. Can write most letters (s)he is likely to be asked to do; such errors as occur will not prevent understanding of the message.
Work	Can follow discussion and argument with only occasional need for clarification, employing good compensation strategies to overcome inadequacies. Can deal with unpredictable questions.	Can understand the general meaning of more complex articles without serious misunderstanding. Can, given enough time, write a report that communicates the desired message.
Study	Can follow up questions by probing for more detail. Can make critical remarks / express disagreement without causing offence.	Can scan texts for relevant information, and grasp main topic of text. Can write a piece of work with a message that can be followed throughout.

Cambridge English: Advanced paper by paper

1 Reading and Use of English

Eight parts, testing vocabulary, grammar and reading skills: candidates must answer all eight parts; there are 56 questions in total; candidates receive one mark for each correct answer in Parts 1, 2, 3 and 8, up to two marks for each correct answer in Part 4, and two marks for each correct answer in Parts 5, 6 and 7.

Part 1: Multiple-choice cloze

A modified cloze test containing eight gaps and followed by eight four-option multiple-choice items. Candidates must choose the option that correctly fills the gap.

Part 2: Open cloze

A modified open-cloze test containing eight gaps. Candidates must write one word to fill each gap.

Part 3: Word formation

Candidates must read a text containing eight gaps. Each gap corresponds to a word. The stems of the missing words are given beside the text and must be changed to the correct word form to fill the gap.

Part 4: Key word transformation

There are six separate questions, each with a lead-in sentence and a gapped second sentence to be completed in three to six words, including a given 'key word'.

Part 5: Multiple choice

A longer text followed by six four-option multiple-choice questions. Emphasis is on the understanding of a long text, including detail, opinion, tone, purpose, main idea, implication, attitude and organisation.

Part 6: Cross-text multiple matching

Candidates have to read four short texts and answer four questions that require them to read across texts. The emphasis is on comparing and contrasting opinions and attitudes across texts.

Part 7: Gapped text

Six paragraphs have been removed from a longer text and placed in a jumbled order, together with an additional paragraph. Candidates have to choose the missing paragraph for each gap. Emphasis is on understanding how texts are structured and following text development.

Part 8: Multiple matching

A text or several short texts is preceded by ten multiple-matching questions. Emphasis is on locating specific information, detail, opinion and attitude in texts.

2 Writing

Two parts: candidates must answer both parts (a compulsory one in part 1, one from a choice of three in part 2).

Part 1: One compulsory question

Candidates will be asked to write an essay based on two points given in the input material. They must write 220–260 words.

Part 2: One from a choice of writing tasks

Candidates can choose one task from a choice of three questions. They may be asked to write any of the following: a letter, a proposal, a report or a review. Candidates must write 220–260 words.

3 Listening

Four parts: each part contains a recorded text or texts and corresponding comprehension tasks. Each part is heard twice. There are 30 questions in total.

Part 1: Multiple choice

Three short extracts, from exchanges between interacting speakers. There are two three-option multiple-choice questions for each extract.

Part 2: Sentence completion

A monologue with a sentence completion task which has eight items. Candidates must complete each sentence with information that they hear in the recording.

Part 3: Multiple choice

A longer dialogue or conversation involving interacting speakers, with six four-option multiple-choice questions.

Part 4: Multiple matching

Five short, themed monologues, with ten multiple-matching questions. There are two tasks to complete.

5 Speaking

In the Speaking test there will be two examiners: one who is both interlocutor and assessor, and one who is an assessor; there will be two or three candidates per group. Candidates are expected to respond to questions and to interact in conversational English. There are four parts to the exam.

Part 1: Introductory questions

A conversation between the interlocutor and each candidate (spoken questions).

Part 2: Individual 'long turn'

An individual 'long turn' for each candidate with a brief response from the second candidate (visual stimuli, with spoken instructions).

Part 3: Two-way conversation

A two-way conversation between the candidates (written stimuli, with spoken instructions).

Part 4: Extension of discussion topics

A discussion on topics related to Part 3 (spoken questions).

1 BEGINNINGS

Unit introduction

The topic of this unit is starting things, beginnings and starting again. It aims to focus on new vocabulary, especially verbs and phrases which are associated with beginnings. As students are beginning a new book, they are probably also beginning a new course (*Advanced*) and they may well be beginning a new school year or period of their education.

Warm-up activity

If you are starting with a new class, try to break the ice by doing a warm-up activity. Write out or photocopy the 'Find someone who ...' activity below, and give one copy to each student. They should move around asking other students questions. When they find someone for whom an item is true, they should write their name next to that item.

Find someone who ...

1 is wearing something new.

2 has joined the class for the first time.

3 likes the same kind of music as you.

4 likes dancing.

5 enjoys eating the same food as you.

Getting started

1 Elicit what the picture shows the beginning of. Place students in pairs and encourage them to think of other beginnings as quickly as possible.

Answers

The picture shows the beginning of a race.
Other possible beginnings: seeds germinating, the launch of a rocket, the kick-off of a football match, a wedding, a ship setting sail, a new baby

2 Ask students to identify words in the box they already know, and ask which of the meanings 1–3 might apply. Help them with unknown words by writing example sentences on the board.

Answers

1 activate, bring about, inaugurate, incite, initiate, inspire, instigate, prompt, provoke, set off, stimulate, trigger
2 conceive, engender, establish, found, generate, launch, originate, produce, set up, spawn
3 embark on, launch into, set about

→   Vocabulary organiser 1, exercises 1 and 2, page 162

Vocabulary organiser answers

1 1 launched   2 inaugurated
    3 set off   4 launched / set up / established
    5 initiated   6 originated
    7 instigated   8 embarked on
2 a inaugurate   b embark on
    c set off (on)   d originate
    e instigate

Reading reading for specific information

As this is the beginning of the *Advanced* course, and the task of working on multiple texts may be unfamiliar to students, aim to do all three texts and their accompanying tasks in class, in order to guide your students and assess their individual abilities.

Ask students to look at the photo of Charlie Chaplin, and elicit information about him, e.g. *Who is he? What is he famous for? Where does he come from? Do you know anything about his background?*

BACKGROUND INFORMATION: CHARLIE CHAPLIN

In 1910, Charlie Chaplin moved to America. By 1914 he had made 35 films. He made another 14 the following year, and 12 short films between 1916 and 1917.

Chaplin's most notable films include *The Gold Rush* (1925), *Modern Times* (1936), and *The Great Dictator* (1940). Chaplin was married four times, and had a total of 11 children. He died in Switzerland on 25 December 1977.

3 Allow students time to read text A. Tell them to underline the information which gives them the answers.

Answers

Chaplin first performed at the age of five. He had to work hard because neither of his parents could support him.

4 Ask students to read sentences 1 and 2 carefully, and compare them to the text.

Answers

1 S   2 D

5 Ask students to do this task individually. Ask them to check their answers with a partner, then elicit answers from the class.

Answers

1 F	2 T	3 T	4 F	5 T

→ Vocabulary organiser 1, exercise 3, page 162

Vocabulary organiser answers

1 invaluable	2 hoarse
3 resounding	4 establishments

6 Students read text B and answer the two questions.

Answers

1 The writer was put off by a teacher who discouraged her from thinking about art college because art was too competitive.
2 Her new interest is photography, not painting and drawing, but it is also an art.

7 Allow students time to read text C before asking them for their summaries.

Answers

The writer seems to believe that people born with a particular talent will not necessarily be successful. Their success also depends on their life experiences.

8 Students now look at all three texts to find the answers to these questions.

Answers

1 text A	2 text A	3 text C	4 text B

9 Elicit words such as *nervous, excited, anxious, enthusiastic*. Then ask students if they feel differently when they return to an activity they have not done for some time.

Student's Book pages 12–13

Language development

starting again

1 Ask students to think about who uses a drawing board (e.g. *architects, designers*). Ask them to guess why someone might have to go 'back to the drawing board'. Then tell students to skim the text again to find two more phrases.

Answers

Back to the drawing board means to begin something again, or redesign it completely, usually because the first attempt has failed or is unsuccessful. Here it can also be used literally to mean to return to drawing sketches. Other phrases in the text are 'make a fresh start', 'start from scratch'.

2 Ask students to do the exercise. They will probably be able to complete most of the phrases. If they have trouble, ask them to refer to their dictionaries.

Answers

1 fresh	2 leaf	3 square	4 scratch	5 slate

3 Elicit suggestions from the class.

Answers

They all convey the meaning of starting again from the beginning.

4 Tell students that this is to give them a closer understanding of the meaning and use of the expressions in exercise 2. Ask them to try and complete the expressions from memory. Check the answers with the group.

Answers

1 started from	2 wipe the slate
3 to square one	4 make a fresh
5 turned over	

5 Ask students to refer back to the texts to find the phrases and read them in context before they attempt the task.

Answers

1 made his debut	2 make a name for himself	3 make ends meet

Key word *make*

6 Ask students to use the context of the sentences to guess the meanings. They should not use dictionaries to help them with this task.

Answers

1 I found it hard to speak loudly enough for people to hear me.
2 I don't know either.
3 I'd like to change that to a large one.
4 Flooding was important enough to be written about in the national papers.
5 He forced me to stay in (though I wanted to go out).

7 Allow students time to guess some of the items here, before asking them to use a dictionary. After checking the answers, refer to the tips for organising vocabulary on page 162 of the Vocabulary organiser section. Encourage students to consider which methods suit their learning style best (exercise 5), and to start recording new vocabulary regularly in a notebook.

Answers	
1 made it	2 made out
3 make-or-break	4 make a go of
5 made the best of	6 make do with

→ Vocabulary organiser 1, exercise 4, page 162

Vocabulary organiser answers	
1 make it up to	2 make for
3 make up	4 make off
5 make out	6 make up for
7 make into	8 make something of

Grammar review of tenses (past and present)

8 This is an opportunity for students to use a mixture of tenses. Accept a variety of answers and encourage discussion to lead into the theme of the grammar section.

9 Students should read text A and underline examples of the tenses. Check their answers with the class.

Answers
1 *we know; is still only speculation; It seems to be*
2 *there have been countless theories; we have collected; we have been able to offer; have only led*
3 *the universe began; we once called*
4 *many people are still questioning and re-evaluating*
5 *we have been searching*

Extension

Write the following question and options on the board, or ask the class to listen as you read them aloud.

Which of the following sentences best summarises the text?

a We have learnt all there is to know about the history of the universe but still want to know more.

b No matter how much we learn about the universe, we cannot answer all the questions.

c We do not understand most of the things we have learnt and scientists always disagree.

(The answer is b.)

10 This exercise offers an opportunity to revise the uses of different tenses and is probably best done as a class activity.

Answers	
1 present perfect continuous	2 present simple
3 past simple	4 present perfect simple
5 present continuous	

11 This text provides an opportunity to revise the past tenses, and compare them to each other. Students should first read the whole text individually to understand the meaning.

Answers
proposed: past simple
was expanding: past continuous
had been assumed: past perfect simple
existed: past simple
had: past simple
had (not) *been trying*: past perfect continuous
knew: past simple
were moving: past continuous
noticed: past simple
were travelling: past continuous
was expanding: past continuous
had: past simple

→ Grammar reference 1, page 208

12 Students should work individually to rewrite the sentences. Tell them they can refer to the Grammar reference section if they need to. Check the answers with the whole class.

Answers
1 He had been looking / had looked at the stars but he hadn't found any new planets.
2 He realised that the universe had been growing for 13 billion years.
3 It all started / It had all started with a big bang, according to some scientists.
4 We have been searching for answers and we are still looking.
5 The universe started to expand a very long time ago.

BACKGROUND

Edwin Powell Hubble (1889–1953) was an American astronomer. He profoundly changed astronomers' understanding of the nature of the universe by demonstrating the existence of other galaxies besides the Milky Way. He also discovered that the degree of redshift observed in light coming from a galaxy increased in proportion to the distance of that galaxy from the Milky Way. This became known as Hubble's law, and would help establish that the universe is expanding.

13 Students can refer back to the text if necessary to answer the questions, but they should summarise the information in their own words.

Answers
The notion that the universe had always existed in the same state, because he realised that the universe was actually getting bigger and so it couldn't have always been the same.

14 Students should complete the text individually. They should read the whole text first in order to understand the context of each gap and the tense required.

Answers

1 was expanding / is expanding	2 had been put forward
3 postulated	4 had sprung
5 has	6 had exploded
7 was / is still going on	8 had / has been expanding
9 was coined	10 was trying
11 stuck	12 is

15 Ask students to form pairs so they can practise talking about the text and asking each other questions.

See *Story: The Shack* photocopiable activity, page 21.

Student's Book pages 14–15

Listening short extracts

INTERPRETING CONTEXT FROM VOCABULARY

Explain to your students the value of reading task questions before they listen in order to anticipate what they are going to hear. They should learn to pinpoint key vocabulary that indicates the subject, speaker's attitude and opinions expressed.

1 Ask students to look at the words in the box and decide what topics they are associated with.

Answers

Books: chapter, extract, first edition, front cover, paperback, scene
Cinema: animation, excerpt, scene, soundtrack, special effects, trailer
Internet: download, extract, online, print out, surfing, web page

2 Ask students to read the questions and underline the key words in each option. Elicit other words the students think they might hear connected with each one.

Answers

1 advertisement, for, book, design, do-it-yourself kit
2 reading from, magazine, catalogue, Internet

3 ⊙ 1 Play the recording once and allow students time to choose the answers in exercise 2. Play the recording again and ask them to check. Check answers before allowing students to look at the audioscript on page 243.

Answers

1 b *by printing out (materials) attached.*
2 c *Shall we download the attachment?*

Audioscript ⊙ 1

Husband:	Mandy! This one sounds good for Joey.
Mandy:	Go on, then. What have you found?
Husband:	'A Child's First Clock ... Most children don't learn how to tell the time until they are in first grade, or beyond, but with this lovely 'no-numbers-needed' clock, even toddlers can learn the basics of timekeeping.'
Mandy:	Mm. Sounds interesting. Tell me more ...
Husband:	'Developed by two mothers – a children's television presenter Noni Anderson and artist Alison Perrin – the woodland clock features a slow painted turtle for the hour hand, a faster grey rabbit for the minute hand, and a speedy red-breasted robin on the second hand' ... Blah, blah, blah. 'You can assemble a clock much like ours by printing out the art materials attached, and applying them to a clock from a do-it-yourself kit.' So, Mandy, what do you think? Shall we download the attachment?

4 As this is the first unit, you may like to do this exercise as a class. Ask students to read the questions, and brainstorm ideas about what they are going to hear. Write the students' suggestions on the board.

Possible answer

two people talking about moving (house)

5 ⊙ 2 Play the recording and give feedback on the rubric suggestions. Then play the recording again for students to answer the two questions in exercise 4.

Answers

1 The husband wants to change their lifestyle. 2 sceptical and uncertain

Audioscript ⊙ 2

Woman 1:	So, what's brought this on, then?
Woman 2:	Yeah, well, Bill's just had enough of living in the city. It's all the stress, you know. Not only at the office itself, but when he's to-ing and fro-ing in all that traffic! He's just sick of it. So, he suddenly decided to pack it all in, and make a fresh start. So, we're off to the Isle of Man, in the middle of the Irish Sea. Middle of nowhere, if you ask me! Still, at least it's not like moving abroad. He's taking up sheep farming, of all things! God knows if it'll work. But you know Bill, when he sets his mind to something, there's no stopping him.
Woman 1:	Well, I never! It seems a bit drastic, though.
Woman 2:	He reckons it'll be good for us, like starting over. All I can think of is sitting alone, with the wind howling outside. I mean, how many people stay there in the winter? We're used to the noise of the traffic. But, I've told him I'll give it a go. Who knows, it may be the making of us!

6 Ask students to turn to the audioscript on page 243, and underline the words that show the speaker's feelings.

> **Answers**
> *middle of nowhere, if you ask me! of all things! God knows if it'll work! All I can think of is sitting alone …*

7 Ask students to do this task individually without listening again.

> **Answers**
> 1 F   2 F   3 T   4 F

8 Refer students back to the boxed words in exercise 1, and ask them what words they expect to hear.

> **Answers**
> animation, chapter, excerpt, extract, scene, soundtrack, special effects, trailer

9 ◉ 3 Play the recording and allow students time to answer the question. Play the track again so they can check their answer.

> **Answer**
> c

> **Audioscript** ◉ 3
>
> Oliver: So, what do you think of our ideas, Jane?
>
> Jane: Well, overall, quite acceptable, Oliver, but I'm not happy about some of the omissions. I mean, ignoring the details in the first two chapters means that members of the audience who haven't read the book will be left in the dark. They won't understand the reasons behind the protagonist's actions in the film.
>
> Oliver: Yeah, but most people have read the book! It was a blockbuster, after all!
>
> Jane: We shouldn't take that for granted, though. I feel that, as it stands, your proposal threatens to focus too much on action and special effects, leaving little room for character development.
>
> Oliver: Huh! Yeah, well, you know, this is only a rough outline of the scenes, as yet …
>
> Jane: OK. But, personally, I would prefer the opening scene to include some sense of Jim's confusion and fear about what he's about to do.
>
> Oliver: OK! … But don't you think hitting the audience with the murder straight away creates suspense?
>
> Jane: Perhaps. But it also looks like a cold-blooded, calculated murder rather than … Look, I don't know what you got out of the book, but I wrote a psychological thriller, Oliver, and I'd like some element of the psychology to come through in the film, and not just the thriller aspect! Jim's character is a complex one, and your plans for him threaten to reduce it to a wooden stereotype!

Use of English key word transformations

> **EXAM SPOTLIGHT**
>
> Ask students to read the information and the question in the Exam spotlight box. Elicit the answer from the class.
> Tell students that sometimes several changes need to be made in order for the second sentence to have a similar meaning to the first. Elicit suggestions as to what changes should be made in the example. (He has been driving / able to drive since he was 17.)
>
> > **Answer**
> > The first sentence means that he finished learning and passed his test when he was 17; the second sentence means that he **is still learning** to drive now – in other words he has not passed his test.

10 Ask students to do this task individually. Elicit the answers, and ask for explanations why the other options are wrong.

> 1 b   2 a
> 1 a = incorrect. It means 'I want a short break, but not a change of job.'
> c = incorrect, as it means 'I've been teaching for some time, and I'm looking for another teaching position.'
> 2 b = incorrect. The reason he went to live on an island was not because he was successful.
> c = incorrect. We don't know if he was successful on the island.

11 Students should do the exercise individually, either in class or for homework.

> **Answers**
> 1 deliver an urgent message to
> 2 make up your mind
> 3 not been easy to
> 4 had not / hadn't expected the test to
> 5 is suspected of killing / having killed
> 6 is she taking karate lessons

> **EXAM SPOTLIGHT**
>
> The true / false statements in this Exam spotlight box encourage students to think about what they should and shouldn't do in this part of the exam. Ask students to discuss the statements in pairs and decide what they think is the correct answer. Check the answers as a class and elicit the reason for each answer.
>
> > **Answers**
> > 1 T   2 F   3 T   4 T   5 F   6 F   7 T   8 F

Speaking talking about new experiences

12 Allow students to comment freely as a class on the pictures before focusing on the question.

> **Answer**
> They all show a new beginning.

13 Ask the class to contribute questions, and write them on the board.

> **Possible answers**
> Why did you decide to do that? What was it like? Did you like it? Were you scared? Was it expensive? Where did you do it?

SOCIAL TALK

Read the information with the class. Emphasise that in Part 1 of the Speaking test, students should avoid giving answers of a few words only.

Student's Book pages 16–17

14 Allow students time to complete this task individually.

> **Possible answers**
> 1 There was a lot to see, but I most enjoyed the section about dinosaurs and prehistoric life.
> 2 In fact, I was so nervous I was shaking, but after the first few questions I calmed down and I managed to answer the questions quite well.
> 3 It was fantastic. The weather was really hot and sunny, and we ate some delicious food.

15 Explain that the purpose of this task is to show students how to expand their sentences in speaking.

> **Answers**
> 1 g   2 b   3 a   4 d   5 e   6 c   7 f

IN OTHER WORDS

This feature appears throughout the book, either in the Speaking section or the Writing section. Its aim is to encourage students to expand their range of active vocabulary when handling these tasks.

16 For the Speaking task, you may find it useful to elicit the full question for Student A, and write it on the board. Remind students to use some ideas from the 'In other words' box in their answers.

See *Try something new!* photocopiable activity, page 22.

Writing a descriptive or narrative piece of writing (letter)

1 Read the information in the box and ask students to put the planning stages of the five-point plan in the correct order. Emphasise that they should use this plan for every piece of writing they do from now on.

> **Answers**
> 1 brainstorming   2 outlining   3 selecting vocabulary
> 4 writing   5 checking

2 Students should read the exam question in the box and answer the questions. Stress that whenever they do an exam task they should think about these questions.

> **Answers**
> A letter. A description of a new or unusual experience and the reasons why it was memorable or significant.

EXAM SPOTLIGHT

Ask students to read the Exam spotlight box. Ask students which types of writing may require narrative or descriptive writing, and what level of formality may be required for a letter to a magazine or a review in a newspaper.

3 Encourage your students to spend a few minutes thinking of ideas. Tell them you want each student to try and think of at least three different experiences.

4 ⊙ 4 Play the recording and elicit answers to the questions from the class. Ask students to check the answers with the audioscript.

> **Answers**
> bungee jumping, travelling to America, swimming with dolphins, going to a rock concert, flying in a helicopter

> **Audioscript** ⊙ 4
>
> **Teacher:** OK, let's brainstorm some ideas. What new experiences have you had that you clearly remember?
>
> **Student A:** I tried bungee jumping once. I'll never forget that!
>
> **Student B:** Really? That must have been terrifying. I don't even like heights. But I did travel to America – a totally new experience for me.
>
> **Teacher:** Good – don't forget you also need to tell us why it was memorable or significant for you.
>
> **Student B:** I was very impressed by the lifestyle there and I decided I wanted to improve my English enough to go and study over there.
>
> **Teacher:** Excellent! What about you Vasilis?
>
> **Student C:** I've been swimming with dolphins in the water. It was amazing. I would love to write about that, because it made me respect animals and nature.

Teacher:	How wonderful! I can't wait to read about it. Massimo, what about you?
Student D:	I, er, haven't had any new or exciting experiences that I can think of.
Teacher:	Well maybe you could make one up?
Student D:	Mm, well I suppose I could say I have been to a rock concert.
Teacher:	Yes, and why would that have been memorable or significant to you?
Student D:	Er – I could say that it changed my life and made me want to become a rock star.
Student A:	Oh, I almost forgot. I have flown in a helicopter too.
Teacher:	Well, we've certainly got a few ideas there.

5 ⊙ 5 Play the recording. Complete the notes with the class and check the answers with the audioscript.

Answers
First paragraph: preparations and background to the experience
Next paragraph(s): the experience itself – description / feelings
Final paragraph: reasons why it was significant / what happened afterwards / how I felt about it later / why it changed my life

Audioscript ⊙ 5

Teacher:	OK, so you've brainstormed some ideas for your writing and chosen one. Now we need to outline the structure. What's the best way of doing that?
Student D:	With paragraphs?
Teacher:	That's right, Massimo. But you need to have an idea about what to say in each paragraph, and they should link together well. What's an easy way to do that?
Student D:	You need to decide what the main purpose is of each paragraph.
Teacher:	Good. Claudine, what would be the main purpose of the first paragraph?
Student A:	Um, I think I would have to write about what made me decide to go bungee jumping in the first place.
Teacher:	OK, so for planning purposes, we could say: 'What led to the experience.' What else could you call that … Svetlana?
Student B:	I would talk about how I prepared for my journey to America, and the hopes and fears I had.
Teacher:	Good, so you could write about the preparations and the background to the experience then. Right, now, what about the main body of our piece? What would we need to focus on?
Student C:	It would have to be about the experience itself. Describing it, our feelings, what happened.
Teacher:	Very good Vasilis, and very important too. And what mustn't we forget?
Student B:	An ending? And the reason why it was significant.
Student D:	I would say what happened afterwards, and how I felt about it later, and why it changed my life.
Teacher:	Excellent – so a good, strong concluding paragraph. Now we're getting somewhere.

6 Students should read the letter individually. Elicit suggestions from the class. Ask them to suggest paragraph breaks.

Answers
There is only one paragraph. It ends abruptly and doesn't answer the second part of question.

→ Vocabulary organiser 1, exercise 6, page 162

Vocabulary organiser answers
1 crisp 2 expanding 3 ascended
4 patchwork 5 buffeting

7 Students can do this exercise alone, in pairs or as a group, depending on how confident you think they are.

Answers
a It was a beautiful summer's day with a fresh crisp wind blowing from the east – ideal weather for a balloon ride.
b the airfield getting smaller and the horizon expanding; it started to look like a toy town; a patchwork of fields and roads.
c I had expected to be frightened; I was amazed at how safe I felt. It was breathtaking. We were reluctant to return to earth.

8 Students should spend a few minutes writing a suitable ending that explains why the balloon ride was significant.

9 Ask students to exchange their answers and look for errors in grammar, spelling, punctuation, structure, etc. in their partner's work.

10 Ask students to plan the letter in class, and check their plans with them. Don't let them spend more than five minutes on this.

CARRYING OUT WRITING TASKS

At this level, students should not waste time writing a rough draft and then copying it out neatly. There will not be time to do this in the exam. However, it is very important that they check their writing carefully. It is their last chance to gain extra points by correcting any mistakes.

Student's Book pages 18–19

Video profiles in exploration

Aim: The main aim of the video and Ideas generator is to help students to prepare for Part 1 of the Speaking test by asking and answering questions around the topic of personal information.

Synopsis: In this video, three explorers take it in turns to talk about their areas of work and why they enjoy it. Alexandra Cousteau is a member of the Cousteau dynasty, which has been involved in diving and underwater exploration for several generations. Johan Reinhard is the archaeologist who discovered the frozen Inca mummy whose nickname was 'the Ice Maiden'. Sylvia Earle is an oceanographer who is interested in the 'big picture' of how fish integrate into the ecosystem of ocean life.

1 Use the photos and the questions to generate interest in the topic.

Before the Spanish invaded in the 1530s the Inca empire controlled large parts of South America. This included most of Ecuador, Peru and Bolivia as well as parts of Chile and Argentina. The Incas are not to be confused with the Aztecs who were from Mexico.

2 Students match the jobs in A to the definitions in B and then watch the video to find out the name of the expert in each field. In feedback explain that the photo shows Johan Reinhard standing on the summit of Nevado Ampato next to the remains of an Incan ceremonial platform.

Answers

an archaeologist: discovers and interprets ancient sites to understand the past, for example Inca mummies and their burial grounds. Johan Reinhard

an environmental advocate: explores the unknown in the natural world and shares the resulting discoveries and stories with other people. Alexandra Cousteau

an oceanographer: spends a lot of time underwater, finding connections between the living systems in the ocean. Sylvia Earle

Videoscript

Alexandra Cousteau: So there's nothing I would rather be than a National Geographic explorer and I'll tell you why. Coming from a family of explorers and growing up travelling all over the world, I learnt to dive with my grandfather when I was seven years old; I got to go snorkelling in tide pools, I've gone swimming with dolphins and diving with whales and I've made films about sharks in Tahiti. And all of these things are … it's like Christmas every day.

There's nothing more exciting than being able to go out, and seeing a wild place or a wild creature or a new kind of culture, or food. The smell of every new place is always a revelation and you learn so much and you're free; you're free to explore anything you want and to talk about anything you want, with anybody – because that's your job. Your job is to explore the unknown and to bring those stories back and share them with your friends and your family and people who are excited and inspired by what you do.

Johan Reinhard: I'm probably best known for having discovered the Ice Maiden. This is on a mountain summit of about over 20,000 feet high. An Inca child had been sacrificed, but later we returned and found several more mummies. And then, eventually, on some other mountains, including up to 22,000 feet on the Argentine border, we found three perfectly preserved Inca mummies.
Probably the things that most excited me for discoveries weren't so much the mummies per se, but what they told us about the past because they were so well preserved. The point that I realised just how important the discovery of the Ice Maiden was, was the moment I saw her face. I realised then that it was indeed a mummy because we weren't a 100% sure what was inside this kind of a dusty covered bundle, an ice-covered bundle. And my companion Miguel Zárate turned it on its side to get a better grip on it to try and lift it up, and all of a sudden we saw this face of this Inca mummy staring at us.

But, in a way, it was tinged with disappointment because the face had dried, and the real moment came when we tried to lift the mummy and realised that it weighed nearly 100 pounds. And that meant that the body itself was frozen, so even though the face had been exposed and dried out, the rest of the body probably was frozen. And what that means is that, we're not only going to get all the textiles and all the other things in, in context, (this is the key thing for archaeology) but we're also going to be able to get DNA studies, and I knew that she was … a she.

Dr Sylvia Earle: The best part of my job is that you never know what you're going to find. It's the joy of … of discovery. It's finding, not just new things but new ideas, to begin to connect the dots. When you spend a lot of time actually in the ocean, as I do, after a while you begin to see things that you might have missed the first time. But, over a period of hours, days, weeks, years, you really begin to understand something about how systems work. You get to see the behaviour of fish, it's not just a fish that swims by, but a fish that has a life, and trying to understand how they spend their days and nights, how long it takes for them to grow.
I think the best part is, just the excitement of … of discovery. It's something anybody can do, everybody should do. To look around, see the natural world, and try to understand not only how it works, but where do we fit in to the systems that keep us alive.

3 Students read the notes and then complete them while watching the video a second time.

Answers

1 explorers	2 grandfather	3 wild
4 inspired	5 discovery	6 three
7 face	8 frozen	9 discovery
10 fish	11 understand	

4 Students watch the video and note possible questions.

5 Students work in groups and speculate on possible answers. Listen in discreetly and check that students are able to use a variety of verbs and phrases for speculating; i.e. could / must / might / can't be / have been rather than simply maybe or perhaps.

6 Allocate roles to students and allow them time to prepare questions to ask each other. If you wish, introduce some useful expressions for social English:

So, tell me about yourself …
I'm so pleased to meet you in person …
I've heard so much about you …
It's been great talking to you …

Read through the Ideas generator box with the students. Explain the rationale behind this feature: to help to prepare students by giving them strategies for navigating the speaking part of the exam and generating ideas on some of the key topics. This section gives students a useful tip for structuring a spontaneous answer.

7   Students decide how they will answer the question, using the suggested structure.

8   Students ask and answer the question in as spontaneous and natural way as possible. Listen in for basic errors and, if necessary, lead a short post-exercise correction spot.

9   Students make notes to answer the further questions following the same structure.

10 Students look at the Useful expressions and expand them into sentences to talk about themselves.

11 Set up the task. Listen in discreetly as students perform the task, and identify three or four important errors. Round off the activity with a short correction spot.

12 Students reflect on how well they performed the task, and how successfully they exploited the respond, expand, example / focus structure, then repeat one of the exchanges that they think they can improve.

Vocabulary organiser 1, page 162

ORGANISING VOCABULARY

Teachers should encourage students to think of how they would like to record the vocabulary they've learnt from this unit:

- by theme: e.g. words connected with beginnings
- grammatically: perhaps create word webs or tables for particular language items, such as phrasal verbs, etc.
- by word association: e.g. word webs with *matter*, *material*, etc.
- by function: placing suitable phrases together for specific speaking tasks, discussion, writing tasks, etc.

BANK OF ENGLISH

Explain that the purpose of the Bank of English feature is to help students think of and group together word families, word partnerships and associations, to develop their use of language. This section can be done at home, but check the answers in class, to make sure students have understood how to use this Bank.

Answers

1
1 launched	2 inaugurated
3 set off	4 launched / set up / established
5 initiated	6 originated
7 instigated	8 embarked on

2
1 inaugurate	2 embark on
3 set off (on)	4 originate
5 instigate	

3
1 invaluable	2 hoarse
3 resounding	4 establishments

4
1 make it up to	2 make for
3 make up	4 make off
5 make out	6 make up for
7 make into	8 make something of

5
1 crisp	2 expanding
3 ascended	4 patchwork
5 buffeting	

Bank of English

1   N COUNT: sewing materials, artist's materials
    N UNCOUNT: writing material
    ADJ: material world, material evidence, material witness
2   N UNCOUNT: printed matter, grey matter, subject matter
    N COUNT: a business matter, personal matter, trivial matter
    PHRASES: what's the matter? a matter of concern / importance / urgency / principle, it's no laughing matter

Photocopiable activity instructions

Story – *The Shack* (page 21)

Aim: to practise storytelling in English.

Instructions:

1   Photocopy the activity and fold the paper so that only the beginning of the story is showing.

2   The first student should read the start of the story and then write their own answer to the second part. The next student should do the same, but without reading what the previous student wrote. Each student should fold the paper before passing it on, so the next student can't see what has already been written.

3   When everyone has finished, the last person should read the (probably strange and wonderful) story aloud.

Try something new! (page 22)

Aim: to make suggestions and convince others.

Instructions:

1   Photocopy the page and cut into individual advertisements.

2   Organise the class into pairs or small groups, and give each one an advertisement. Ask them to prepare a presentation to persuade other students to sign up to their activity.

3   Students give their presentations to the class. The rest of the class should listen and ask questions about the activity.

4   Students vote on which activity they would prefer to do.

Story – The Shack

Beginning	Billy and Jo always walked home from school along the footpath that ran through the old wood, but one day, as they were walking, they noticed a small wooden shack that seemed to have suddenly appeared in the middle of the path. It definitely hadn't been there the day before and there was definitely something strange about it.
Why did it look strange? Describe it.	
What did Billy say to Jo?	
What did they do next?	
Where did they suddenly find themselves?	
Who or what did they meet there?	
How did they react?	
What did Jo say?	
What did they do next?	
How did it end?	

Try something new!

Come fly with us in our beautiful balloon!

Feeling daring? Want excitement? Try rafting!

Feel free as a bird... fly like one!

World Balloon Tours

- Approved balloon ride company
- Operate our own balloons
- Checked regularly
- Experienced, qualified pilots
- Ride lasts about one and a half hours, but allow four hours for the whole experience
- Dependent on weather conditions
- Minimum age limit of 6 years; passengers aged 6–14 must be accompanied by an adult
- Fly to approximately 6,000 feet
- Excellent opportunity for photographers

Price: $220–275

Water Rat Rafting Ltd

- Approved rafting company
- Equipment provided – new rafts, top quality Coast Guard approved life jackets, helmets for more difficult waters, waterproof bags and boxes
- Age no problem
- Day trips offered – introductory gentle floats down the river, or more adventurous ones for a white water novice
- Groups of four on each raft, with two instructors
- All instructors are qualified, and experienced in the local waters
- Trips dependent on weather conditions

Price: $100 for one day trip

Condor Tours

- Approved paragliding company
- Choice of introductory tandem flight:
  1 fly with the instructor on one glider or
  2 a one-day introductory lesson
- Age no problem
- Choice of coastal or mountain flight, lasting at least 20 minutes
- Amazing views – tandem passengers may bring a small camera
- Should wear protective footwear, and warm clothing
- Trips dependent on weather

Price:
1 tandem flight $150–180
2 introductory lesson $200

2 A CHILD'S WORLD

Unit introduction

The topic of this unit is children, playing and childhood experiences. The Writing section focuses on writing a review.

Warm-up activity

This activity will get students thinking and talking about their early childhood, and provide oral practice without preparation. You may like to record what the students say.

Prepare slips of paper beforehand with a suggested topic written on each one. Ask students to randomly choose a slip, and take turns to present a one-minute spontaneous speech about the topic.

Possible topics: your earliest memory, your favourite toy, a frightening experience you had as a small child, your first day at school, an exciting experience you had as a small child, learning to ride a bike, your favourite children's story, your favourite children's TV programme, things you didn't like as a small child, an important person in your childhood.

Getting started

1   Students talk in pairs about the activities they did when they were children, using the verbs in the box. Many of the verbs may be new to them. To pre-teach the meanings, allocate one verb to each student or pair of students. Ask them to find the meaning in a dictionary and then mime the word to the rest of the class. Exercise 1 in the Vocabulary organiser section on page 163 also checks the meanings of these words, and could be completed before students do this speaking activity.

TEACHING IN PRACTICE: MOTIVATING CLASS DISCUSSION

Students are often reluctant to speak in the early stages of a new course, particularly if the teacher is new to them. One way of getting them to respond is to tell a story of your own experience as a child that your students may relate to. For example, in this unit, telling them tales of you and your siblings or friends playing outside, and the kinds of games you used to play, would encourage them to respond in kind.

→   Vocabulary organiser 2, exercise 1, page 163

Vocabulary organiser answers

| 1 clambered | 2 bounded | 3 wrestling | 4 waded |
| 5 hopped | 6 slide | 7 paddled | 8 heaved |

Reading gapped text

BACKGROUND INFORMATION: OUTDOOR NURSERIES

The idea for outdoor nurseries first developed in Denmark in the 1950s and has spread across Scandinavia and to Germany and Switzerland. In Germany there are 700 *Waldkindergärten*, or 'woodland nurseries'. None of the countries where they've taken off experience anything like 'tropical weather', but the nurseries are increasingly popular with parents worried about the cloistered, sedentary lifestyle of the modern child.

2   Ask students to look at the newspaper headline and predict what they think the article will be about.

Answer

The article is about an innovative kind of nursery that looks after children in an out-of-doors environment, in all kinds of weather conditions.

Reading extension

Give students help with vocabulary if necessary. Ask them questions such as:

What is a nursery? What kind of building or location are nurseries usually run in? Why do you think the parents are enthusiastic about this particular nursery? What is an 'antidote' to something? Why is the word used here?

TEACHING IN PRACTICE: PREDICTING INFORMATION

Being able to predict what a text is about is a useful skill that students should aim to develop. Looking at clues such as key words, headlines, pictures or headings can help students predict the content of a text or a listening tapescript.

3   Ask students to read the two paragraphs and summarise the content of each. Encourage them to underline any words or phrases in the second paragraph that seem to have a connection to the first. Then ask them to answer the question.

Answers

The middle paragraph would probably contain more information about the two boys, Freddie and Alastair, and the reasons why they are playing outside.

4 & 5 Ask students to complete the two exercises. This will help them to identify the connectors in the paragraphs before they choose the missing paragraph in exercise 6. Check the answers with the class.

Answers

4 1 Freddie and Alastair   2 the pair   3 their childminder
5 1 Cathy Bache   2 their   3 the children
   4 nursery or kindergarten

6 Students should now read the three paragraphs on page 241 and decide which belongs in the gap in exercise 3. They can do this task individually or in pairs. Stress that they must read all three options before making their choices. When they have finished, take a class vote – how many people chose each option? Ask students to justify their choice.

Answer

Option B. It is the correct paragraph because it focuses on the two boys and what they are wearing, and introduces the nursery project that is described in more detail in the next paragraph. Also the descriptive style of writing seems to fit.
Option A focuses too much on the uniform, which does not tie into paragraph 3, or link back the to the second half of paragraph 1.
Option C suggests that the boys' attitude is strongly negative (*cold, irritable, demonstrated a marked disinclination to …*), which does not fit in with the positive connotations of the first paragraph (*snugly, earnestly, bounding*) where the boys are portrayed as enthusiastic about their activities.

7 Ask students to read the rubric. Explain that normally in this part of the exam, students would need to find the paragraph that fits each gap, but first, they are being asked to choose one of two headings, a or b, which best summarises what might be missing in each gap. They should read each of the six paragraphs and decide what information would fit best in the paragraph before it.

Answers

1 b   2 a   3 b   4 a   5 a   6 a

8 Ask students to look back at their answer for exercise 7, paragraph 1 – Monimail Tower. Ask them to quickly scan the missing paragraphs to see if they can find one that matches this theme. Explain that 'scanning' is another useful technique to use when you are looking for specific information in a longer text. They should be able to find G quite quickly as the first word of the paragraph stands out.

Answer

G Key word: *Monimail* (first word of the paragraph). Other key words that tie in with the paragraphs are: *donor, £20,000, sum raised* (link to previous paragraph); *Secret Garden* (links to following paragraph).

9 Ask students to read the remaining paragraphs more carefully, and employ the techniques they've already learnt to find which paragraphs go where. This could be done in class as a timed activity, or set for homework.

Answers

2 D   3 C   4 A   5 E   6 B

10 Discuss the questions as a class.

→ Vocabulary organiser 2, exercise 2, page 163

Vocabulary organiser answers

1 ruddy   2 pioneers   3 curriculum   4 oblivious to
5 thrive   6 frustrated   7 toxin   8 sedentary

See *Do you see what I see?* photocopiable activity, page 31.

Student's Book pages 22–23

Language development parts of the body idioms

1 Ask students to look back at paragraph D on page 21. Elicit how the children seem to feel about playing outside in the rain. Demonstrate how students can guess the meaning of unknown words and phrases by using the context.

Answer

1 The children aren't concerned about the weather, they don't think it is a problem.

2 Allow students time to read the sentences and look up the meaning of the idioms in a dictionary. Encourage them to try to guess the meanings first.

Answers

a have a good idea
b ignore somebody, be cold and unfriendly towards them
c look unhappy or depressed

3 Tell students there are many idioms relating to parts of the body. Ask them to look at the idioms in the box and use them to complete the sentences.

→ Vocabulary organiser 2, exercises 3 and 4, page 163

Vocabulary organiser answers

3
1 neck   2 foot   3 mouth   4 head   5 shoulder
4
a pain in the neck   b wet behind the ears   c tongue in cheek
d see eye to eye   e (don't) bat an eyelid

Extension

Draw the figure of a person on the board, with arrows to the parts of the body mentioned in the idioms. Write in the phrases from exercise 2 on page 22. Then, elicit the other idioms covered in exercise 3. Ask students to draw the figure in their vocabulary notebooks, and add the idioms around it. Having a visual representation of the parts of the human body and the phrases connected to them will help visual learners to remember them.

Ask student pairs to find more body idioms using their dictionaries, e.g. *pull someone's leg, play it by ear, lose heart, put someone's back up, pay through the nose, an eyesore, off someone's head*, etc.

→ Vocabulary organiser 2, exercise 5, page 163

Phrasal verbs *pick up*

4 Encourage students to look back at the text to find the sentence. They should then try to find the definition that best matches the meaning.

Answer

9 to lift someone or something up from a surface

5 Students should do this exercise individually or in pairs. Encourage them to use a dictionary whenever they need to.

Answers

a 2   b 4   c 8   d 1   e 7   f 6   g 5   h 3   i 9

→ Vocabulary organiser 2, exercise 6, page 163

Vocabulary organiser answers

1 do what you can to recover from a bad situation
2 ask for help with a problem
3 choose from a group
4 criticise something
5 walk very carefully to avoid obstacles
6 something someone does or has when they are feeling tired or unwell
7 a thief who steals from your person
8 someone who is difficult to please
9 examine something closely
10 look through something

Key word *run*

6 Read out the sentence from the text. Ask the students to tick the words in the box that can be used with *run*. Remind them to make notes of new meanings or usages of common words, especially in idioms or fixed phrases. More obscure meanings are sometimes tested in the Reading and Use of English paper, Parts 1, 2 and 4.

Answer

The following words **cannot** be used: a bus, a conversation, an idea, a message, a party, politics.

7 This exercise can be done individually or in pairs.

Answers

a run an errand   b run counter to   c run a story
d run for office   e run a risk

Grammar passive forms

8 Read through the sentences with the class. Elicit the passive structures. Make sure that students notice there are two in the first sentence.

Answers

the children will be taught and entertained
their curriculum will be devoted to

9 Ask students to look back at the text on page 21. The sentence appears in the final paragraph before gap 6. Allow students time to consider the contextual meaning of *can* here.

Answer

3

10 Ask students to complete the task individually before checking the answers as a class.

Answers

1 d   2 b   3 a   4 c

VERBS WITH PASSIVE FORMS

Explain to the students that there are some verbs that can be used in more than one passive construction. The object in the active sentence may become the subject of the passive sentence, (Construction 1) or a construction with *it* can be used (Construction 2) You may like to direct them to the Grammar reference section now, for further examples before they do exercise 11.

11 Ask students to complete exercise 11 by rewriting the sentences in two different ways.

Answers
1 Children have been reported stealing from the school cafeteria
  It has been reported that children have been stealing from the school cafeteria.
2 A dolphin is believed to have rescued the baby
  It is believed that a dolphin rescued the baby.

12 Tell students to rewrite the sentences using a suitable passive form.

Answers
1 is considered to be too young
2 has been rumoured that the children's playground is going
3 against underage drinking are thought to be
4 is suspected of breaking into
5 is estimated to have increased
6 is said that the missing boy was a loner and didn't have
7 is believed that she went missing somewhere between the bus stop

→ Grammar reference 2.1, page 209

passive form with *have* and *get*

13 Elicit the uses of *have* in each case. Explain that *get* can be used to replace *have* as a causative form.

Answers
1 b   2 a

14 Elicit passive sentences with similar meanings to the sentences given. Make sure that your students understand that *let* has to become *be allowed* in the passive, and that *make someone do* becomes *be made to do*.

Answers
I am allowed to have friends to stay at the weekend.
I was made to do my homework before I could go out.

TEACHING IN PRACTICE: USING THE GRAMMAR REFERENCE SECTION

Encourage your students to make use of the Grammar reference at the back of their books whenever they address the Grammar section in each unit. They may also find it useful for reference when attempting the exercises in the Exam Booster.

See *Find the accomplice* photocopiable activity, page 30.

Student's Book pages 24–25

Listening sentence completion

Read through the information, rubric and questions with students. Make sure they understand what the task requires of them. Point out that several answers are possible. Read through the tips and discuss the different ways that the answer can be narrowed down.

Possible answer
temperature, weather, conditions, light, etc.

1 Again, point out that there are many possibilities here. The point is to get students to focus on various options, so they know what to listen out for.

Answers
1 an adjective, positive (suitable, safe, reliable, interesting, etc.)
2 an adverb / adverbial phrase (temporarily, at the moment, etc.)
3 a noun (pollution, radiation, chemicals, etc.)

2 ⊙ 6 Ask students to read the rubric and then read through the sentences in the same way as they did for exercise 1. Check to see what information they can predict. Then they should listen to the recording and complete questions 1–8.

Answers
1 silence	2 (practical) use	3 exposed to
4 four or five (years)	5 communicate	6 countries
7 first	8 relationship	

Audioscript ⊙ 6

We still don't fully understand how or why human language came about, although there are certainly a good number of theories. One main theory suggests that when men became hunters, they needed to develop a language in order to share hunting tactics with one another during the chase, despite the fact that most carnivorous animals – even those that hunt in packs – find silence to be a distinct advantage. And yet historians are agreed that the first spoken languages must have been very crude. How then could they have been of any practical use?

There is, however, one theory that proposes that it wasn't men who first used language. It wasn't even women. It was in fact children who invented it, and taught it to their parents. The truth is that fully grown adults actually lack the ability to learn to speak. Only children can do it. People that have never been exposed to any kind of spoken language before the age of five (and there are a handful of documented cases) have never been able to learn to speak at all, despite concerted efforts to teach them. Similarly, children that are born deaf may have difficulty learning to make verbal sounds because they've never heard them.

Children's natural propensity for learning languages is taken as read. They don't have to be taught their first language – they only have to hear it spoken around them. During the first four or five years of life a child can learn several languages simultaneously, without being taught, without any apparent effort.

Newborn babies all over the world have their own repertoire of involuntary sounds which are useful for communicating to the mother their most basic needs – hunger, pain or the need for attention. This is true of the young of most mammals. However, between three and four months of age the human baby begins to emit new sounds and before long, will start to 'babble'. This baby talk varies from country to country, suggesting that the baby is responding to, and trying to imitate, the sounds around him. Before long, he learns to control the sounds. He gets a response. He says 'ma' and mother responds. This could be the reason why the word for mother is so similar in almost every language. It's one of the first syllables a human child can voluntarily produce. Can we be so sure that baby is really imitating mum or could it be the other way round? Next, he is inventing his own words for objects and his mother is using them too. Language is born. Perhaps this is why girls often learn to speak sooner and more fluently than boys, because at one time the ability to develop language was essential to the mother-infant relationship.

Speaking using visual prompts

3 Ask the students to look at the pictures on page 231, and give their opinions about the questions.

EXPRESSING OPINIONS

Having discussed the pictures in exercise 3, students should have had the opportunity to collect their thoughts and form their own clear opinion. Exercise 4 gives them the chance to practise in an exam situation, and gain an idea of the timing. Make it clear to them that the examiner will only allow them a specific amount of time to speak before interrupting them. Students should not worry if they are stopped before completing what they want to say.

4 After Students 1 and 2 have had a chance to talk about their pictures, ask the students to change roles. The new interlocutor should ask the question again, to imitate the exam as closely as possible.

Use of English multiple-choice cloze

EXAM SPOTLIGHT

The aim of this Spotlight box is to highlight the different types of options commonly found in a multiple-choice cloze test. Read the rubric and go through the options with the class. Encourage students to make notes in their vocabulary notebooks.

Type 1: Focus on how these words have a similar meaning but are not all used in the same context.

Answers

1 Not aware or conscious of something, having no knowledge, oblivious to.
2 d cannot be used in the sentence; a, b and c can all be followed by 'of'.
3 d can be used as it is usually followed by a noun.

Type 2: Focus on how these words look or sound similar but have quite different meanings. For 2, ask students to consult their dictionaries and find the meanings of the words before writing their own sentences.

Answers

1 d (recollection = memory)
2 Students' own answers

Type 3: Focus on the lexical contexts of these words, which are all followed by a particular preposition.

Answers

1 d   2 b   3 a   4 c

Type 4: Focus on the grammatical requirements of the sentence (singular and plural verbs).

Answers

4 a, b and c could be used. d could not be used as it requires a singular verb.

Extension

Ask students to find an article or piece of writing in English of a suitable length (about 170 words) and to choose eight items of vocabulary within the text that could be tested. For each word they choose, they should use their dictionaries to find one correct synonym that can be used to replace it, and one word that is similar in some way, but which would be incorrect if used in the same context.

5 Ask students to read through the text and do the task individually, then compare their answers with a partner. Elicit the meanings of known words and distractors, and explanations of why they are wrong. Then ask students to use their dictionaries to find the items that were difficult, and give explanations of why the distractors don't work in this context. Follow up with a discussion of students' experiences with colour when they were small. Did their parents try to dress them in particular colours, for example?

Answers

1 A   2 D   3 A   4 B   5 A   6 C   7 B   8 A

Student's Book pages 26–27

Writing a review

It is often a good idea for students to see examples of authentic pieces of writing relating to the kind of task they are going to do. Most students will be aware of and may have read reviews of films, books and music, but they might not have seen reviews of places to visit, or of exhibitions, concerts, etc. Try to show them examples of different types of review, some positive, and some slightly more critical.

1 Ask students to read the question, and underline the two things they need to do when answering it.

Answer

Students should underline the following: *describing what there is to see and do there and saying whether or not you recommend it to other people and why.*

2 Emphasise the importance of answering the whole of the question. Write the following items on the board: *organisation, use of language, full answer to the question.* Ask students to comment on these areas when looking at the sample answer.

Answers

Organisation – there is not a clear structure to the writing; it moves from topic to topic in a disjointed and confusing way. The paragraph breaks are not logical: the third paragraph begins with an example illustrating the point at the end of the previous paragraph. These two sentences belong together. The sentences could be reorganised into paragraphs which group information on a particular aspect of the museum.
Use of language – there is some good language, but the structures lack variety. 'They' is used throughout, but it is not clear who it refers to, so a passive construction would be much more appropriate.
Does it answer the question fully? No, because the student fails to include a recommendation in his answer.

SENTENCE DEVELOPMENT

The aim of this box is to draw students' attention to the need to vary their language and style when writing. Advise them that use of the passive can help them achieve a more formal style, but they should avoid overusing it!

3 Ask your students to look at the underlined sentences in the review in exercise 2 and rewrite them using suitable passive structures. For weaker classes, provide them with the first one as an example.

Answers

They have dedicated it → it has been dedicated to
they have built the museum → the museum has been built
They made toys mainly out of wood or metal → Toys were made mainly out of wood or metal
they gave us → we were given
people encouraged us to fill it → we were encouraged to fill it
They designed each room → Each room was designed
they have created one room → one room has been created
they encourage children to play → children are encouraged to play
some people show the children → the children are shown

4 Tell students to choose the most suitable conclusion for the sample review. Elicit from them what the conclusion should include, e.g. a recommendation.

Answer

3 It is the only one which actually recommends the museum to others. The style is also formal and more appropriate than the style in 2. 1 is inappropriate as it does not summarise the writer's opinion, and the first sentence would be more suitable to an introduction.

5 Ask your students to make the review from exercise 2 more descriptive, by varying the language presented in brackets. Students don't need to use all the words and phrases in the box, but should aim to use some of them effectively.

Possible answers

My family and I recently visited a toy museum. It has been dedicated to a local family who were among the earliest toy makers in my country, and has been built on the site of the family's factory. Their toys were constructed mainly out of wood or metal, but the museum exhibits reflect developments in toy making over the past 200 years.
The Bryant Toy Museum is an innovative, interactive playground for children. When we arrived, we were presented with a notebook called 'My Toy Scrapbook.' The cover shows a photograph of the original factory. As we wandered through the museum, we were encouraged to fill it with pictures, stamps and notes, if we wanted.
Each room is cleverly designed to look like scenes from particular periods in history. For example, one room has been created to look like a scene from a Charles Dickens novel, another from around the time of the Second World War, and then suddenly, you're in a room filled with all kinds of electronic games. My brother and I found this room particularly fascinating. In every room, children are encouraged to play creatively with some of the toys, and when they come to the final room, they are shown how to design and construct their own toys, if they want.

TEACHING IN PRACTICE: WORD LIMIT

Remind students of the word limit for this task. Note that if you add paragraph c from exercise 4 to the suggested answer above, you have a total of 249 words, which is well within the word limit. If your students are experiencing difficulties, you may like to present this as a model answer.

6 Check that your students know the meaning of the words provided.

7 Set this exercise as homework, but perhaps ask the students to underline the points they need to include in their answer before they go away to tackle the task.

Vocabulary organiser 2, page 163

Photocopiable activity instructions

Find the accomplice (page 30)

Aim: to practise the use of passive structures for speculation – *he is thought to be* ... etc.

Instructions:

1 Divide the class into pairs. Give each pair a copy of the page.

2 Tell them to read the information about the theft, and look at the 'photofit' of one of the suspects.

3 The students must give a description of the man's accomplice. They should choose someone else in the class, without that person knowing, and create a description of them, using structures like 'It is believed the suspect had an accomplice. This person is thought to be ... , etc.'

4 When all the pairs are ready, choose one to stand in front of the class and give a description of the accomplice. The rest of the class has to guess who is being described. Then the next pair does the same, and so on.

Do you see what I see? (page 31)

Aim: to practise speaking, giving descriptions and making comparisons, and to practise using the verbs of movement learnt in this unit.

Instructions:

1 Organise the class into pairs and give each student in each pair one part of the photocopy – either A or B. They shouldn't see each other's page.

2 Tell the students that there are eight differences between the two sets of pictures. Students should take turns describing what they can see in each picture, for example: I can see a little boy climbing a tree, there are two boys arm wrestling.

3 They continue until they have identified eight differences in the two sets of pictures.

4 They should aim to use as many of the verbs from the unit as they can. (You have the option of not including them when you cut the photocopy.)

FIND THE ACCOMPLICE

This man is believed to have broken into the local school last night. Items of sports equipment were stolen, and several classrooms were vandalised. The suspect is believed to be of average height, approximately 1.65 m, and is thought to have been wearing jeans and a black sweater. It is believed the suspect had an accomplice. Not much is known about this person, and witnesses did not get a clear view of them, but this person is thought to be ...

_____

_____

_____

_____

DO YOU SEE WHAT I SEE?

A

Verbs to use: bound, clamber, climb, heave, hop, jump, leap, march, paddle,
skip, slide, stride, stroll, swing, tiptoe, wade, wander, wrestle

- ✂

B

Verbs to use: bound, clamber, climb, heave, hop, jump, leap, march, paddle,
skip, slide, stride, stroll, swing, tiptoe, wade, wander, wrestle

3 ARE YOU GAME?

Unit introduction

The topic of this unit is endurance sports and taking risks.

In recent years, there has been a rapid increase in fascination for endurance sports and extreme sports. Some of your students may do such activities, but others may not like them at all. This unit endeavours to take both groups into account, by focusing on the question of risk taking in general.

Warm-up activity

Write the following list of activities on the board:

cycling, sailing, kayaking, horse riding, aerobics, dancing, jogging, motor racing, swimming, football, tennis, mountaineering, hiking.

Ask your students to place them in order, from the most to the least dangerous. Then elicit from them which activities they already do, and which they would be willing to try. Discuss how daring they think they are.

Draw their attention to the first page of the unit. Elicit the meaning of the title, *Are you game?* Explain that if you are *game* you are willing to try something new, dangerous or risky.

Getting started

1 ⊙ 7 Ask students to look at the activities listed in the box. Check the meanings of the more difficult words. Then, tell students to listen to the recording and identify which of the activities in the box are being talked about.

Answers
Speaker 1: white-water rafting
Speaker 2: yacht racing
Speaker 3: kite landboarding

Audioscript ⊙ 7

Speaker 1:   So, I said, well, I'm game, if you are. But I wish I hadn't. It was terrifying! The water flows so fast, with rocks appearing out of nowhere ... There's no time to think. I was petrified! Never again!

Speaker 2:   Well, the long hours without sleep were exhausting, and the loneliness got me down occasionally, but I was determined not to give up, and would keep myself busy, by repairing sails and ropes, or sending faxes to folks back on dry land. Also, listening to music had a way of relaxing me, and was quite reassuring.

Speaker 3:   That was awesome! Absolutely incredible! A real adrenalin rush! Everything happens so fast, you've got to be on your toes, and, like, keep control of both the board and the kite, otherwise you'll overturn ... and ... man, it was so exhilarating!

2 Ask the students to look at the words in the box. Tell them to listen to each speaker again, and circle the words they hear. Play the recording.

Answers
adrenalin rush, awesome, determined, exhausting, exhilarating, incredible, loneliness, petrified, reassuring, relaxing, terrifying, tiredness

→   Vocabulary organiser 3, exercise 1, page 164

Answers to Vocabulary organiser
1 awesome	2 terrifying	3 reassuring
4 exhilarating	5 exhausting	

3 Ask students to talk about their experiences. Explain that it doesn't have to relate to one of the activities depicted. It could be their first day at school, for example.

4 The questionnaire is on page 241 of the Student's Book. Have students complete the quiz individually.

Reading multiple choice

BACKGROUND

The extract is taken from Pete Goss's amazing book, *Close To The Wind*. In 1996, while competing in the Vendée Globe single-handed round-the-world yacht race, he turned back into hurricane-force winds in order to rescue fellow competitor Raphael Dinelli, ruining his own chances of success in the race. Dinelli was almost dead when Goss found him, but he nursed him back to health, and the two men became firm friends.

UNDERSTANDING THE WRITER'S / NARRATOR'S ATTITUDE

Read through the box with the class before students do exercise 5, which asks them to identify the narrator's feelings in the text.

5 Ask students to read *A Close Encounter* on page 29, and decide how the narrator feels.

Answer
b *I had to go, I knew that. The fight began. ... the anger helped to strengthen my resolve. I knew that we would do it somehow. I decided to take no prisoners.*

6 Ask the students to read through the multiple-choice questions before they do the task. Then ask students to justify their choices.

Answers

1 D 2 C 3 A 4 B 5 C 6 B

DIFFICULT WORDS IN A READING TEXT

Explain that sometimes when we read, we encounter words which are technical or very specific to the topic. Students should not be put off by this. An understanding of specialist language will not be required to answer exam questions. The context often helps to give an idea of the type of word it is, e.g. a piece of equipment on a boat (*satcom system*, paragraph 1, line 3) or a technical sailing term (*jibe*, paragraph 3, line 3).

→ Vocabulary organiser 3, exercises 2 and 3, page 164

Answers to Vocabulary organiser

2
1 stakes   2 strengthen his resolve
3 atrocious   4 put on the line
3
1 din   2 distress call   3 extricated
4 daft   5 atrocious   6 put on the line
7 the stakes   8 strengthen my resolve

Student's Book pages 30–31

Language development phrases
with *up* and *down*

1 Elicit ideas about the meaning of the phrase.

Answer

It means the speaker is wondering if he is physically and mentally capable of what he has to do.

2 Students do this in pairs. Suggest they write their initial answers down in a separate notebook, rather than on the page, in case they make any mistakes. Set a time limit for the task.

Answers

1 What are you doing nowadays?
2 We must concentrate on working.
3 It's your choice what you do.
4 The cancellation was Brian's decision.
5 I've only got a few pennies left.
6 The children do a lot of mischievous / adventurous things at their grandmother's.
7 What's wrong?
8 I'm not very happy at the moment.
9 Five (letters) completed, and four still to do.
10 That film wasn't very good.

→ Vocabulary organiser 3, exercises 4 and 5, page 164

Answers to Vocabulary organiser

4
1 I'm down to   2 get up to something   3 get down to (work)
4 I'm feeling down   5 not up to much   6 be down to
5
we've been having our problems

phrasal verbs with *take*

3 Ask your students to find the target phrase in the text on page 29 and share their ideas about its meaning.

Answer

He automatically acted according to his training.

4 Ask students to complete the sentences. Ask if they know any other phrasal verbs with *take*.

VOCABULARY: PHRASAL VERBS WITH *TAKE*

take on (responsibility): agree to do a task or duty
take over (from someone): take someone else's position when they leave
take back (something you've said): apologise for something you've said, and admit you were wrong
take out (a subscription): order and pay for a number of magazine issues to be sent to your home
take (something) *apart*: separate an object such as a machine into pieces
take to (someone): immediately like someone when you meet them
take down (notes): write information in a notebook
take (someone) *for* (someone else): mistakenly believe that a person is someone else
take after (someone): look or be very similar to someone else in your family
take up (an activity): start a new activity on a regular basis

Answers

1 on   2 over   3 back   4 out   5 apart
6 to   7 down   8 for   9 after   10 up

→ Vocabulary organiser 3, exercise 6, page 164

Answers to Vocabulary organiser

1 take for   2 take back   3 take after
4 take down   5 take on   6 take up
7 take over   8 take out   9 take to
10 take apart   11 take back   12 take out

phrases with *take*

5 Ask students to find the phrases in the text. Encourage them to use the context to help them choose the meaning. You may find it useful to give a further example sentence for each phrase:
He glanced briefly at his sister, and then did a double take. She looked so different with her new haircut!
He decided to take no prisoners and do everything in his power to beat the world record.

Answers	
1 a	2 b

See *Take it or leave it!* photocopiable activity, page 40.

Key word *game*

6 Students do this exercise in pairs. Give feedback on their answers and explain any phrases if necessary.

Answers				
1 c	2 h	3 j	4 f	5 g
6 i	7 b	8 d	9 a	10 e

7 Ask students to complete this exercise and then check their answers as a class.

Answers

a the name of the game	b gave the game away
c Are you game?	d The game's up
e play games with me	

Grammar modal auxiliaries (1)

8 Ask your students to look at the picture and speculate about what it shows, using the modals indicated. The possibilities are quite limited, so encourage them to create negative ideas as well, such as *It can't be a ... , because ... .*

SPECULATION AND SUGGESTION, DEDUCTION, ASSUMPTION

Read through the information with students, and provide an example sentence for each type of modal.
→ Grammar reference 3, page 210

9 Ask your students to read the rubric and the sentences. Allow them time to consider their answers. Elicit answers.

Answers

1 suggestion	2 suggestion	3 deduction	4 assumption
5 speculation	6 deduction	7 deduction	8 suggestion

10 ⊙ 8 Tell your students they are going to hear a couple talking about why their daughter is late. Read the questions with them. Play the recording twice if necessary.

Answers

1 She might have missed the bus.
2 She would have phoned to say she'd be late, and she wouldn't have forgotten her mobile.
3 Something must have happened.

Audioscript ⊙ 8

Man:	... Right! That's everything. Are we ready to go?
Woman:	Jane still hasn't arrived. It's not like her to be so late.
Man:	She might have missed the bus.
Woman:	I don't think so. She would have phoned to say she'd be late.
Man:	She may have forgotten to take her mobile phone with her. You do that all the time!
Woman:	Yeah, much to your annoyance! No, Jane's so organised. She wouldn't have forgotten her mobile, and even if she had, she would still be able to use a payphone! No. Something must have happened.
Man:	Oh, come on, love. Don't worry so much. There's always a first time for forgetting things, you know. I'm sure it's ... There! That'll be her now!
Woman:	Hello, Jane, is that you? ... Oh, sorry ... Yes ... Oh no! When? How did it happen? Yes, I'm on my way.

Extension

Ask your students to speculate what might have happened to Jane using the constructions in the speculation box.

11 Make sure the students understand *refute* and *qualify*. If you *refute* something you argue strongly against it. If you *qualify* something, you partially agree, but make some reservations, e.g. *I might have been terrified, but I did what I could to help.* (qualify)
I might be small, but I'm not a child! (refute)
Now ask your students to complete exercise 11.

Answers

1 ... I specialised in the twentieth century! (qualify)
2 I might talk a lot, ... (refute)

12 Ask the students to read the rubric. Remind them that in the exam this task would include a range of constructions, not all modals as in this exercise.

Answers

1 may / might have forgotten my birthday
2 can't have written that note
3 will have phoned to tell
4 would have called (me) to say
5 might not have won
6 may be good with

See *Intrepid explorers* photocopiable activity, page 41.

Student's Book pages 32–33

Listening multiple choice

1 Ask the students to look at the rubric, and tell them you are going to say the phrase in the different tones of voice indicated. Do so, using a random order. They must identify your tone of voice each time. Students should then try this in pairs. Observe from a distance, and correct only when the intonation is wrong.

2 🔘 9 Ask the students to read the rubric. Check they understand the meaning of each attitude option (A–E). Play the recording. Allow students time to consider their answers before replaying the recording.

Answers
Speaker 1: E	Speaker 2: C	Speaker 3: D	Speaker 4: B

Audioscript 🔘 9

Speaker 1:	Well, naturally, I was disappointed, but ... nothing I could do about it. Just one of those things, I suppose.
Speaker 2:	Honestly, you could have told me about it beforehand. Then I wouldn't have gone to all that trouble, not to mention expense!
Speaker 3:	Who? James? Well, I wouldn't like to say, really. I mean, I don't know him all that well ... Why are you asking?
Speaker 4:	Oh, don't let him worry you! He's just a nobody. Don't take any notice of him, dear.

TEACHING IN PRACTICE: LISTENING STRATEGIES

Advise your students to try and answer as many questions as possible on the first listening. They should listen carefully the second time round, and check every question again, in case they misheard something.

3 🔘 10 Tell your students to look at the pictures at the top of the page. Find out what they think is happening. Tell them they are going to listen to an interview with a mountaineer. Ask them to read through the questions, and elicit any unknown words.

Answers
1 B	2 A	3 D	4 A	5 A	6 C

Audioscript 🔘 10

Interviewer:	Right! My next guest is someone who I personally admire very much. Tom Masefield has done it all! Whether it be climbing the highest peaks, such as Everest, trekking to the South Pole or kayaking along the coast from Alexandroupolis, on the Greek-Turkish border, to the town of Agria in Central Greece, where he now lives ... a mere 505 kilometres ... You name it, he's probably done it! Tom, welcome. Tell me, how did all this start?
Tom:	Well, Tracy, I started rock climbing ten years ago, near the town where I now live. Agria is at the foot of Pelion mountain, so there are lots of places to climb there. I trained as a P.E. teacher, and I'm not only a climbing instructor for the town council, but I also teach handball and skiing for them, and watersports such as kayaking and swimming in the summer months. Two summers ago, we took a group of nine teenagers and kayaked down the coast from Alexandroupolis to Agria. That was an amazing experience for all of us.
Interviewer:	Wasn't it a little dangerous, being on the open sea in a canoe?
Tom:	Well, um, I suppose it was a little risky, but we were all experienced, and the kids did really well.
Interviewer:	Did you see any interesting sea life on your voyage?
Tom:	We saw lots of dolphins. They liked swimming alongside us, but from a distance. Then one day, the leader thought he saw what looked like a sunken ship floating under the surface, but as we approached for a closer look, we realised it was a huge sea turtle. The guys in front were so surprised by the size of it they nearly overturned! It was an amazing feeling.
Interviewer:	So, is the sea your true love?
Tom:	I enjoy being on the water, certainly ... but *climbing* is what I really love. The feeling when you're hanging from a rope, 300 metres from the ground ... There's nothing like it. It's the closest we can get to being a bird.
Interviewer:	Is it easy being a member of an international team, Tom?
Tom:	Not always. At Everest, I was with a Kuwaiti, an American woman, two Belgians and two Japanese. That often caused misunderstandings, obviously, some amusing, some frustrating. But on the whole, we got on well and became good friends. You're in close proximity with each other 24 hours a day, under extreme conditions ... There's going to be friction, but also you form strong bonds. Climbing is about teamwork – you have to rely on the next person holding the rope. Every mountaineer understands that, and everyone is working towards a common goal.
Interviewer:	Did you experience any difficulties during the climb?
Tom:	Well, the worst thing that happened was that two of the team got very bad frostbite, and had to have the ends of two of their fingers chopped off. That meant returning to base camp for a while. But they recovered and carried on. It's one of the recognised hazards of mountaineering. Experienced climbers accept it as a risk they take.
Interviewer:	I wouldn't like to have been in their shoes, though! Now, the trip to Everest was just part of a bigger project, wasn't it?
Tom:	Yes. We've just managed to complete the ascent of the 'Seven Summits', as it's known. These are the highest peaks in each continent, including Everest. The last one we

attempted, Carstensz Pyramid, Papua New Guinea, proved the most difficult to climb, due to problems beyond our control. We had a struggle to raise enough sponsorship money, but then we had to abandon an attempt because of helicopter failure. The next time we planned to climb it, there was an earthquake shortly before we were due to arrive! However, we succeeded in March of this year, and it was a special achievement for me, as not that many people have ever climbed all seven summits. This time, we had a tough climb in a snowstorm, but when the Belgian climber, Robert Huygh, and I reached the top, it was a moment neither of us will ever forget. The culmination of a lifetime dream …

Interviewer: Very impressive! And I believe you've written a book …

4 Discuss the questions as a group.

Speaking interacting

5 Ask the students to read the exam task on page 232. This task could be done as an open pair task, to give students an idea of what is expected. Ask students how they feel about these activities.

Use of English open cloze

6 This exercise allows students to practise using the different structures mentioned in the box. Ask them to read through the rubric and complete the task.

Answers

1 After / Once	2 Before
3 which	4 dancing / listening
5 this / it	6 Nevertheless / However
7 on	8 into

Degree of difficulty

Decrease the level: for weaker groups, allow students to work on exercise 6 in pairs.

Increase the level: with stronger students, see who can find the answers first.

7 Ask students to read the text quickly, ignoring the gaps. Elicit what the text is about and what *Beyond the pain barrier* means. Explain any unknown words. Then ask students to carry out the exam task individually.

Answers

1 its	2 one	3 being	4 in
5 as	6 themselves	7 few	8 Whatever

Student's Book pages 34–35

Writing a formal letter

Aim: to make students aware of the importance of using the input material in a Part 2 question effectively, by identifying the target reader, the reason for writing, the information to include and the expected outcome of the letter.

1 Ask students to read the rubric, and elicit their views.

2 Ask students to read the exam task and decide whether the task requires a formal or informal answer.

Answer
formal

3 Students do this in pairs. Ask them to read through the exam task again, and discuss possible arguments they could make. Explain that they will need to use their imagination for this, and present ideas from the point of view of a teacher. Only one of them needs to make notes. Elicit ideas and give feedback.

Possible answers

1 The trip was well organised and risk assessments had been carried out. The students had been given clear instructions which would have ensured their safety, had they followed these instructions correctly.
2 Many school trips of this kind have taken place in schools in our region, and this is the first time there has been an accident.
3 Our school also organises local trips to museums and places of interest, but while these are valuable, they cannot fully replace longer residential trips.

---

4 Ask the students to read the sample answer. They are asked to consider register and organisation, and whether the points in the Spotlight box have been considered. Students should do this task individually.

Answer

The student considers points 2 and 4 in the Exam spotlight, but uses phrases lifted from the question.
The student has not considered who the letter is written for: the register is inconsistent, and sometimes informal language is used, which is inappropriate. The information does not address the second point in the exam question. The letter is not well organised and reads like a list of points. The student doesn't use enough examples to support her points. Also, the answer is too short.

---

5 Ask the students to read the rubric and the expressions in the box. For weaker students, you might find it useful to elicit the inappropriate phrases first, and then ask students to rewrite them. Elicit answers, and give feedback.

Answers

Inappropriate phrases	Suitable alternative
Dear Newspaper	*Dear Sir / Madam*
… I want to give my view of what happened.	*… I would like to present my own account of the occurrence.*
Something like this had never happened before!	*This event was unprecedented, and occurred as a result of …*
… but this is often boring	*Unfortunately, these activities do not always interest students.*
So, I think you are wrong to suggest that …	*Therefore, I feel it would be a mistake to suggest that …*
Please print my letter …	*I would be grateful if my letter could be published in the next issue of …*

---

6 Read the information in the box about using your own words, then ask students to read the sentences. Elicit ideas for rewriting the first sentence.

Possible answers

1 I work as a teacher myself.
2 First, the students in question were under proper supervision …
3 In my opinion students need to do more than visit museums and tourist sites …
4 In my view this incident is not typical of most school trips.

---

7 Ask students to read through the sample answer in exercise 4 again, and decide what is missing.

Answer

The answer does not contain enough examples to support the points made, so it reads like a list of notes.

---

8 Ask the students to read through the exam task and letter extract. Ask them to explain the points that they need to include in their answer. Set the task for homework.

Student's Book pages 36–37

Video frozen search and rescue

Aim: The main aim of the video is to stimulate interest in problem solving. The Ideas generator pursues the idea of using brainstorming as a preliminary stage in discussing and solving the kind of problems that appear in Part 3 of the speaking test.

Synopsis: This video is about an Alaskan helicopter rescue mission to track and save a snowmobiler called Dave who had become separated from his fellow snowmobiler in a blizzard (snowstorm). The helicopter crew eventually find Dave alive and un-injured, but exhausted by his ordeal.

1 Generate interest in the topic by asking students to look at the photo.

Possible answers

1 climbing / mountaineering
2 remote, sheer mountainside, extreme conditions, very cold, dangerous and unforgiving
3 falling, hitting your head, rope breaking, getting stuck, getting hypothermia / frostbite

---

2 Read through the different sports and check the students' pronunciation, in particular with regard to word stress (stressed syllables are underlined in the answer key). Students discuss the sports and give them a mark out of ten according to how dangerous they are.

Possible answers

1 <u>dog</u>sled <u>rac</u>ing	2 <u>snow</u>mobiling
3 <u>cross-country skiing</u>	4 <u>kite</u> skiing
5 <u>ski</u>ing	6 <u>snow</u>boarding
7 mountai<u>neer</u>ing	8 <u>ice</u> climbing

---

3 Turn down the sound, and allow students to watch the first part of the video before they decide what the rescue alert is.

Answer
3

4 Play the rest of the video with the sound, and ask students to answer the question.

Answer
The helicopter crew locate and rescue the man they are looking for. Dave, the missing snowmobiler, is unharmed but exhausted.

Videoscript

Narrator: The unforgiving weather and terrain means time is running out to find a man who has been lost on the mountain overnight.

State trooper (ST) 1: OK, let's go find this guy now.

Narrator: In the air, Helo 1 scours the terrain for any signs of Dave. But with no leads, the possibilities of where he could be are endless.

ST 1: Did John give you guys a pretty good idea of where he might be?

Rescue Base: He has no idea whatsoever.

Narrator: To make matters worse, Dave's tracks could be covered by last night's snow storm, making it impossible to track him.

Rescue Base: He said the wind was covering up the tracks as fast as they'd made 'em.

Narrator: From the air, they can easily mistake the trees and rocks for a human, or, just as easily, overlook him entirely.

ST 1: There's a few dark spots up there.

ST 2: Got 'em.

ST 1: They're just some rocks sticking out.

ST 2: Yeah, pretty small.

Narrator: Then, Helo 1 spots a set of faded tracks. But they lead up the crest of the mountain. If Dave went over the edge, it would mean a fall to almost certain death.

ST 1: If he got turned around he could easily have dropped down in there.

ST 2: They wouldn't have wanted to drop down into any of this.

ST 1: What's that to the left there?

ST 2: I think that's his snow-machine right there.

ST 1: Rescue Base to Helo 1. We've located a second snow-machine at the following co-ordinates – North 6, 1 ...

Narrator: Dave has seemingly abandoned his snow-machine. But spotting footprints from the air will be nearly impossible. Now, rescuers hope he hasn't strayed too far.

ST 1: Subject is on foot, but not with machine.

Rescue Base: So confirming, you saw the machine, but not the subject, over?

ST 1: That's affirmative.

ST 2: Nothing out there?

ST 1: No, I don't see anything out there.

ST 1: What's that out there?

ST 2: Got one dark spot over to the left there, see it? Right here.

ST 1: There he is, there he is.

ST 2: Rescue Base, Helo 1. We have the subject in sight.

Rescue Base: Is subject vertical and moving?

ST 1: That's affirmative.

Rescue Base: Team 3, Base, do you copy?

Team 3 leader: Go for Team 3.

Rescue Base: Do you copy the Helo is going to be picking up our subject?

Team 3: Roger, Roger.

ST 1: Rescue Base, we're landing at this time.

Rescue Base: Roger.

ST 2: Dave? Dave? Dave, how you doing?

Dave: Tired.

ST 1: You doing OK?

Dave: Any word from John?

ST 1: Yeah, we've got him down at the …

ST 2: He's back at the truck.

Dave: I tracked him for, last night, picked up his trail this morning; it came to the point I had to get the hell out of here.

ST 2: Yeah, you guys were kind of chasing each other round from the looks of the tracks.

Dave: You couldn't see anything.

ST 2: I understand. Yeah, it was a white-out last night. How you doing?

Dave: Well last night wasn't no party.

ST 1 and ST 2: Yeah.

Dave: It was blowing so hard.

ST 1 and ST 2: OK, yeah.

Dave: I was up on that ridge; did you see where I camped?

ST 2: I didn't see where you camped but we were looking.

Dave: I couldn't get off that ridge. You get on the edge and it was just – phew!

ST 2: Well this is it, we'll get you out of here.

Dave: We tried coming out, couldn't see five feet in front of you going up the hill.

Dave: Well, that wasn't no party last night, that's for sure. Wind blowing like … man it was cold. It was cold.

Narrator: Dave is finally on his way home. If not for the Alaska state troopers and volunteers, he may not have made it off this Talkeetna mountain top alive.

5 Students watch the video from beginning to end and decide if the statements are true or false.

Answers
1 T   2 T   3 F   4 F   5 T   6 T   7 T   8 T   9 F

6 Lead a short whole-class discussion about the relative dangers of snowmobiling.

7 Students work in pairs and decide what they might do. Listen in and check that they are familiar with the more common ways of making suggestions and coming up with ideas, e.g. *How about making an igloo? We should stay close together. We could always …* This leads into the ideas in the Ideas generator box.

This box focuses on the technique for brainstorming ideas. This is a way of coming up with a large number of ideas in a short space of time. The classic technique is not to discuss each idea as it comes up, but to generate your ideas first before ranking them or discussing them afterwards. Remind students that they shouldn't be rude or dismissive of their partner's initial ideas. When discussing topics in the exam, there has to be an obvious link between their ideas and the task that they have been given.

8 Students discuss the sports in exercise 2, but in relation to the topic given. They can reuse ideas that were discussed earlier as long as they relate to whether the sports are appropriate for school children. Elicit other factors they might want to take into account, e.g. whether the activities would be fun, expensive, difficult to organise, etc.

9 Students work alone and generate as many ideas as they can. The bullet points will guide students by helping them to consider the activities in the context of raising money.

10 Students discuss the three questions for a minute each, then choose the best activity.

11 Students reflect on their performance in exercise 10. It is important that students have a reasonably wide topic vocabulary for the type of topics that are likely to come up in the examination.

Vocabulary organiser 3, page 164

Answers

1
1 awesome	2 terrifying	3 reassuring
4 exhilarating	5 exhausting	

2
1 stakes	2 strengthen his resolve
3 atrocious	4 put on the line

3
1 din	2 distress call	3 extricated
4 daft	5 atrocious	6 put on the line
7 the stakes	8 strengthen my resolve	

4
1 I'm down to	2 get up to something	3 get down to (work)
4 I'm feeling down	5 not up to much	6 be down to

5
we've been having our problems

6
1 take for	2 take back	3 take after
4 take down	5 take on	6 take up
7 take over	8 take out	9 take to
10 take apart	11 take back	12 take out

Bank of English
Do not use *take*: (look on) the bright side; (make) a mountain out of a molehill; (make) or break it

Photocopiable activity instructions

Take it or leave it! (page 40)

Aim: to revise the different uses of phrasal verbs with *take*.

Instructions:

1 Photocopy page 40 and cut out each of the phrasal verbs and the definitions.

2 Organise the class into two teams and share the phrasal verbs between them, making sure that *take to* goes to one team, and *take down* goes to the other. Keep the definitions to read out yourself.

3 Tell the teams that the phrasal verbs they are holding can be used with more than one meaning according to the context. They must listen to each definition as you read it out, and decide, in their team, whether the definition fits one of their verbs or not. If they think it does, they shout 'take it'. If they think it does not, then they shout 'leave it'. Whichever team shouts correctly first, receives two points. Record their points on the board.

4 If a team shouts 'take it' correctly, then give them the definition, if a team shouts 'leave it' first, then place the definition on your desk.

5 Each phrasal verb has three definitions, except for *take to* and *take down*, which have only two. The winners will be the team that gains the highest number of points, or the first one to find all the definitions for their phrasal verbs.

Answers
a take up	b take off	c take on
d take in	e take down	f take to
g take back	h take off	i take in
j take on	k take out	l take off
m take in	n take to	o take on
p take out	q take back	r take up
s take on	t take off	u take out
v take back		

Intrepid explorers (page 41)

Aim: to practise using modals for speculation and suggestion.

Instructions:

1 Organise your students into three groups (or two, if your class is small).

2 Give each group a photocopy of one of the situations.

3 Ask them to read the information for their situation. Then, as a group, they should speculate and suggest possible solutions to their problem.

4 When they have discussed various possibilities, they should reach a decision about what to do next.

5 Each group reads out its situation, then reports and explains its decision to the rest of the class.

Take it or leave it!

take up	take out
take back	take in
take off	take to
take down	take on

a	start doing a new activity regularly
b	If someone's career does this, it suddenly becomes very successful
c	accept responsibility for something
d	If you do this to someone, you fool them or trick them
e	make notes (during a lesson, perhaps)
f	you like someone the first time you meet them
g	you regret saying something, and apologise
h	remove something from a shelf
i	allow someone who is in trouble to stay in your house
j	accept a new challenge or offer
k	invite someone to go with you to a restaurant, the cinema etc
l	an aeroplane leaves the ground
m	pay attention to something you hear and understand it
n	begin doing something as a habit
o	employ someone to do a job
p	obtain something by applying for it and paying the necessary fee
q	return something you have borrowed
r	use a particular amount of time or effort to do something
s	develop a new appearance
t	go away suddenly and unexpectedly
u	remove something, like a tooth, permanently
v	If something does this to you, it reminds you of the past

Intrepid explorers

Situation 1

You are a team of mountaineers taking part in an international competition to climb Everest. You were caught in a snowstorm, and have lost contact with base camp. Your tents have been almost completely covered by snow. One of your members has broken her ankle and needs medical attention. You have an emergency first aid kit and mountaineering equipment (skis and rope). Discuss your options and decide upon the best course of action.

Situation 2

You are a group of survivors from a plane crash. You have landed on an island which is covered in dense forest, but you don't know where you are. One of your group is badly injured and needs medical attention. It is mid-afternoon, and you need to decide what to do before nightfall, to make yourselves safe. You have an emergency first aid kit and a tool box. Discuss your options and decide upon the best course of action.

Situation 3

You are part of an environmental expedition team exploring the Amazon jungle. Your small group became interested in a particular kind of plant, and were collecting samples, when you got left behind by the rest of the team. The density of the jungle means that mobile phones cannot pick up a signal, and you have no compass with you. Your supplies of food and water are limited, but you have an emergency first aid kit and camping equipment. Discuss your options and decide upon the best course of action.

Situation 4

You are a group of friends who are out at sea on a small fishing boat. The captain of the boat has been taken ill (you think he has had a heart attack) and he is too unwell to drive the boat. You can't see land and you don't know where you are. None of you have any experience with any of the equipment. You have some supplies of water and food, and plenty of fresh fish! Discuss your options and decide upon the best course of action.

4 EUREKA!

Unit introduction

The topic of this unit is science and discovery. It covers anything to do with scientific discovery, technology, the past, the future, inventions, predictions, robots and dinosaurs. Most students are interested in some aspects of discovery and will probably enjoy using their imaginations.

Warm-up activity

Ask students to each think of one important scientific invention or discovery that is very important in their lives. Have a class vote as to which is the most important and discuss the reasons.

Getting started

1 The aim of this exercise is to generate interest in the subject, to see how much students already know and to introduce some important vocabulary. Students have to decide their own categories that can be used to organise the words. There is no one correct answer.

Possible answers

archaeology, palaeontology, prehistory (history)
biology, medicine, genetics, forensic science (biology)
electronics, inventions, IT (computers)
physics, mathematics, astronomy (mathematical)
chemistry, geology, forensic science (chemistry)

BACKGROUND: EUREKA!

Ask students if they understand the unit heading. Explain that 'Eureka' is an exclamation used as an interjection to celebrate a discovery. It is most famously attributed to Archimedes who is said to have uttered the word when, while bathing, he suddenly realised that the volume of an irregular object could be calculated by finding the volume of water displaced when the object was submerged in water. After making this discovery, it is said that he leapt out of his bathtub and ran naked through the streets of Syracuse.

→ Vocabulary organiser 4, exercise 1, page 165

Answers to Vocabulary organiser

1 palaeontology 2 forensic science 3 astronomy 4 prehistory

Reading multiple-matching texts

SCANNING TEXTS FOR INFORMATION

The purpose of this section is to teach students how to approach Part 8 of the Reading and Use of English paper, where they have to scan a number of texts for specific information. Emphasise that scanning is a useful technique, especially when you need to find something quickly.

2 Read the rubric with the class and ask students to read reviews A and B (on page 39) individually to scan for the information requested. Tell them to raise their hands as soon as they have finished, in order to encourage them to do the task quickly.

Answers

1 B   2 A   3 both

TEACHING IN PRACTICE: PRACTISING READING SKILLS

The reading texts provided are meant to be used in such a way that they develop the skills needed for students to pass the relevant part of the exam. By following the instructions and doing the tasks, students will learn how to handle any text in the exam, not just these. Therefore, it is not so important to analyse other aspects of the text, such as vocabulary, although this can be done later after the main tasks have been finished.

Degree of difficulty

Decrease the level: for weaker groups, allow students to work in pairs.

Increase the level: for stronger students, see who can find the answers first.

BACKGROUND: DINOSAURS

Dinosaurs were the dominant animals on land for over 160 million years, from the late Triassic period (about 230 million years ago) until the end of the Cretaceous period (65 million years ago), when most of them became extinct in the Cretaceous-Tertiary extinction event. Most paleontologists today regard birds as the only surviving dinosaurs. The term *dinosaur* was coined in 1842 by Sir Richard Owen and means 'terrible, powerful, wondrous lizard'.

3 Before students read the rest of the article on page 39, elicit as much information about dinosaurs as possible. Students should then do the exam task individually. Check the answers with the group and ask students to quote from the text directly to justify their answers.

Answers				
1 B	2 E	3 A	4 A	5 E
6 C	7 B	8 B	9 D	10 C

→ Vocabulary organiser 4, exercises 2 and 3, page 165

Answers to Vocabulary organiser
2

1 vague	2 avian	3 swift	4 predators
5 eroding	6 serpents	7 gestating	8 fertile

3
1 produce an image in someone's mind
2 an unpleasant death
3 to show that they were big and heavy and made a loud noise when they moved
4 to show that birds are small and light, unlike the dinosaurs
5 ducks, geese or even small children
6 beneath their physical appearance

Student's Book pages 40–41

Language development colourful language

1 Elicit answers from the group. Encourage them to refer back to the text if necessary.

Answer
A bolt from the blue means something that is very sudden and unexpected.

2 Encourage students to use their dictionaries for the next exercise. They should work alone or in pairs.

Answers				
1 b	2 c	3 a	4 a	5 b

→ Vocabulary organiser 4, exercise 4, page 165

Answers to Vocabulary organiser

1 black and blue	2 the black	3 red-handed	4 green with envy

Key word *tell*

3 Students should do this exercise individually or in pairs.

Answers						
1 b	2 f	3 a	4 g	5 c	6 d	7 e

VOCABULARY: *TELL*

If you **tell someone something**, you give them information.
Later, I returned to tell Phyllis our relationship was over.

If you **tell something** such as a joke, a story, or your personal experiences, you communicate it to other people using speech.
His friends say he was always quick to tell a joke.

If you **tell someone to do something**, you order or advise them to do it.
A passer-by told the driver to move his car so that it was not causing an obstruction.

If you **tell yourself something**, you put it into words in your own mind to persuade yourself about something.
'Come on', she told herself, 'you can do it!'.

If you can **tell what is happening**, you're able to judge correctly what is happening or what is true.
It was already impossible to tell where the bullet had entered the body.

If you can **tell one thing from another**, you are able to recognise the differences between them.
I can't really tell the difference between their policies and ours.

If you **tell**, you reveal or give away a secret. (INFORMAL)
Many of the children know who they are but are not telling.

If **facts or events tell you something**, they reveal certain information to you through ways other than speech.
The facts tell us that this is not true.

If an unpleasant or tiring experience **begins to tell**, it begins to have a serious effect.
The pressure began to tell as rain closed in after 20 laps.

Phrases

As far as I can tell or *so far as I could tell* indicates that what you are saying is based only on the information you have.
As far as I can tell, Jason is basically a nice guy.

I tell you, *I can tell you*, or *I can't tell you* adds emphasis to what you are saying. (INFORMAL)
I tell you this, I will not rest until that day has come.

You never can tell means that the future is always uncertain.
You never can tell what life is going to bring you.

If someone disagrees with you or refuses to do what you suggest and you are eventually proved to be right, you can say *I told you so*. (INFORMAL)
Her parents did not approve of her decision and, if she failed, her mother would say, 'I told you so.'

I'll tell you what or *I tell you what* introduces a decision. (SPOKEN)
I tell you what, I'll bring the water in a separate glass.

4 ⊙ 11 Students should read the dialogue before they listen. Ask if they can predict any of the phrases that may fill the gaps. After they listen, check their answers.

Answers		
1 a tell tale	2 Tell you what	3 kiss and tell
4 I told you so	5 you can never tell	6 can't tell you
7 As far as I can tell	8 only time will tell	

Audioscript 🔘 11

Kate: Hi Sally. I wanted to tell you about what happened to me yesterday, but I don't want you to think I'm being a tell tale.

Sally: Tell you what, why don't you tell me about it and I promise I won't kiss and tell.

Kate: I'll try. But I don't want you to say 'I told you so'!

Sally: Well, you can never tell …

Kate: I can't tell you how much it means to me that you're my friend.

Sally: As far as I can tell you're my friend too!

Kate: Yes, but only time will tell!

→ Vocabulary organiser 4, exercise 5, page 165

Answers to Vocabulary organiser
1 off, a   2 apart, b

Grammar the future

5 Students should underline the future forms in the sentences individually. Check answers with the group and ask students to name the future forms.

Answers
1 The icebergs <u>will melt</u> within the next 40 years. (future simple / *will*)
2 By the end of this week I <u>will have been working</u> here for ten years. (future perfect continuous)
3 This time next week <u>we'll be flying</u> to Mexico. (future continuous)
4 The match <u>starts</u> at 2.00 so you'd better hurry. (present simple)
5 <u>I'm going to visit</u> Julie after I've picked up my son. (future – *be going to* + inf)
6 James <u>will be</u> here for another hour. (future simple / *will*)
7 I <u>won't forget</u> to write to you. (future simple / *will* + *not*)
8 By the time you're ready everyone else <u>will have left</u>. (future perfect)
9 It looks like <u>it's going to be</u> one of those days! (future – *be going to* + inf)
10 <u>I'm meeting</u> Mark outside the cinema. (present continuous)

6 This task can be done as a whole class to check students' understanding of the different future forms, or students can attempt it first individually or in pairs.

Answers
a 4   b 6   c 1   d 7   e 10
f 5   g 9   h 3   i 8   j 2

→ Grammar reference 4.1, page 210

7 Do the first sentence with the class, then ask students to complete the exercise individually or in pairs.

Answers
1 about to pick; the point of picking
2 bound to pass; certain that John will pass
3 should be; time he was
4 chance that everyone will; doubt that anyone won't

Read the information in the box with the class. Ask them to identify which is the main clause and which is the subordinate clause in each sentence in exercise 9. Point out that the main clause is not always the first clause, but is usually the one that contains the subject and the main verb (for example, in sentence 3 the second clause is the main clause).

8 Read the rubric with the students. Students should do this individually.

Answers
1 while   2 By the time   3 As soon as   4 until
Main clause tenses:
1 future (*will*)   2 future perfect   3 future (*will*)   4 future (*will*)
Subordinate clause tenses:
1 simple present   2 simple present   3 simple present
4 present perfect

9 Students should do this individually.

Answers
1 b   2 d   3 c   4 a

→ Grammar reference 4.2, page 211

10 Students should attempt the task alone or in pairs. Then make sure everyone has understood the grammar here.

Answers
1 is (has been), will move   2 will not leave, tell
3 decide, will stop   4 will phone, arrive
5 get, will have left

11 Students can do this alone or in pairs. Check the answers with the whole group.

Answers
1 There ~~will have been~~ > There will be
~~are wanting~~ = will want (will be wanting)
2 ~~will be disappearing~~ > will have disappeared
spelling ~~will have been~~ > will be
Russian ~~will have come~~ > will come second
3 Automobiles ~~are~~ > will be cheaper
~~are going to be becoming~~ > will become (will have become)
4 ~~are to be used~~ > will be used
5 Cameras ~~will have been~~ > will be connected
telephones ~~are going to provide~~ > will provide
6 Strawberries ~~will be being as large~~ > will be as large
~~it won't not~~ > it will not (it won't)

12 Discuss the question with the class.

13 Brainstorm ideas for predictions and discuss the topic with the whole class to finish the lesson.

See *The Time Machine* photocopiable activity, page 49.

Student's Book pages 42–43

Speaking three-way task

1 Discuss this question with the whole class. Notice that there will usually be more fluent speakers who will offer their views. Other students may be more reticent. The teacher should encourage the students who have not spoken to express their opinions. With gentle prompting, all students should be able to participate in the discussion.

Audioscript ⊙ 12

Interlocutor:	In the future, do you think it will be essential to know how to use a computer to get a job in your country, Fernando?
Student A:	No, I think there will always be a need for people who don't know how to use a computer. Computers cannot do everything – for example, we still need bus drivers, and shop assistants, farmers, erm … craftsmen, and, although technology may help them, it's not an essential aspect of those jobs.
Interlocutor:	What do you think, Maria?
Student B:	I agree with that point. Er …
Student A:	And … erm, I also think that at some point, technology will have given us all it has to offer, and after that, people will be looking for alternatives. I mean, even today, you see that more and more people actually want to cycle to work instead of driving, or go to the gym more instead of watching TV. Technology has taken over our lives so much, we are almost fed up with it. What do you think?
Student B:	Yes, er … that sounds like an interesting point. Erm …
Interlocutor:	Thank you. That is the end of the test.

2 Organise the class into pairs to discuss the question. Wherever possible try to have one confident speaker with one less confident speaker. Tell the class that you want each student to try to speak an equal amount and that they should try to help each other if necessary.

3 Students remain in their pairs and discuss the topic as instructed. The student who started second last time should now begin first. Go round the class listening to each pair, and give encouragement. After they have all practised discussing the point, ask for volunteer pairs to demonstrate to the rest of the class.

See *The Nutty Professor* photocopiable activity, page 50.

Listening getting the gist

4 Discuss the topic with the class. The purpose is to lead in to the listening topic of exercise 5: scientific inventions.

5 ⊙ 13 Play the recording. Students complete the task individually. Check the answers with the group. Point out that not all of the key words they hear will accurately describe the invention. Some words will probably be distractors

> **Possible answers**
> Speaker 2: rich had them, big things, size of briefcase, now fit in palm / hand
> Speaker 3: greatest invention ever, no vehicles without it, except monorails
> Speaker 4: amazing, fun, housework, zoom round the house, toy
> Speaker 5: opportunities for research, communication, kids, homework, library

Audioscript ⊙ 13

Speaker 1:	Well, I don't know where I'd be without it, to tell the truth. There's just no other way to get around these days, unless you want the stress and pollution brought on by driving in the city.
Speaker 2:	At first, I hated them. Only the rich and pretentious seemed to have them – do you remember what they were like then? Great big unwieldy things, almost the size of a briefcase. Now of course they fit in the palm of your hand and I'd be lost without one.

Speaker 3:	It's probably the greatest invention of all time because just imagine where we'd be without it. I mean, there wouldn't be vehicles of any kind – except monorails perhaps.
Speaker 4:	It's amazing – and great fun too. First time I've actually enjoyed doing the housework. Marjory can get on with her writing and I just zoom round the house with my new toy!
Speaker 5:	As far as my family is concerned, it's the best invention there's ever been, because it's really made a difference to our lives. It gives us so many opportunities for research, plus we use it all the time for communication, and the kids can do their homework without having to go to the library. But I know not everyone feels the same way.

6 ⊙ **14** Tell students to read the rubric. Ask them what they should do next and elicit that they should read the questions, underline key words and predict what they think each person might talk about. Then play the recording once. Students should work individually to complete both tasks.

TEACHING IN PRACTICE: LISTENING AGAIN

After one listening ask the class to raise their hands if they managed to complete all the questions. Ask how many students feel they don't need to listen again. Some students may well raise their hands, confident that one listening is enough. However, very often students do not check their work and they do make mistakes. Tell the class that you are going to play the recording a second time anyway and that they should all check their answers. Afterwards, ask if anyone changed any of their answers during the second listening.
Play the recording again. After the second listening check the answers with the class. Tell students to turn to the audioscript on page 244 and underline the correct answers.

Answers

1 B	2 E	3 C	4 A	5 F
6 B	7 G	8 E	9 A	10 C

Audioscript ⊙ 14

Speaker 1:	Well, I don't know where I'd be without it, to tell the truth. There's just no other way to get around these days, unless you want the stress and pollution brought on by driving in the city. I live out in the suburbs, so it's good exercise. And of course, ecologically speaking, I know I'm doing my bit to save the planet. I'm setting an example for the kids I teach as well, although you do occasionally get one of them shouting out something clever as their teacher goes by. Just because they're stuck on a double-decker bus in rush hour traffic. I know which one I'd rather use.
Speaker 2:	At first I hated them. Only the rich and pretentious seemed to have them – do you remember what they were like then? Great big unwieldy things, almost the size of a briefcase. Now, of course, they fit in the palm of your hand and I'd be lost without one. I have to spend so much of my day visiting sites, negotiating with clients, co-ordinating workers and then back to the office to go over designs, or tweak a plan. I use it to check the time, do quick calculations, store

reminders. And then of course wherever I am, Harry or the kids can find me if they need to tell me something or to find out what time I'll be home for dinner. In the old days they would just have had to leave messages all over the place.

Speaker 3:	It's probably the greatest invention of all time because just imagine where we'd be without it. I mean, there wouldn't be vehicles of any kind – except monorails perhaps. Boats would be OK, but planes wouldn't be able to take off. We'd all be riding horses – good for the environment, maybe, but not very convenient these days. In fact, it's quite obvious that we'd still be stuck in the dark ages if some bright spark hadn't come up with it. I know most people would probably say the most important invention was television, or the computer, or something, but I don't think we would even have them if this hadn't come first.
Speaker 4:	It's amazing – and great fun too. First time I've actually enjoyed doing the housework. Marjory can get on with her writing and I just zoom round the house with my new toy!. Compared to our old one, this has loads of advantages. For one thing, you don't have to carry a heavy load around the house with you; secondly, there are no bags to change – you just empty the bin every now and then; thirdly, it doesn't smell out the house because the actual engine is down in the basement; and fourthly, it's quieter too. There are several outlets in the house that automatically switch on when you plug in, but the hose is nine metres long anyway, so it reaches every corner.
Speaker 5:	As far as my family is concerned, it's the best invention there's ever been, because it's really made a difference to our lives. It gives us so many opportunities for research, plus we use it all the time for communication, and the kids can do their homework without having to go to the library. It provides entertainment as well as knowledge, and they enjoy it too. It keeps them off the streets, off the TV and I think they learn a lot. OK, granted, there is a downside, because you don't always know how accurate the information is, and some people seem to get a kick from being abusive, but we try to teach the children how to deal with all that.

Use of English prefixes

PREFIXES

Ask the class if they know what a prefix is and then draw their attention to the definition and examples in the box.

7 Students can work in pairs or individually. For each group they need to find one prefix that can be used to complete all the words.

Answers

1 il	2 im	3 en	4 in	5 ir	6 multi
7 un	8 re	9 ultra	10 sub	11 pre	12 dis

Do this as a class activity and check the answers with the class.

Answers

1 imprisonment	2 resurfaced	3 unhappily

8 Tell the class to read the text once through before they do the exam task. Elicit that the text is about a mysterious ancient Greek computer that was discovered in a shipwreck.

Answers

1 reconstruct	2 astronomical	3 precision	4 inscriptions
5 Astonishingly	6 complexity	7 comparable	8 disappeared

→ Vocabulary organiser 4, exercise 6, page 165

Answers to Vocabulary organiser

1 e	2 f	3 h	4 a	5 d/g	6 c	7 g/b	8 b

Student's Book pages 44–45

Writing an essay – using the notes provided

1 Have a class discussion about the questions. Then ask students to read the Exam spotlight box. Make sure they realise that Part 1 is always an essay, always takes the same form, and that students have to answer this question.

2 Ask students to read the rubric and underline the relevant words and phrases.

Possible answers

research scientist, lecture, future, statistics, survey, two areas, future development, benefit humans most, provide reasons, own words

3 Ask students to read the rubric, then complete the task and discuss the opinions in pairs.

Answers

automation: robots will get all the best jobs in the future
medical advances: couples should be allowed to choose the sex of their babies
improved life expectancy: society cannot support increasing numbers of old people.

4 Ask students to read the two paragraphs, then elicit answers to the questions.

Answers

Paragraph 1 argues that improved life expectancy in the population is mainly going to cause problems.
Paragraph 2 sees improved life expectancy as a positive development.

5 Ask students to follow the instructions in pairs.

Answers

Paragraph 1: a number of problems for society; the difficulties health services will face in their efforts to care for elderly people with dementia and Alzheimer's; reports in the media about the poor quality of care.
Paragraph 2: people would like to live longer; the good thing is that people will be healthier in their old age and fewer resources will be needed.

6 Ask students to work in pairs and discuss the information in the essay.

Answers

The second paragraph: '… finding a cure for diseases such as malaria and cancer would be more advantageous to humans than any other aspect of scientific progress'. The reasons: 'because it would save so many lives'.

7 Ask students to complete this task individually.

Answers

There are examples of *going to*, present continuous, future simple, future perfect, hypothetical forms *would* and *should*, future passive, future continuous.
The differences in meaning – sometimes very subtle – help the writer to express nuanced opinions.

8 Ask students to look back at exercises 4 and 6 and find the phrases that correspond to the percentages.

Answers

65%: the majority of people / most people
40%: quite a few people / a considerable number of people
20%: not many people

9 Students should read the task, discuss the comments and give their own opinions. Elicit the number of features that they must discuss in the essay, and what else they have to do. (They must write about two of the three features, explain whether they think the changes will be negative or positive, and provide reasons to support their opinions. They should also use their own words as far as possible, and write between 220 and 260 words.) Then they should plan an outline for an essay, and either write it in class or as homework.

Student's Book pages 46–47

Review 1

Answers

1

1 B	2 D	3 B	4 A	5 C
6 D	7 B	8 C	9 A	10 C

2

1 have moved, went, hadn't been, decided, have opened / opened, is doing
2 am going, was coming, forgot, will have to, are going to, really liked, made
3 did it happen, was riding, was, was shining, could, came, crashed

3

1 skipped	2 provoked	3 instigating
4 bounded / leapt / clambered	5 hop	6 prompted
7 marches	8 embarking on	9 wades
10 initiated		

4

1 get, will have finished	2 will be conducted
3 has finished / finishes, will be able	4 am going to tell, will believe / believes
5 will be trekking	6 will no longer use / be using
7 am seeing, are thinking	8 is taking, is bound to

5

1 has been able to dance	2 might have been friends for
3 has been rumoured that	4 they had been engaged for
5 may be regarded / viewed with	
6 can't have seen Paul with	

6

1 as	2 ago	3 like	4 Instead
5 there	6 in	7 so	8 might / may

7

1 down	2 an eyelid	3 the slate clean	4 rein
5 take	6 down to	7 wild	8 scratch

Vocabulary organiser 4, page 165

Answers

1

1 palaeontology	2 forensic science	3 astronomy	4 prehistory

2

1 vague	2 avian	3 swift	4 predators
5 eroding	6 serpents	7 gestating	8 fertile

3

1 produce an image in someone's mind
2 an unpleasant death
3 to show that they were big and heavy and made a loud noise when they moved
4 to show that birds are small and light, unlike the dinosaurs
5 ducks, geese or even small children
6 beneath their physical appearance

4

1 black and blue	2 the black	3 red-handed	4 green with envy

5

1 off, a	2 apart, b

6

1 e	2 f	3 h	4 a
5 d / g	6 c	7 g / b	8 b

Bank of English

1 technophobe	2 technique	3 technology	4 techno
5 technical support	6 technician	7 Technicolor	8 technicality

Photocopiable activity instructions

The Time Machine part 1 (page 49)

Aim: to use the future tenses and forms as much as possible.

Instructions:

1 Organise the class into pairs and give each pair a copy of the photocopiable activity.

2 Tell them that they have to take turns imagining that they could travel forward in time to the dates in the pictures but before they go, they should tell their partner what they expect to find when they get there. One partner should be pessimistic, and expect only the worst, while the other should be full of optimism about what they will find.

3 Student 1 uses future forms to discuss the future concerning the points shown. For example: *Fifty years from now I think the Earth's climate will …*

4 Student 2 should ask questions to establish as much as possible about what Student 1 expects to find. Student 2 should also express disagreement: *I don't agree with you. In 200 years I think …* They should then swap roles for the next picture.

The Nutty Professor (page 50)

Aim: to practise paraphrasing and expressing ideas in different ways.

Instructions:

1 Organise the class into two teams. Explain that a Nutty Professor wants to tell the world about his work, but he can never remember the right words to use.

2 Photocopy the activity and cut out each list of words. Select one person from each team to be 'speaker' and give them one list of words. Keep a copy of the lists yourself and have a stopwatch to time them.

3 The first speaker begins. He or she has one minute to communicate as many of the words on the list as he or she can, using synonyms or definitions only.

4 As soon as someone on the team shouts out the right word the speaker moves on to another word on the list. He or she can choose any word in any order. If they do not know what a word means or how to communicate it, they should say 'pass' and move on.

5 Keep score of the number of words correctly communicated and cross them off your list.

6 When a minute is up, the other team repeats the game, with another list.

The Time Machine (part 1)

50 years from now

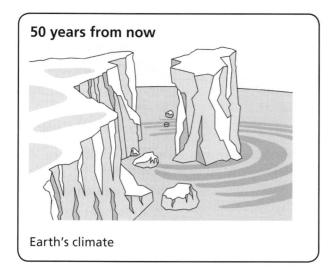

Earth's climate

200 years from now

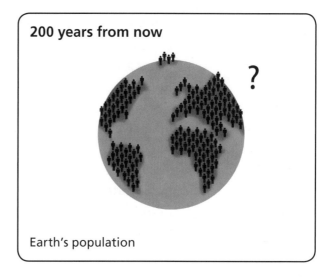

Earth's population

500 years from now

Earth's resources

1,000 years from now

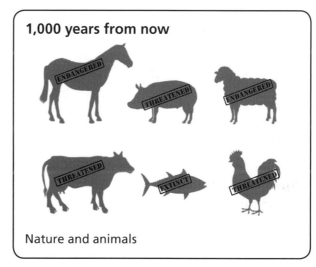

Nature and animals

5,000 years from now

Technology

10,000 years from now

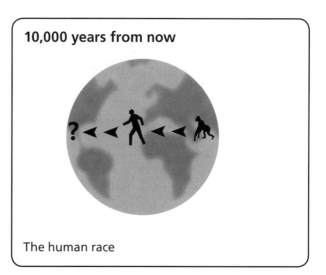

The human race

The Nutty Professor

Nouns	Verbs and phrasal verbs	Adjectives	Expressions
android	astound	aerial	a bolt from the blue
archaeology	construct	anatomical	black card
aristocracy	detect	avian	black list
artificial life	disintegrate	bureaucratic	black mark
astronomy	dissolve	compelling	blue around the gills
automobile	emit	concise	blue in the face
complexity	envision	contrasting	blue moon
device	eradicate	cyber	bring to an abrupt end
diversity	erode	extensive	catch someone red handed
eclipse	expose	fertile	eureka
evolution	flutter	kinetic	green fingers
extinction	inscribe	legendary	green with envy
flora and fauna	meditate	legible	in the red
forensic science	observe	legitimate	playful spirit
fossil	preoccupy	literate	red herring
galaxy	preserve	marine	red tape
genetics	resemble	medieval	seeing red
geology	salvage	mobile	sticky end
graphite	scan	mutable	the grass always looks greener on the other side
impact	seek	obscure	to take something lightly
inhabitant	span	pessimistic	under the skin
intervention	thunder	polluted	
inventions	unpick	profound	
mammal	unravel	provincial	
mercury	conjure up	radioactive	
meteorite	date back to	rational	
Milky Way	get on with	redundant	
mollusc	get through	resolute	
natural selection	give rise to	rigorous	
orbit	gloss over	sane	
organism	jot down	simultaneous	
palaeontology	put back together	soaring	
phenomenon	section off	superfluous	
philosopher	tell apart	swift	
predator	tell off	vague	
prediction	wipe out	vast	
prehistory		viral	

Unit introduction

The topic of this unit is internet crime, DNA profiling, road and fire safety.

Internet crime is the fastest growing type of crime in modern society. As students make regular use of the Internet, we decided to focus on this aspect of crime. Similarly, DNA profiling is a very fashionable theme in many TV detective series.

Warm-up activity

This activity revises vocabulary connected with crime.

1 Write the following list of crimes on the board: *arson, burglary, fraud, hacking, kidnapping, manslaughter, mugging, murder, shoplifting*. Students should be familiar with these terms.

2 Organise the class into two groups. Tell them you are going to describe several different crimes that have taken place recently. In their groups, they have to identify each crime. The first team to identify the crime gets a point. If a team identifies a crime incorrectly, they lose a point. Use this dialogue as a model.

Teacher: *On Thursday evening, someone set fire to the local secondary school. It is believed to have been a student.*

Student: *Is that arson?*

Getting started

1 Ask your students to look at the photo. Elicit what is happening in it. Discuss the meanings of the words in the box.

Answer
computer hacking

Reading gapped texts

2 Ask your students to read the rubric and the headline. Make sure they know the literal meaning of *worm* and *woodpecker*. Elicit ideas about the subject of the article. Do not give a definite answer yet.

3 Tell students to read through the first paragraph fairly quickly, and find out who the *woodpeckers* are. Now ask students who or what *worms* might be.

Answers
Woodpeckers are members of an anti-virus team of experts, and worms are self-replicating computer programs, which use a network to send copies of themselves to other nodes (computers on the network). They are able to do this without any user intervention.

EXAM SPOTLIGHT

Explain that in the gapped text task more than one option sometimes appears to be suitable for a particular gap. This is the case with options a–c on page 241. This is intentional. The aim is to highlight the fact that students must also look at the paragraph which follows the gap, and not make rash judgements when making their choices. Allow your students time to make their choices before giving feedback. The aim of exercises 3–6 is to encourage students to consider the options for each gap carefully, and to highlight the importance of checking their choices.

Answers
a possible: 'they' refers to the 'team of young computer programmers'
b not possible: 'Inspired by such impressive surroundings' contradicts the reference to the 'gloomy tower block'
c possible: 'It' can be the 'gloomy tower block', which also corresponds with 'this dark skyscraper'

4 Tell your students to read the paragraph in the text which follows the gap, and decide which option of a and c on page 241 is correct.

Answer
C is correct. A is not correct, as the programmers are working to eradicate crimeware, not develop it. The paragraph which follows defines the new kind of 'power struggle' they face.

SUPPORTING POINTS IN AN ARGUMENT

Tell students to read the information in the box. In connection with point c, explain that an article often includes references to experts' opinions, in order to strengthen a point the writer is making. The full name and title will be given the first time they are mentioned.

5 Tell students to read the rubric for exercise 5 and consider what sort of supporting information they would expect to follow such a paragraph.

Answers

The following information might be expected to give more details on how the task 'is proving increasingly difficult', e.g. background information or statistical examples.

6 Ask the students to read the main text and predict which of the types of supporting points they would expect in each gap. Allow students to discuss their choices and ask questions.

Possible answers

1 a or b
2 c (it follows on from *with good reason, say experts*)
3 a (it follows on from *research published last year*)
4 b or c (information about *Brain*, or an expert commenting on *Brain*)
5 a or c (more statistics, or the response of another expert)
6 c (it follows on from *some experts say*)

TEXT ORGANISATION FEATURES: COMPARISON

Tell your students to read the information in the box and find the example in the text.

Answer

After missing paragraph 3: 'It is all a far cry from the earliest days of hacking'.

7 Ask your students to read the exam task rubric and complete the task. Allow them time to do this. In feedback, point out that in gap 4, paragraph E initially appears to be possible. Students' attention needs to be drawn to the fact that the paragraph which follows doesn't really tie in with it, so paragraph F is the correct choice.

Answers

1 D	2 B	3 G	4 F	5 A	6 C

→ Vocabulary organiser 5, exercise 1, page 166

Vocabulary organiser answers

programmer: a person who creates and develops computer programs
virus: a computer program that introduces itself into a system, and alters or destroys information
crimeware: computer software which introduces viruses into a system
antidote: a solution to the problem of a computer virus
cyber-criminal: a person who perpetrates crime on the Internet
cyber-crime: crime connected with the Internet
hacking: the act of illegally breaking into computer systems in order to gain secret information

See *How to avoid catching a virus* photocopiable activity, page 60.

Student's Book pages 50–51

Language development

phrasal verbs

1 Remind students of the warm-up activity they did. Elicit a list of crimes, and then quickly elicit any words students know to do with punishment (e.g. *arrest someone for, charge someone with, sentence someone to* etc).

Tell students to quickly read through the report. Elicit what it is about. Students work in pairs to complete the report with the particles from the box. Allow three minutes for this.

Answers

1 of	2 with	3 to	4 of	5 in	6 of
7 with	8 for	9 to	10 to	11 of	12 to

→ Vocabulary organiser 5, exercise 2, page 166

Vocabulary organiser answers

1 suspected Larry Jones of committing
2 accused Wayne of stealing
3 arrested Jones
4 confessed / admitted to robbing
5 denied helping
6 charged the couple with committing
7 convicted Larry of
8 sentenced him to three years imprisonment.

phrasal verbs with *turn*

2 Ask students to match the phrasal verbs to the definitions without referring back to the text. Elicit answers and give feedback.

Answers

1 turned out to be   2 turned (them) into

3 Ask your students to read through the sentences and complete them.

Answers

1 in	2 to	3 over	4 in	5 down	6 on	7 off	8 out

→ Vocabulary organiser 5, exercise 3, page 166

Vocabulary organiser answers

1 to	2 in	3 off	4 over	5 down

Key word *law*

4 This task can be done as pairwork in class, if dictionaries are available, or as homework. Check student's answers using the definitions in the box.

VOCABULARY: KEY WORD *LAW*

above the law: believing yourself to be too important to obey the law: *One opposition member of parliament accuses the government of wanting to be above the law …*

against the law: illegal: *It is against the law to park your car on double yellow lines in Britain.*

break the law: disobey a law: *You have broken the law by speeding.*

by law: the law states what you can or can't do: *By law all restaurants must display their prices outside.*

enforce a law: ensure it is obeyed: *It is the responsibility of the police to enforce the law in this country.*

lay down the law: insist upon the law: *They were traditional parents, who believed in laying down the law for their offspring.*

obey the law: follow the rules: *As a police officer, you should set an example, and obey the law at all times.*

take the law into your own hands: refuse to wait for the legal system to work: *The speeding motorist was pinned to the ground by angry locals who took the law into their own hands.*

a law-abiding person: someone who obeys the law rightfully: *The Prime Minister said: 'I am anxious that the law should protect decent law-abiding citizens and their property …'*

Law and order: generally accepted laws: *If there were a breakdown of law and order, the army might be tempted to intervene.*

Law-enforcement agencies: officials responsible for catching criminals: *We need to restore respect for the law-enforcement agencies.*

Lawsuit: a case in court concerning a dispute: *The dispute culminated last week in a lawsuit against the government.*

Within the law: not doing anything unacceptable to authorities: *I've always kept within the law, I just avoid paying more tax than I need to.*

5 This exercise offers practice using items from exercise 4, so you may wish to set the two exercises together as homework.

Answers

1 law enforcement	2 breaking the law	3 are above the law
4 lawsuit	5 by law	6 law and order
7 is against the law	8 laying down the law	

→ Vocabulary organiser 5, exercise 4, page 166

Vocabulary organiser answers

1 B	2 C	3 D	4 A	5 B

Grammar verbs followed by infinitive or *-ing*

6 Ask students to read the verbs in the box and categorise them according the structure that follows. You may wish to do this exercise in open class, eliciting the structures in turn, to ensure that students categorise the verbs correctly.

Answers

a advise someone, agree, arrange, ask, attempt, choose, dare, decide, encourage, expect, fail, invite, order, persuade, pretend, refuse, remind, threaten

b dare (= modal) *'Don't you dare do that!'* and *'How dare you say that?'*; let

c appreciate, avoid, deny, enjoy, face, involve, practise

TEACHING IN PRACTICE: ELICITING INFORMATION

This section aims to revise and consolidate structures that your students should already be familiar with. Elicit things such as definitions and example sentences from them as much as possible. For example, in exercise 6, if some students don't know the meaning of a word, ask if anyone else in the class can explain it before doing so yourself.

7 Tell students to complete the sentences with a verb from exercise 6. Make sure they realise that more than one verb may be possible.

Answers

1 practise	2 threatened	3 decided / arranged / agreed
4 contemplated	5 denied	

8 Ask students to read each pair of sentences, and work out the difference in meaning or use between them. This could be done as pair work or individually.

Answers

1 *I don't like doing* is a statement about something you enjoy or don't enjoy. *I don't like to …* means I don't think it is right to do something in this way.

2 *I remember doing* means I have a memory of something I did. *I remembered to do* means that I didn't forget to do something I had planned to do.

3 *go on doing …* means to continue doing something for a long time. This implies criticism; *go on to do …* means to move on to another activity.

4 *I mean to do …* means that I intend to do something. Used in the past tense, it usually implies that I forgot. *It means doing …* means an activity involves doing something, or requires you to do something.

5 *stop to do something* means to interrupt one activity in order to do something else; *stop doing something* means to stop the activity I'm doing at the moment.

9 Ask students to read the exam rubric and complete the exercise. Remind them to check the context in order to ensure that they use the correct structure in each case. Allow them five minutes for this.

Answers
1 threatened to shoot the old lady
2 denied taking / having taken the wallet
3 Mrs Smith remembered noticing anything unusual
4 don't like to phone her
5 didn't mean to set
6 persuaded his wife to

→ Grammar reference 5, page 211

See *Verb noughts and crosses* photocopiable activity, page 61.

Student's Book pages 52–53

Listening sentence completion

1 These introductory tasks introduce some of the abbreviations used in the listening activity. Elicit what students know about forensic science and DNA analysis.

Possible answer
Forensic science is the study of physical evidence found at the scene of a crime in order to help the police in their investigation. DNA analysis is the study of human tissue to see if a person is connected with a crime.

2 Students do this in pairs.

Answers
1 b   2 b

3 ⊙ 15 Tell students to read the rubric. The talk they are going to hear describes the different methods forensic scientists use to analyse DNA samples, and contains quite a lot of technical information. Tell them they only need to extract the information relevant to the task. Play the recording.

Answers
1 PCR testing   2 STR testing   3 RFLP testing

Audioscript ⊙ 15
... The three main types of forensic DNA testing, then, are all extremely useful, but each has its own limitations. The first type, RFLP testing, requires large amounts of DNA from a recent sample. Therefore, old evidence from a crime scene is quite unlikely to be suitable for RFLP testing. Furthermore, warm and moist conditions usually cause DNA to become degraded quicker, so samples from crime scenes near water are unsuitable. The second type, STR testing, can be used on smaller amounts of DNA, but is still subject to the same limitations as the first type.

The third type, PCR-based testing, has certain advantages over the other two, in that it requires smaller amounts of DNA, and the sample may be partially degraded. However, it still has limitations which must not be ignored. PCR testing can easily become contaminated, both at the crime scene and in the lab. This can affect the test results, particularly if lab regulations are not strict.

4 Ask students to read the rubric. Play the recording again. Allow students time to consider their answer.

Possible answer
There are limitations to DNA testing and it is open to error.
No, it is not necessary to understand all the terminology.

5 ⊙ 16 Tell the students to listen to the short extract and decide which word they think would be the most likely to have been missed out in the exam exercise.

Answer
(DNA) database or (strong) deterrent

Audioscript ⊙ 16
Personally, I see the idea of a national DNA database with everyone's DNA on record as a necessary evil. Yes, it has its risks, and there would need to be strict legislation to protect people, but if it were universal, surely it would eliminate the possibility of suspects being picked out at will.

More importantly, the risk of almost certain detection would act as a powerful deterrent to first-time offenders, and so reduce the risk of innocent people becoming the victims of a violent crime.

6 Ask students to read the sentences in exercise 7. Elicit the type of word needed for each gap, such as a noun, verb, adjectival phrase, or a statistic.

Answers
1 noun (an investigation technique)   2 year
3 noun (a group of people)   4 adjective (possibly negative)
5 adjective (possibly negative)   6 adjective or phrase
7 a number   8 adjective

7 ⊙ 17 Explain that students are now going to complete the exam task. Play the recording. Pause for ten seconds, then play the recording again. Allow the students time at the end to finish writing in the gaps.

Answers
1 fingerprinting   2 1983   3 media   4 idealistic
5 unreliable   6 degraded   7 37 million   8 perfect

Audioscript ⊙ 17
Since the mid-1980s, when Sir Alec Jeffreys first discovered that every human being has his or her own unique genetic make-up, DNA profiling has replaced fingerprinting as the chief forensic tool in criminal investigations. Technological advances enable new techniques for testing DNA to be

developed all the time, and forensic scientists are now able to solve cases from years ago. The recent conviction of John Lloyd, who attacked a number of women between 1983 and 1986, is a case in point.

As a result of all the media attention, the discipline has come to be seen as glamorous, with forensic scientists now occupying centre stage in TV detective series, rather than detective inspectors. Many people assume that DNA testing provides unquestionable proof of a person's guilt or innocence, leaving no room for error. Yet the controversy now surrounding the case of Barry George, convicted in 2001 for the murder of TV presenter Jill Dando, brings to light a number of problems with this idealistic point of view. One of the jurors expressed doubt about the conviction, and gained support from several forensic experts who believe the forensic evidence presented in the case should be regarded as 'unreliable' and therefore inconclusive. And this is not the only example where forensic evidence has led specialists to the wrong conclusion.

Don't get me wrong, I'm not trying to suggest that DNA profiling has no place in criminal investigations! But what we need to clarify from the outset is not simply the merits of DNA profiling – and they are indeed many – but also, its limitations. We must dispense with the idealised, glamorous view presented on TV, and rather examine in an objective manner exactly what DNA testing can and cannot do. The processes involved in DNA testing are complex.

The most effective DNA testing procedure to date is STR analysis. It has a greater ability to distinguish differences than the earlier type of testing, RFLP analysis, yet can be used on a smaller sample. This method analyses a DNA sample in greater detail, so there is less chance of two individuals giving the same results. STR analysis is now used together with the 'polymerase chain reaction', or PCR, as it is commonly known, a process which enables DNA contained in a degraded sample to be analysed. The present technology allows scientists to find DNA matches with odds estimated at 1 in 37 million, but this does not mean that it is not possible for individuals to have similar matches.

For this reason, strict rules must be maintained within the laboratory, and while technology has enhanced the level of accuracy, it is not perfect, nor should we rule out the possibility of human error during the process. Forensic scientists are often under pressure to produce results quickly, and this can lead to errors in judgement.

8 Organise the class into four groups and ask them to brainstorm arguments for and against the DNA database.

Extension

Organise the class into two groups, and allocate the arguments in favour of the database to one group, and those against to the other. Ask each team to present their arguments, then take a vote.

Use of English gapped sentences

Ask students to read the Exam spotlight box, and point out that prepositions are one of the areas of language tested in Part 2. Stress the importance of learning new words along with any prepositions that normally follow them.

9 Ask students to complete the exercise in pairs. Elicit and check answers.

Answers

1 in	2 from	3 at	4 to	5 of

10 Elicit the preposition that can be used in each gap, and ask students to provide examples (e.g. *I'm grateful to my family for being very supportive*).

Answers

1 to	2 of	3 in	4 at	5 to

11 Ask students to complete the exercise in pairs. Elicit and check answers.

Answers

1 for	2 by	3 on	4 over	5 to

12 Ask students to read the rubric and do the task in pairs. Point out that fewer prepositions would be tested in the actual exam. Elicit answers and give feedback.

Answers

1 of	2 however	3 for	4 for
5 comes	6 out	7 from	8 order

→ Vocabulary organiser 5, exercise 5, page 166

Vocabulary organiser answers

1 to	2 from	3 to	4 of	5 for

Speaking giving personal information

13 🔘 18 Ask your students to read the rubric. Tell them to listen carefully to how the two candidates answer each question, and to compare how well they both perform.

Answers

Beret is fluent, and gives full answers, whereas Juan doesn't say very much, and gives very short answers.

Audioscript 🔘 18

Interlocutor:	Hello. My name is Jill Simpson, and this is my colleague, Helen Jones. And your names are …?
Juan:	Juan.
Beret:	Beret.
Interlocutor:	OK. First of all, we'd like to know something about you. Where are you from, Juan?
Juan:	Spain.
Interlocutor:	And you, Beret?
Beret:	I'm from a small village on the edge of the Norwegian fjords.
Interlocutor:	And what are you doing here in England, Beret?

Beret:	I'm studying accountancy at the London School of Economics, and generally having a good time!
Interlocutor:	And you, Juan?
Juan:	Er, I'm working, and trying to improve my English.
Interlocutor:	So, how important is sport and exercise to you, Juan?
Juan:	I play football every Saturday, and I train twice a week.
Interlocutor:	And how about you, Beret? Is sport and exercise important to you?
Beret:	Oh yes, very important. I think we all need to do some form of exercise to stay healthy. Personally, I do aerobics at a gym three times a week, and also I cycle to my lessons every day … I wear, um a … how do you say, scarf over my nose and mouth, to stop breathing the smoke from the cars.
Interlocutor:	If you had the opportunity to take up a new activity, what would you like to do … er, Beret?
Beret:	Well, there are lots of things I'd like to do if I had more time … and money, of course! … But, I think I'd really love to go horse-riding. I love horses, and I like being out in the fresh air. It's difficult here in London, though, and very expensive.
Interlocutor:	Yes, indeed. How about you, Juan? What would you choose to do?
Juan:	Er … Can you repeat the question, please?
Interlocutor:	What new activity would you like to do, if you had the chance?
Juan:	I'd like to play water polo.
Interlocutor:	That's interesting. Why?
Juan:	Er … because I like swimming.
Interlocutor:	… OK. Now, in this next part of the test, I'm going to show you …

EXAM SPOTLIGHT

Ask students to read the information in the Exam spotlight box. To check they have understood the advice given, ask a few of them a personal question about themselves.

14 Tell your students to listen to the recording again and make notes on how Beret expands her answers.

Answers

1 Beret gives information about the location of her village, not just the country she's from.
2 She doesn't just give the reason for being in Britain, but also includes personal information.
3 She expresses an opinion about the importance of exercise, and then says what she does to keep fit.
4 She not only says what she would like to do, but also why.

15 Students should use their imagination to expand on Juan's answers. Elicit answers and give feedback.

Student's Book pages 54–55

Writing a report

1 Ask your students to read the questions. Elicit answers, and allow some discussion.

2 Ask students to read the box about accuracy and organisation. Explain that the task question often indicates how students should organise their answer. Ask students to read the exam task and write four paragraph headings, based on the question.

Possible answers

1 Introduction
2 Traffic in the area
3 Existing safety measures (or Signals, crossings and cycle lanes)
4 Recommendations

3 Ask students to read the paragraphs and decide which one is the most suitable, and why. They should think about the purpose of an introduction and how appropriate the language is.

Answer

c

4 Elicit what is wrong with the other two options and give feedback.

Answers

a is an introduction more suitable for an essay
b doesn't give the reason for writing the report, and the language is more informal

IN OTHER WORDS

look at – examine, study, scrutinise, investigate

consider – assess, evaluate, analyse

suggest – recommend, propose, put forward

Noun forms: evaluation, provision, consideration, effect / effectiveness, scarcity, recommendation, improvement

5 Ask students to rewrite paragraph b in exercise 3 using more formal language from exercises 5 and 6.

Possible answer

The purpose of this report is to assess the level of road safety in this area, by examining the amount of traffic, and the effectiveness of existing traffic signals, pedestrian crossings and cycle lanes. It will also make recommendations for improvements.

6 Ask students to read the rest of the report on page 55 and comment on how well it answers the question.

7 Elicit suitable headings for each paragraph of the sample answer. Give feedback.

Possible answers

1 Problems caused by traffic
2 Present level of road safety
3 Recommendations / Conclusion

8 Students do this in pairs. Read through the instructions with them. Allow them to read through the exam task, and discuss a plan for the answer.

Possible answers

1 Introduction
2 Existing safety measures
3 Foreseeable / Potential problems
4 Recommendations

9 ⊙ 19 Ask students to read the rubric, and elicit what they have to do. Make sure they have their notebooks ready. Play the recording through twice if necessary.

Answers

See underlined parts of audioscript.

Audioscript ⊙ 19

Now, I think we'd all agree that prevention is better than cure, particularly in the case of fire. So, it is vital to establish a fire safety plan in your school. Teaching staff must be instructed on what to do in case of fire. <u>Fire alarms and fire exits must be clearly marked, and all teachers should be aware of their location.</u> Teachers must know where the nearest fire exit is at all times, and must be able to evacuate students efficiently. Therefore, it is advisable to hold regular fire drills for the whole school, so that students can also be made aware of procedures.

In case a fire does break out, teachers should always <u>sound the alarm at the first sign of smoke or flames.</u> Even if it turns out to be nothing, you will have ensured the safety of everyone in the building. Instruct your students to leave the room in an orderly fashion, and <u>move towards the nearest fire exit. If you are able to, use the nearest fire extinguisher</u> to put out the fire. If you are unable to control the fire, leave immediately, and <u>close all doors behind you, to prevent smoke from spreading.</u> Once outside the building, teachers must check that all students are accounted for. Students must stay in their classroom groups, to avoid confusion.

Teachers should learn how to use the fire extinguishers in the school, and all equipment should be checked regularly by the local fire department. <u>Doorways and fire exits must be clearly marked, and kept clear at all times.</u> This last point is most important. Now, I'd just like to demonstrate how …

10 Set this writing task as homework. Emphasise the fact that this is a Part 2 question, and remind students that they must write 220–260 words.

Student's Book pages 56–57

Video the world in a station

Aim: The main aim of this video is to discuss where the first human beings came from. This leads into language of speculating, and practice for Part 2 of the Speaking test.

Synopsis: This video is about a research programme into the origins of human beings. This project, called the Genographic project, analyses the DNA of hundreds of thousands of volunteers from all around the world. It shows that every human being has a common ancestor who originated in east Africa 60,000 years ago.

The Ideas generator focuses on different ways of interpreting pictures, and how it can be useful to create scenarios based on them.

1 Ask the students to read the statements and decide which piece of information is false.

3 is incorrect (all cells contain DNA)

2 Allow students a couple of minutes to read the paragraph carefully. Play the first part of the video and ask them to underline the errors in the text. Take feedback and ask for the correct information.

Answers

1 The study was about people **from all around the world.**
2 The study aimed to trace human DNA back to ancestors in **East Africa.**
3 They took samples from hundreds of thousands of / **over 200,000** people.
4 They took samples of cells from people's cheeks.

3 Students say how they would feel about participating in this kind of experiment. Elicit what questions students would like to ask Dr Wells.

4 Students watch the rest of the video and underline the correct answers.

Answers

1 Minnesota	2 the Middle East	3 California
4 Aztec	5 a survivor	6 South East Asia
7 New York City	8 proud	9 police officer
10 connected		

Videoscript

Narrator: There are seven billion people around the globe, from many different backgrounds. But we're more similar and more connected than you might think. Who were our ancestors? Where do we come from? And how did we get here? In April 2005, National Geographic and IBM worked together on a joint project to find out.

Wells: I wanted to draw people together, to make people realise that we're all part of an extended family and that our DNA connects all of us.

Narrator: National Geographic and IBM wanted to conduct a study to show that as a human species, we're all part of one big family and that our DNA connects all of us. So they started the Genographic Project. The goal was to trace our human DNA back tens of thousands of years to our first ancestors in East Africa.

National Geographic and IBM are working with hundreds of thousands of people around the world and gathering DNA samples, so they can learn about our human history. They need to create the world's largest database of DNA. To do this, they have to get samples from hundreds of thousands of people around the world.

There's no better place to show that we're all connected than here at Grand Central Station, a huge train station in the middle of New York City. Here, you can find people from all over the world.

Wells: My name is Spencer Wells.

Dee Dee: Hello, Spencer.

Wells: I work with National Geographic. I direct a project for them called the Genographic Project.

Frank: Yeah?

Wells: And we're using DNA as a tool to study how people all over the world are related to each other. Would you be interested in maybe giving us a sample and becoming a part of it?

Cecile: Oh definitely, yes, I'd love to contribute my DNA.

J.W.: Absolutely.

Wells: Maybe getting yourself tested?

J.W.: 100%

Wells: What do you think you might find out? What is your family history?

Cecile: Well, I have a lot of questions because my last name is not common in the country where I was born.

Frank: We have Aztec Indian in ours. Because my basic heritage is Mexican as far as I'm concerned, but we traced it back to Spain.

Wells: Fascinating. So you'd be interested in maybe getting yourself tested?

Narrator: Wells explains that the test is very simple. People swab the inside of their cheek to get some DNA cells. Then, they send the cells to a lab anonymously. The lab analyses the DNA and puts the results on a website in a few weeks.

Wells: Well let's get you started swabbing.

Dee Dee: Don't look at any of my fillings!

Narrator: Wells explains that the DNA research shows all people are related. Humans all started out in Africa about 50,000 years ago. They only started separating and moving to other parts of the world about 2,000 generations ago.

Wells: What do you know about your family history?

J.W.: I know a lot of my relatives. Some of them look as you do and then I have, like, for example, my mother's father was very dark.

Wells: We all started off in Africa around 50,000 years ago. So you are African, I'm African.

Dee Dee: So, like, you and I are related?

Wells: We could be related. How do you feel about that?

Dee Dee: Oh, fantastic! I can't wait for my Christmas present!

Narrator: In just a few weeks, Cecile, J. W., Frank and Dee Dee will get the results of their DNA tests and learn about the mysteries of their past. So far, the Genographic Project has collected over 200,000 samples. Dr Ajay Royyuru is Computational Director at IBM. He is helping analyse the results.

Dr Royyuru: This is our first chance in the history of human civilisation to look within and learn something that actually was not knowable before.

Narrator: Analysing this DNA helps us understand how we're all connected. Like our four participants from Grand Central Station. They are about to learn about their distant past.

Dee Dee lives near Minneapolis, Minnesota.

Dee Dee: Oh hi Spencer the scientist, from National Geographic!

Wells: Hi Dee Dee. How's it going? It's good to see you again!

Dee Dee: Nice to see you. Great! How are you?

Wells: You start off in Africa …

Narrator: Wells explain that Dee Dee's ancestors, like all other humans, started out in Africa. Around 45,000 years ago, a small group of her ancestors left Africa. They moved north to the Middle East. It was very cold and dangerous.

Wells: Suddenly you're living in this icy wasteland with things like that walking around, and you've got to figure out a way to kill them to make a living and survive.

Dee Dee: Mmm.

Wells: What would you have done?

Dee Dee: Well, I would have killed him. No, I would've found a guy to do it for me. Yeah!

Narrator: Frank lives in Southern California. He discovers that his ancient relatives were the first humans in the Americas. He might really have Aztec ancestors.

Frank: It's quite interesting. Up to the last 15–20,000 years, our ancestors were extremely adaptable, who survived by hunting large mammals. It kind of makes me understand why I feel I'm such a survivor. Because I am, I can create, you know, things out of nothing. I've always been that way.

Narrator: Cecile Nepal's results show that her ancestors were some of the first humans to live in South East Asia. Now Cecile lives and works in New York City. But she still feels connected to her Philippine roots.

Cecile: There's something that we still have, that we carry on. And it's something to be proud about.

Narrator: J. W. is a police officer in New York City. He lives there with his wife and son. His DNA results show that he has Puerto Rican, Spanish and ancient African ancestors. But that isn't all. J.W. finds that some of his early ancestors were probably the first farmers.

J.W.: Coming from grandparents who were farmers themselves, I kind of see the relation there so, pretty interesting.

Wells: Everybody that we met at Grand Central that day ultimately traces back to an ancestor in Africa.

J.W.: I feel connected because we all have one common place of origin. East Africa.

Wells: The cool thing that comes out of this research is obviously that we're all connected to each other and that we scattered to the wind, if you will, to populate the world over the last 60,000 years.

5 Students watch the entire video again and write a brief summary using the words in the box.

Possible answer

The project took samples of DNA from more than 200,000 people around the world and created a database of DNA. The results traced the human species back to its origin in East Africa, and showed that we are all connected to one another genetically, with a single common ancestor who lived 50,000 years ago.

6 Ask the students to work in pairs and to speculate what these people might be doing in Grand Central Station. Ask students where they would choose to do the study in order to get a wide range of DNA samples.

7 Students use the useful expressions to speculate about what the people in the photographs are doing in the station.

8 Students talk for one minute about the people in the photo.

9 Students look at the photos and do the activities. Point out that it is good if students can use synonyms rather than repeating the same word. This helps to show that a candidate has a wide vocabulary and recognises the value of variation in speech.

10 Students select one of the photos and answer the questions by talking for half a minute.

11 Students reflect on their performance in exercise 10. Discuss ways that students can develop their vocabulary, e.g. using connotation, e.g. *thin,* versus *slim, skinny* or *emaciated*; descriptive verbs e.g. *look: glimpse, stare, peer; walk: stride, stroll, limp;* the use of different registers, e.g. *encourage, urge.*

12 Students flick through the book and find other photos they can use to practise speculating.

Vocabulary organiser 5, page 166

Answers
1
programmer: a person who creates and develops computer programs.
virus: a computer program that introduces itself into a system, and alters or destroys information
crimeware: computer software which introduces viruses into a system.
antidote: a solution to the problem of a computer virus
cyber-criminal: a person who perpetrates crime on the Internet
cyber-crime: crime connected with the Internet
hacking: the act of illegally breaking into computer systems in order to gain secret information
2
1 suspected Larry Jones of committing
2 accused Wayne of stealing
3 arrested Jones
4 confessed / admitted to robbing
5 denied helping
6 charged the couple with committing
7 convicted Larry of
8 sentenced him to three years imprisonment.

3				
1 to	2 in	3 off	4 over	5 down
4				
1 B	2 C	3 D	4 A	5 B
5				
1 to	2 from	3 to	4 of	5 for

Bank of English
battle cry: phrase used to encourage support for a protest or campaign
cry out for: need something desperately
a far cry from: something very different from something else
for crying out loud: spoken phrase showing annoyance or impatience
a shoulder to cry on: someone to listen sympathetically
cry off: say you cannot do something you have agreed to do
cry wolf: ask for help when you don't need it
cry foul: protest that something is wrong or unfair
a crying shame: say that something is very sad or upsetting
it's no use crying over spilt milk: don't waste time feeling sorry about a mistake that cannot be changed

Photocopiable activity instructions

How to avoid catching a virus (page 60)

Aim: to consolidate and develop awareness and use of language connected with safety on the Internet.

Instructions:

1 Make sure you have one photocopy per student. Hand these out.

2 Explain that there is no real right or wrong order for the advice items. The aim is to make sure you get the correct items under the 'Do' column, and the correct ones under the 'Don't' column.

Answers
Do: A, C, D, G   Don't: B, E, F

Verb noughts and crosses (page 61)

Aim: to revise and consolidate use of some of the verb structures covered in this unit.

Instructions:

1 Separate the class into two teams: a noughts team and a crosses team. Make sure each student has a copy of the game image. Toss a coin to see which team will have the first go.

2 The team chooses a word in a suitable square, and makes a sentence with the word. If the word is used correctly, then the team places its mark – O or X – in the square.

3 Tell the students that they have a time limit of one minute to choose their square and make a sentence. If their sentence is incorrect, then the square will be left open, and the other team can try. The winning team is the one which creates a line of its marks, horizontally, vertically or diagonally.

How to avoid catching a virus

You are a representative from an anti-virus company. You have been asked to create a leaflet giving advice to PC users on how to protect their computer from viruses. You must complete the table below, by adding the notes A–G to the appropriate boxes.

Do ...	Don't ...
delete any email you suspect may be infected, and empty your 'Deleted items' folder regularly.	open any attachment you are not sure about, even if you have a virus scanner.
1	2
3	send an email about a 'new virus' without checking it out. Visit sites to check for hoaxes.
send any email you think is infected to an anti-virus company (you may have to own a copy of their virus software). They can tell you if it is a virus or not.	4
5	6
7	relax, even if you have a virus scanner. You will still need to keep your eyes open for any new viruses.

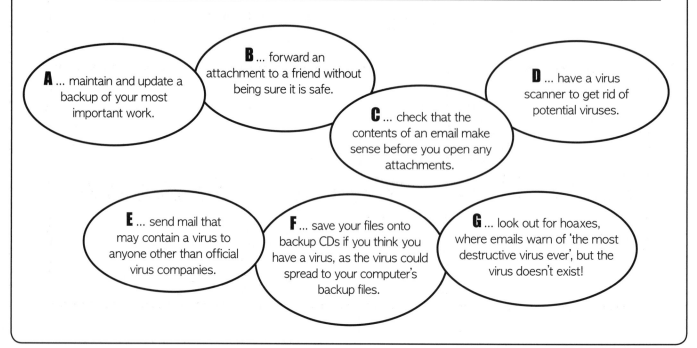

A ... maintain and update a backup of your most important work.

B ... forward an attachment to a friend without being sure it is safe.

C ... check that the contents of an email make sense before you open any attachments.

D ... have a virus scanner to get rid of potential viruses.

E ... send mail that may contain a virus to anyone other than official virus companies.

F ... save your files onto backup CDs if you think you have a virus, as the virus could spread to your computer's backup files.

G ... look out for hoaxes, where emails warn of 'the most destructive virus ever', but the virus doesn't exist!

Verb noughts and crosses

advise	CONVICT	dare
deny	**confess**	**contemplate**
appreciate	remember	**threaten**

6 HALE AND HEARTY

Unit introduction

The topic of this unit is good health and nutrition. One of the most important aspects of our lives is good health. More and more these days we are told how important diet is to good health, and that prevention is better than cure.

Warm-up activity

Decide who the healthiest person in the class is. Ask questions and write down the name of the person who gives the 'healthiest' answer for each question, e.g.
What did you have for breakfast this morning?
When was the last time you exercised?
How often do you eat vegetables or fresh fruit?

Getting started

1 This exercises aims to generate interest in the subject of a healthy lifestyle, and introduces some topic vocabulary. Students can work in pairs or alone to put the lifestyle factors in order of importance. Discuss the topic with the whole class and try to agree an order. Brainstorm any other ideas about what constitutes a healthy lifestyle.

2 ⊙ **20** Play the recording. Students should be able to hear some key words that they can match to the topics in exercise 1. They can check their answers in the audioscript on page 245.

Answers

Speaker 1: 8   Speaker 2: 6   Speaker 3: 7

Audioscript ⊙ 20

Speaker 1: Well, my old man was always going to the doctor for this, that or the other reason, but never for any life-threatening cause. Whatever the doctor said was gospel. No questions asked. Didn't have a clue what he was putting into his system, poor man. If the doc' said it was the thing to take, you can bet he believed it. Sometimes it worked, but more often than not the problem just got worse. I've read up quite a bit about conventional medicine since then and discovered that prescription meds, more often than not, just tend to treat the symptoms, never the root cause. 'Course, that's what made me interested in holistic medicine and the like, right.

Speaker 2: We live in an age where synthetic compounds surround us on a daily basis, from the solvents in our woodwork, to the ingredients in our shampoo. I read somewhere that we are exposed to over 70,000 different chemicals every single day. Did you know the same ingredients in our toothpaste can be found in car engine oil? Some of these have of course been classified as carcinogens, so it's hardly surprising that the more domestic products we use in the home, the more we see an increase in cancer rates. If you're worried about your health, there are alternatives to chlorines and bleaches. In pre-industrial eras, our grandmothers used vinegar and lemon juice, salt and bicarbonate of soda to clean the house! You can do the same.

Speaker 3: I first started doing it about three years ago when I heard about how it can reduce stress and therefore decrease heart rate and blood pressure. I also read about how in some cases, simple visualisation exercises have caused the regression of cancer. It is said to boost the immune system and is often used in hospitals with patients who are terminally ill. The medical community tends to agree that if mental factors such as stress were significantly reduced, a person's physical health would be much better. There's a growing movement in mainstream science to fund research into this kind of exercise. Personally, I do it because I find it so relaxing on both my mind and body, and because it keeps me fit and healthy. I don't need any equipment, just a quiet room or a spot in the garden where no one will disturb me.

→ Vocabulary organiser 6, exercise 1, page 167

Vocabulary organiser possible answers

1 plenty of fresh fruit
2 foods high in fats or sugar
3 your immune system is to eat raw vegetables
4 much healthier for you
5 fighting off any viruses or bacteria
6 if you have a serious illness
7 exercise and meditation
8 cause of the problem

Reading identifying opinions

3 Students should do this individually. Ask them to read the tips in the box and number them in order. Elicit suggestions from the class.

4 Students should read the text individually and answer the questions using techniques a and b.

EXAM SPOTLIGHT

Ask students to read the first paragraph in the Exam spotlight box. Make it clear that the task involves comparing the opinions of four writers in an academic context. It differs from Reading and Use of English Part 8, which requires candidates to match an opinion or statement with a specific text.

5   Ask students to read the exam task about the article. Ask them to identify each writer's opinion relating to questions 1 to 4. (See the Teaching in practice box below.)
When they have had time to identify these opinions, check their answers, and then elicit the answers to each of the four questions.

TEACHING IN PRACTICE: JUSTIFYING ANSWERS

Students should get into the habit of justifying all their answers by reference to the text itself. Ask students to underline the parts of the text that give an answer or refute an incorrect option.

A's opinions:

1   scientific research is credible (*Research indicates*)
2   the motives of food companies are regarded negatively (*companies are simply using as a means to more profit. Whether the food has special nutrient value seems barely relevant to them*)
3   supports modern and traditional advice because both stress the importance of nutrients (*Hardly a new approach, but rather a resurrecting of ancient wisdom*)
4   no mention of personal opinions or experience

B's opinions:

1   scientific research into 'superfoods' is not always credible (*research into the benefits of many of these foods is often based on preliminary studies open to multiple factors that can skew the results*)
2   the motives of food companies aren't regarded negatively (*something that suppliers and manufacturers understandably continue to promote*)
3   doesn't mention traditional advice
4   yes (*We all know certain foods are better for us than others*), but this isn't presented as being personal

C's opinions:

1   scientific research into 'superfoods' is not always credible (*it isn't a scientifically-defined term; Researchers just don't call them 'super'; the leap from testing foods in a lab to witnessing the actual benefits of including them in our daily diet is simply too great to be scientifically sound*)
2   the motives of food companies aren't regarded negatively (*It's easy to see why the concept is marketed by food companies so successfully*)
3   modern and traditional advice about eating isn't discussed
4   the writer says they personally used to believe this (*one I foolishly allowed to seduce me*)

D's opinions:

1   scientific research into 'superfoods': the writer mentions *new research* without expressing a view
2   the motives of food companies are not mentioned
3   modern and traditional advice about eating are similar (*General dietary research shows … , just like mother always said*)
4   there is no reference to the writer's own opinions or experience

6   Ask the students to read the box about analysing unknown words, and discuss whether they already consciously use any of these techniques. Ask them to apply these techniques as they do the exercise.

Student's Book pages 60–61

Language development
expressions with food

1   🔘 21 Ask students to read the information in the box about using idioms in speech. Students then listen to the recording and note the food idioms. Afterwards they should work in pairs to find the idioms in the audioscript and discuss their meaning.

Audioscript 🔘 21

1

Man:	I found a box of abandoned kittens by the side of the road the other day.
Woman:	Oh no! That's terrible! What did you do?

| Man: | Well, I took them to the cat rescue centre of course. They were a bit hungry but basically OK. |
| Woman: | Well that was good of you. Anyone worth their salt would have tried to give them a chance. But what heartless person could have left them there in the first place? |

2

Woman 1:	Did Sally tell you that she's been having a hard time at work?
Woman 2:	No, why? What's been happening?
Woman 1:	She's been putting in all this overtime and is just fed up of being taken for granted. Everyone expects her to run around for them all the time.
Woman 2:	Why doesn't she complain to her supervisor?
Woman 1:	She'd never do that. She's the next in line for promotion so she knows which side her bread is buttered!
Woman 2:	Yeah, I suppose you're right.

3

Man:	Emily got into trouble at school yesterday.
Woman:	No! You're joking? Whatever for?
Man:	Well apparently she was accused of breaking a window.
Woman:	No! I don't believe it. What did she say?
Man:	She denied it of course and I think the headmaster believed her story.
Woman:	Well of course he did. How could anyone suspect Emily of lying? She looks as if butter wouldn't melt in her mouth! And it's true. It wouldn't.

4

Woman:	Hello Bob! How's business?
Man:	Not so bad. Pretty good in fact.
Woman:	Really? That's fabulous. I always knew you'd make a good salesman.
Man:	It's not me – it's the book. Everyone just wants a copy. The first 1,000 sold like hotcakes. I'm already half way through the second shipment. How about you? Why don't I try and interest you in …
Woman:	Oh no you don't! I certainly don't need any more books, thank you!

2 Students should read the questions and choose the answer they think is right. Elicit answers, then ask them to check their answers in their dictionaries.

Answers
1 d   2 d   3 a

3 The point of this task is to show students that very often it is possible to work out what an idiom means using logic. Elicit suggestions from the class.

Answer
Any situation where important changes need to be made that might cause small problems or upset people.

4 Students can work in pairs. They should use a dictionary to find as many idioms as they can.

Possible answers
bacon: bring home the bacon, save someone's bacon
butter: fine words butter no parsnips (archaic), bread and butter
cake: you can't have your cake and eat it, piece of cake
egg: to have egg on one's face, to put all of one's eggs in one basket, a chicken and egg situation, a nest egg, a bad egg, an egghead
salt: salt of the earth

→ Vocabulary organiser 6, exercise 2, page 167

Vocabulary organiser answers
1 i ✗ c   ii ✗ a   iii ✗ b
2 d   3 a   4 b

See *Food idioms* photocopiable activity, page 69.

Key word *life*

VOCABULARY: PHRASES USING *LIFE*

If you *bring something to life* or if it *comes to life*, it becomes interesting or exciting. *The cold, hard cruelty of two young men is vividly brought to life in this true story …*

If you say that someone is *fighting for their life*, you mean they may die as a result of an accident or illness. *He was in a critical condition, fighting for his life in hospital.*

For life means for the rest of a person's life. *He was jailed for life in 1966 for the murder of three policemen …*

If you tell someone to *get a life*, you are suggesting that they have nothing better to do than interfere in other peoples affairs, or fuss over things that are unimportant. *'Really Natalie, why don't you just go and get a life?'*

If you say that someone or something is *larger than life*, it means that they have a strong personality, e.g. very noisy or flamboyant. *Throughout his career he's always been a larger than life character.*

If someone *lays down their life* for another person, they die so that the other person can live. (LITERARY) *Man can have no greater love than to lay down his life for his friends.*

If someone *risks life and limb*, they do something very dangerous that may cause them to die or be seriously injured. *Viewers will remember the dashing hero, Dirk, risking life and limb to rescue Daphne from the dragons.*

If you refer to someone as *the life and soul of the party*, you mean that they are very lively and entertaining. *Lilla was in such a good mood – she really was the life and soul of the party!*

Expressions such as to *come to life*, to *spring to life*, and to *roar into life* indicate that a machine or vehicle suddenly starts working or moving. (LITERARY) *To his great relief, the engine came to life …*

5 Ask students to do this in pairs. Check the answers with the group.

Answers
1 b / c / d   2 a   3 a   4 b   5 d   6 d   7 c

6 Students use their dictionaries to find which words in the box cannot be used with *life*.

Answers
dream, killer, vision

→ Vocabulary organiser 6, exercise 3, page 167

Vocabulary organiser answers
1 fact   2 matter   3 lay

Grammar conditionals

7 Students should turn to the audioscript on page 245 and underline the conditional sentences, then match each one to a description a–c.

Answers
a If you are worried about your health there are alternatives to chlorines and bleaches
b … if mental factors such as stress were significantly reduced, a person's physical health would be much better.
c If the doc' said it was the thing to take, you can bet he believed it.

8 Students work individually or in pairs. The aim is to make sure that students know the appropriate use for each conditional type.

Answers
1 d   2 c   3 b   4 a   5 f   6 e

TEACHING IN PRACTICE: CHECKING CONDITIONALS

In order to check that students have understood the function and meaning of a conditional sentence ask questions about the sentence. For example, for the sentence:
If it rained we took the bus, but if the sun came out we always walked.
Ask:
'Did it rain?' 'Yes.'
'How often?' 'Sometimes.'
'What did we do when it rained?' 'We took the bus.'
'What did we do the other times?' 'We walked (when it was sunny).'
'Did we do this more than once?' 'Yes.'
'When?' 'In the past.'
Therefore elicit that we use this structure to talk about past habits.

9 Students work individually or in pairs. The aim is to refresh their memories of the different conditional types. They may not be familiar with mixed conditionals, zero conditionals and false conditionals.

Answers
a 4   b 3   c 2   d 5   e 6   f 1

→ Grammar reference 6, page 212

10 Students work individually or in pairs. Do the first sentence as an example. Check the answers with the class.

Answers
1 Unless   2 If I should   3 Provided
4 As long as   5 Even if   6 If you were to
7 Had it not been for 8 Supposing   9 But for
1 c   2 b   3 d   4 g   5 f   6 i   7 a   8 e   9 h

11 Students attempt the task individually as this is an exam-type question. Time them and give them no more than ten minutes.

Answers
1 goes down / drops / falls / decreases, I intend to call
2 had had time I would have
3 for William's advice
4 happen to come to
5 had been taller I would have
6 you to cut down on

See *The Time Machine* photocopiable activity, page 70.

Student's Book pages 62–63

Listening multiple-choice questions

1 Read the information in the Exam spotlight box with the class. Students should underline key words in a question that may help them identify the correct answer.

Answer
<u>According to the speaker</u>, why are <u>enzymes essential</u> in our diet?

2 ⊙ 22 Play the recording. Elicit from the class the speaker's main point.

Answer
Her main point is that enzymes are needed for many functions, they keep us healthy and even help our bodies to cope with serious diseases.

Audioscript ⊙ 22
Raw foods, such as fresh fruit and vegetables, nuts and seeds, are foods which contain enzymes, the living energy of plants. Enzymes are of vital importance to our health because without them we would get sick and many of our bodily systems wouldn't be able to function properly. We need enzymes to digest our food, to strengthen our immune systems, to flush out toxins and to regenerate our cells. In fact, clinical tests have shown that enzyme-rich diets can even help people suffering from some serious illnesses.

3 ⊙ 23 Make sure students spend about a minute reading the questions and underlining key words before you play the recording. Students should listen to the recording twice, as they would in the exam. Remind them to check their answers even if they think they are correct.

Answers
1 C   2 A   3 D   4 A   5 D   6 C

Audioscript ⊙ 23

Interviewer: Today we are in the studio with Dr Maureen Cunningham whose latest book, *Raw Power*, has raised a few eyebrows. Dr Cunningham, your book advocates that a diet rich in raw fruit and vegetables is the healthiest diet of all. Can you tell us a little bit more about it?

Maureen: Raw foods, such as fresh fruit and vegetables, nuts and seeds, are foods which contain enzymes, the living energy of plants. Enzymes are of vital importance to our health because without them we would get sick and many of our bodily systems wouldn't be able to function properly. We need enzymes to digest our food, to strengthen our immune systems, to flush out toxins and to regenerate our cells. In fact, clinical tests have shown that enzyme-rich diets can even help people suffering from some serious illnesses.

Interviewer: I think most people are aware that fresh fruit and vegetables are good for us. But in your book you mention that eating too much cooked food can actually be bad for us and this has caused some strong reactions. Can you tell us why you advocate reducing our intake of cooked food?

Maureen: I'm certainly not suggesting that anyone should suddenly switch to a strictly raw food diet, but most of us do rely far too heavily on cooked meals to fulfil most of our nutritional requirements, which it simply can't do because cooking destroys so many of the nutrients. Obviously, if we're always eating cooked food, then we can't be eating enough raw plant food.

Interviewer: In your book, you cite a famous experiment involving about 900 cats I think.

Maureen: Yes, that's right. Half of the cats, which were studied over four generations, were fed a diet of raw meat (which is of course the natural diet of cats), while the other half were fed cooked, processed meat (tinned cat food). Within only one generation this second group had started to develop a variety of pathological problems, similar to the health problems that so often afflict even humans today. The second generation of cats suffered even more and with each subsequent generation, the problems increased so that by the fourth generation the cats were displaying all kinds of problems. Conversely the majority of cats in the first group lived healthy long lives in each generation, with very few of them developing serious illnesses.

Interviewer: But surely humans are not cats – and our bodies react differently to cooked foods?

Maureen: Yes, but we all need enzymes to digest our food, which unfortunately suffer complete and total destruction by cooking. This means we have to draw on our own limited reserve of enzymes, which puts enormous strain on our bodies. Similarly, as most people are aware, much of the vitamin content of foods is destroyed by cooking. But that's not all; a great deal of protein is damaged or destroyed when we cook our food, so that it becomes either completely useless or worse still, toxic to us.

Interviewer: Well, how are we supposed to get enough protein then?

Maureen: Well – fortunately most raw foods contain protein in easily digestible form. All nuts and beans are rich in protein, and in fact the richest source of protein is found in sprouted seeds and beans.

Interviewer: So does that mean that we don't need to worry about eating two square, home-cooked meals every day, as long as we eat a salad or some fruit?

Maureen: Well, basically, I would recommend eating plenty of raw food salads and vegetables with every meal. Further evidence is showing that the majority of our health problems are related to an ineffective immune system that has been weakened by a bad diet: too much junk food, not enough raw plant food. In fact, it is has been shown that the body's response to cooked food is to suddenly increase the number of white blood cells in our blood, something that usually happens when our bodies are attacked by alien invaders. By mixing our cooked food with at least 50% raw, we can reverse this reaction and keep our immune system on standby for when it's needed.

Interviewer: So your advice to anyone who hates boiled carrots, as I do, would be ...?

Maureen: That's simple. Eat them raw!

Degree of difficulty ▰▰▰▱▱▱

Decrease the level: for weaker groups pause the recording after each section that provides the answer to a question.

Increase the level: for stronger groups, tell students to read the questions and options once and then to close their books while they listen.

Speaking comparing pictures

4 Read the information in the Exam spotlight box with the class. Tell students to look at the pictures on page 233 and think of things they have in common, and how they deal with the themes.

Possible answers

Set 1: all three pictures show one person eating on their own. All the people are showing an emotional reaction.

Set 2: all three pictures show people doing exercise. Some forms of exercise are good for fitness, others are better for strength or mental health. They are carried out in a team, as a group or individually.

TEACHING IN PRACTICE: TALKING FOR A MINUTE

Tell your students not to waste time explaining which pictures they are going to talk about as this will become obvious when they begin the task. It may also make it harder for them if they change their minds about which picture they are going to talk. Advise your students against using 'closure' techniques such as, *I've finished!* They should keep talking until the interlocutor says *Thank you*.

5 Arrange the class into groups of three. Students should time each other to speak for one minute for the main task, and for 30 seconds to answer the question about their partner's pictures.

Extension

Ask your students to collect pictures from newspapers and magazines, group them into sets and imagine what they might be asked to talk about in a Part 2 task.

Use of English identifying collocations

IDENTIFYING COLLOCATIONS

Elicit from the class what a *collocation* is. Get them to give you examples of some and write them on the board. Read the information in the box.

6 Students can work in pairs or individually. Give them two minutes to note down as many collocations as they can find in their dictionary.

Possible answer

can't stand, won't stand for, stand in someone's way, stand still, stand a chance, stand in someone's way, take a stand, etc.

7 Ask students to underline or tick the noun phrases they know to be correct. They may be familiar with some of the collocations. For any they are unsure of, they should use a dictionary.

Answers

1 fault   2 luck   3 a process   4 justice   5 fortune   6 off power

8 Remind students that before attempting to answer any of the questions they should read through the whole text to gain a general understanding of it. You could ask some general comprehension questions to check this. Tell students to then look at each option individually and check the sentence before and after the gap for evidence of collocations. Students should spend no more than eight minutes on this. Check the answers with the class.

Answers

1 D   2 B   3 A   4 D   5 B   6 C   7 C   8 D

BACKGROUND: NATUROPATHIC MEDICINE

Naturopathic medicine (also known as naturopathy, or natural medicine) is a complementary and alternative medicine which emphasises the body's intrinsic ability to heal and maintain itself. Naturopaths prefer to use natural remedies such as herbs and foods rather than surgery or synthetic drugs. Practitioners emphasise a holistic approach to patient care – one that treats the whole patient rather than just the symptoms – and may recommend patients use conventional medicine alongside their treatments.

→   Vocabulary organiser 6, exercise 4, page 167

Vocabulary organiser answers

1 take   2 do   3 run   4 make   5 give   6 fall   7 fall   8 let

Student's Book pages 64–65

Writing developing an argument in an essay

Aim: The purpose of this section is to introduce students to the techniques needed to write and plan an essay, especially the development of an argument.

1 Discuss the topic with the class. Try to give everybody a chance to put forward ideas.

2 Read the Exam spotlight box with the class. Students can then do exercise 2 individually or in pairs. Or, you might like to ask one student to read the paragraph out loud. This would highlight the problems with it. Elicit comments on whether it meets the requirements for the introduction.

Answer

No, it is not well organised: it has no introduction or clear development, and the writer doesn't give reasons for their views.

DOING AN ESSAY PLAN

Read the information with the students, or ask them to read it to themselves. Afterwards ask them to close their books and tell you the order of the essay plan from memory.

3 Students work alone or in pairs. Check answers with the class.

Answers

1 c   2 b   3 d   4 a

4 Students read the introductory paragraphs. Elicit opinions from the class about which would be the best paragraph, and reasons for their choice.

Answers

Paragraph 1 is quite simple and doesn't explain the meaning of the title.
Paragraph 2 is a good introduction to the topic.
Paragraph 3 is repetitive and the language is basic and limited.

5 Explain that students now have to write the main body paragraphs for the essay. They should use the notes in the boxes to help them. Remind students to look back at exercise 3 and to use the paragraph summaries as topic sentences.

6 This task highlights how students can develop their points and strengthen their arguments. Read through the table and the example statement with the students, and then tell them to rewrite the second statement on their own. Elicit the best answers from the group and write them on the board.

Possible answer

Eating too much junk food can make you feel bad about yourself. For example, someone who eats too much junk food is likely to be overweight, and therefore less likely to exercise. Exercise releases endorphins which promote a sense of well-being and happiness.

7 Students carry out the task individually or in pairs. Check the answers with the class.

Possible answer

You are what you eat in that if you eat good food then you feel good, whereas if you eat bad food, you feel awful. If you eat lots of junk food you will get fat, and therefore you won't be able to go out to exercise, which is why you'll feel heavy. Furthermore, you'll be tired all the time. Subsequently, you'll just sit on the couch watching even more TV. Moreover, you'll eat lots of pizzas and drink fizzy drinks, as a result of which you'll get even fatter. However, if you eat lots of healthy food like fruit, vegetables, beans or rice then you will have lots of energy. Also, your food won't all turn into fat so you'll have more energy to do the things you want to do. Consequently, you'll feel really great.

8 Ask a student to read the conclusion out loud. This will highlight how bad it sounds. Students should attempt to rewrite the sentence as two or three sentences. They can make any structural changes they need to.

Possbile answer

Therefore, if we want to live long healthy lives, we should follow a number of general guidelines, like, for example, not smoking and exercising more, but also we must be aware of the food we eat and aim to eat more of the right foods. Good health is fundamental to our sense of well-being and feelings of happiness and, as good food equals good health, we should make every effort to eat well.

9 Students write the essay for homework. If time allows, elicit a brief discussion about it, just to brainstorm a few pertinent points.

→ Writing guide, page 222

Vocabulary organiser 6, page 167

Answers

1
1 plenty of fresh fruit
2 foods high in fats or sugar
3 your immune system is to eat raw vegetables
4 much healthier for you
5 fighting off any viruses or bacteria
6 if you have a serious illness
7 exercise and meditation
8 cause of the problem

2
1 i a   ii b   iii c
2 d   3 a   4 b

3
1 fact   2 matter   3 lay

4
1 take   2 do   3 run   4 make   5 give   6 fall   7 fall   8 let

Bank of English
1 healing, healer, health, healthful, healthy, healthily, healthier, healthiest, unhealthy
2 bus, provider, school
3 a incorrect = get better, improve   d incorrect = make me better

Photocopiable activity instructions

Food idioms (page 69)

Aim: to learn some new food idioms and use them in an appropriate context, while emphasising the absurdity of using too many idioms at once!

Instructions:

1 Organise the class into pairs and give each pair a copy of the worksheet.

2 Tell them they are going to do a little role-play activity, and they will each play one of the female gossips.

3 Students rehearse the script. At each gap they have to say the correct food idiom, but they shouldn't write it down.

4 Give them a few minutes to practise rehearsing their characters and learning their script as much as possible.

5 Afterwards students should take turns to stand in front of the class and act out their plays. They can refer to their scripts as much as necessary. Finally, the class votes for the best act.

Answers

1 you're going to turn into a couch potato
2 the apple never falls far from the tree
3 he's a hard nut to crack, that one
4 it wouldn't be my cup of tea I'm afraid
5 he had his hands in the cookie jar
6 that really takes the biscuit
7 he gave her some half-baked story about what he'd been up to
8 he was as cool as a cucumber
9 it's no use crying over spilt milk
10 he had to eat humble pie

The Time Machine part 2 (page 70)

Aim: to practise using the second and third conditional.

Instructions:

1 Organise the class into pairs and give each pair a copy of the photocopiable activity.

2 Tell each pair that they have to take turns imagining that they could travel back in time to the situations in the pictures and that their aim is to change history.

3 Student 1 has to tell their partner which time they would go back to and what they would have done there in order to change history. Student 2 should ask questions to establish how their partner would have changed history. Write the following useful phrases on the board for students to use:

Student 1: *If I could go back in time, I would …*
If I had been there at that time, I would have …

Student 2: *How would you have … ? What would you have … , if you could have … ?*

FOOD IDIOMS

- he's a hard nut to crack, that one

- you're going to turn into a couch potato

- that really takes the biscuit

- he was as cool as a cucumber

- it's no use crying over spilt milk

- that wouldn't be my cup of tea I'm afraid

- he had to eat humble pie

- the apple never falls far from the tree

- he had his hands in the cookie jar

- he gave her some half-baked story about what he'd been up to

---

The Gossips … Vera and Betty

Vera: Did you hear about Mrs Rogers and her son Tony? No. Oh, well, if you've got nothing better to do love, why don't I tell you what I heard from Nora in the corner shop. Well, it goes like this … Mrs Rogers was getting fed up with her Tony being on the dole, lounging around at home, doing nothing. I mean, he is 22 and he's finished college and everything. So she says to him: '[1]_____ if you don't get off your behind and go out and get yourself a job!'

Betty: Just like his father. You know what they say: [2]_____!

Vera: That's right. Anyway, Nora – that's Mrs Rogers – sends him off without another word to get a job, although months go by and he still can't find anything he likes.

Betty: [3]_____! He never was satisfied about anything, even when he was little.

Vera: In the end, Nora's going to throw him out on his ear unless he gets himself a job, so he finally accepts a job in a sports shop, stocking shelves.

Betty: [4]_____!

Vera: No, mine neither, but what can you do? Anyway, before long, guess what happens? Tony's given the sack, isn't he? And do you want to know why? According to his boss, he'd been helping himself to free stuff! Not that it could be proved mind you, but that's what the rumour is.

Betty: What, you mean [5]_____?

Vera: That's right.

Betty: Well, I'm shocked! Of all the things he could've done, [6]_____. What did he tell his mother?

Vera: Oh, you know, [7]_____. He told her he'd been made redundant due to a shortage of work, that kind of thing.

Betty: Did she believe him?

Vera: Of course she did. After all [8]_____ when he told her. She was very upset. Not that it would've done any good. You know what they say: [9]_____!

Betty: That's right Vera. But what happened in the end?

Vera: Well, she found out the truth eventually didn't she? She went ballistic at him! Of course [10]_____ after that, didn't he? He apologised to her, and he's been a good boy ever since. Got himself a good job in a lawyer's office.

Betty: I say!

The Time Machine (part 2)

1

'The town of Pompeii, beneath Mount Vesuvius, a few days before the eruption, AD 79.'

2

'SS Titanic, 14 April 1912, shortly before hitting an iceberg in the North Atlantic.'

3

'Extinction of the dodo, mid 17th century.'

4

'The assassination of Archduke Ferdinand of Austro-Hungary, one of the key events leading to the start of World War I, 28 June 1914.'

5

'A bakery on Pudding Lane, source of the Great Fire of London, 2 September 1666.'

6

'Mr and Mrs Hitler (Adolf's parents) marry, 7 January 1885'.

7 WISH YOU WERE THERE ...

Unit introduction

The topic of this unit is travel, cities, virtual worlds, tourism.

Travel is a very broad subject, and due to the Internet, opportunities for new kinds of travel experiences are becoming increasingly available.

Warm-up activity

Write the following quiz on the board or photocopy it. Students can do this in pairs or groups of three.

Quiz: Know your geography

1 The world's highest waterfall is in ...
  a Brazil   b Venezuela
  c Colombia   d Canada

2 What is the world's longest river?
  a The Danube   b The Amazon
  c The Nile   d The Yangtze

3 If I have just entered the city of Cuenca, which country am I in?
  a Argentina   b Italy
  c Spain   d Ireland

4 I am walking down the Spanish Steps. Which city am I in?
  a Rome   b Madrid
  c Lisbon   d Argentina

5 I visited Ayers Rock yesterday, and I'm going to the Taronga Zoo next week. Which country am I in?
  a Canada   b South Africa
  c Australia   d New Zealand

Answers
1 b   2 c   3 c   4 a   5 c

Getting started

1 ◉ 24 Ask your students to read the rubric. Play the recording. Elicit answers, and if necessary, play the recording again.

Answers
airship hotels, eco-friendly holidays, virtual tourism

Listening ◉ 24

Well, I think you're going to see airship hotels. You know, like cruise ships, but in the air. That's likely to be big business, because it'll be affordable for most people. Space hotels are a possibility, but they'll be pricey, so accessible only to the few. What's really taking off are eco-friendly holidays, as people are becoming more concerned about how they affect the environment. They're going to be really big, I reckon.

Another thing in the offing is your holiday down under. Hydropolis is being designed for an area off the coast of Dubai, an underwater paradise, but again, this is not going to do your bank balance a lot of good. Also, we shouldn't forget that you're still going to get the traditionalist tourist who wants to see the world as it is at ground level, who still yearns to walk the streets of cities of old. You know what I mean. What I can't see happening is this so-called virtual tourism being popular. I mean, you like travel because you want to leave home for a while. That's the whole point, isn't it? I don't think computers will ever be able to really capture that feeling of excitement you get as you climb on board a plane or a ship to go somewhere new, do you?

---

2 Ask for students' views on the different types of travel.

Reading multiple-matching texts

3 Ask students to read the rubric, then describe their city to their partner. This is a topic they should be able to respond to in a personal way. Monitor from a distance. Then, give general feedback to the class.

4 ◉ 25 Ask students to read the rubric. Play the recording twice. Allow students time to finish writing in their answers. In feedback, point out that Fiona is not used as an answer at all in the exercise. Emphasise that students should be careful not to be misled by their expectations about a task, e.g. expecting each of the speakers to be used once.

Answers
1 N   2 N   3 B

Listening ◉ 25

Nick: ...You know, I think of all the places we've been to, Edinburgh was my favourite.

Fiona: Really? It's certainly one of my favourites, but compared to Prague, and Amsterdam ... I don't really think I've got one particular favourite.

Nick: No? Well, for me, Edinburgh's got it all. Amazing architecture, culture, great shops and this warm, friendly air about it.

Fiona: I have to agree with you on that point. You feel safe walking about. Perhaps because it's a small city, and everything's easy to get to. Personally though, I found the architecture rather

---

intimidating. All those tall, stark buildings and dark stone. You can really believe all the ghost stories that come out of Scotland!

Nick: That's exactly what's so amazing about it! The setting and buildings make you feel you've walked onto a Charles Dickens film set, with their medieval and Georgian facades. Then, you walk inside, and you're hit with vibrant colours and the innovative designs of modern life.

Fiona: Umm ... I think what I liked about the place most were the coffee shops and art cafés. As you say, they were colourful, but I was struck by the friendliness of the people. Did you notice how chatty everyone was? And the laughter ... I seem to remember lots of animated conversation and laughter. Fantastic!

Nick: Yes, they were very helpful, too, weren't they? And I remember the aroma of fresh coffee and bread in the shops, while outside, the crisp sea breeze left a faint taste of salt in my mouth.

Fiona: Yes ... Definitely worth a return visit, possibly around Festival time ...

5 Read the rubric and allow the students time to read texts A and B. Elicit one thing each writer likes about their city.

Possible answers
Text A: a sense of belonging, the White Nights, the historic buildings, the Hermitage Museum
Text B: feeling at home, the cosmopolitan aspect of the town, the improvements

EXAM SPOTLIGHT

Explain that a very important part of reading comprehension lies in understanding what information the question is asking you for. Questions are sometimes phrased in a manner that students might find confusing. Students should make sure they understand each question before answering.

6 Ask students to read the rubric for exercise 6. Allow students to discuss their answers, and justify their choice. Give feedback.

Answers
1 means that they have family ties with the place, but were not necessarily born there.
2 means that they were actually born in that place.
Sentence 1 is true of both texts.

7 Tell your students to read the rubric and consider the wording of each question carefully before answering. Allow them time to complete the exercise.

Answers
1 T 2 F 3 F 4 T

8 Explain that this is an exam-style task, and students will need to refer to the four texts, A–D, in order to answer the questions. Ask them to read the rubric and questions, and elicit any unknown words.

Answers
1 C 2 B 3 D 4 C 5 D 6 C 7 D 8 C 9 A 10 B

9 Students do this exercise in pairs. Draw their attention to the fact that they are told which text each vocabulary item is taken from.

Answers
1 surge   2 overawed
3 chains   4 haunt
5 sprawl   6 trepidation
7 bring something to a standstill   8 autonomy
9 bustling

→ Vocabulary organiser 7, exercise 1, page 168

Vocabulary organiser answers
1 sprawl   2 overawed   3 bustling   4 surge
5 autonomy   6 trepidation 7 chains   8 haunt

Student's Book pages 68–69

Language development
describing places

1 Ask students to read the rubric. Elicit any unknown words in the box. Suggest that students write the three lists in their notebooks.

Answers
a buildings: amazing, crumbling, disgusting, dusty, eerie, gothic, grandeur, horrible, magical, old, threatening, run down, shoddy, slums, sober, sparking, unique
b atmosphere: eerie, grandeur, horrible, industrious, like home, lovely fresh air, magical, snow, threatening, sober, touristy
c personal reaction: amazing, breathless, it has it all, like home, magical, open mind, passion, the essence of

→ Vocabulary organiser 7, exercise 2, page 168

Vocabulary organiser answers
a Positive description: amazing, appealing, breathless, cosy, grand, industrious, magical, passionate, remarkable, sparkling, unique
Negative description: crumbling, disgusting, dusty, eerie, horrible, run down, shoddy, sober

phrasal verbs and phrases with *look*

2 Ask students to explain what the phrasal verb means in the quote, which is taken from text C on page 67. Check answers as a class.

Answers
taking care of, showing consideration for

3 Students do this in pairs before discussing the answers as a class.

Answers

1 c   2 e   3 a   4 g   5 b   6 h   7 f   8 d

4 Students read the sentences explaining the meaning of phrasal verbs with *look*, and decide if they are true or false. They should do this exercise individually.

Answers

1 T   2 F   3 F   4 T   5 T

→ Vocabulary organiser 7, exercise 3, page 168 (students' own answers)

5 Tell students to write out the complete sentences in their notebooks.

Answers

1 f   2 g   3 a   4 b   5 c   6 d   7 e

Key word *road*

6 Students do this exercise in pairs. Allow them time to choose the correct endings.

Answers

1 b   2 a   3 a   4 b   5 b

7 Tell students to make a list in their notebooks.

Answers

block, hog, house, map, rage, side, sign, show, works, worthy

→ Vocabulary organiser 7, exercise 4, page 168

Vocabulary organiser answers

1 F (A road hog is a driver who drives selfishly and doesn't consider other drivers.)
2 T
3 F (We say a vehicle is roadworthy when it is in a good condition and can be driven.)
4 T
5 F (A roadshow is a touring TV or radio programme, which broadcasts from a different town each day or week.)
6 F (A road block is when the police stop cars at a certain point on the road in order to search them.)
7 T

8 Ask students to read the exam rubric. Explain that this is a word formation exercise, and that Blackpool is a town on the northwest coast of England. Allow them time to read the email and complete the task.

Answers

1 outing   2 seaside   3 touristy   4 grandeur
5 investment 6 lookalike   7 unforeseen   8 memorable

Use of English open cloze

9 Read the information in the Exam spotlight box with the class. Ask students to read the questions in exercise 9 and allow them time to complete the task before giving feedback.

Answers

1 hardly   2 many   3 Despite   4 without
5 However   6 with   7 often   8 Few

10 Ask your students to read the rubric and text for the exam-style task. Ask if any students have heard of or played games like this. If so, get further information from them. Check such difficult words as *simulated* and *proxy*.

Answers

1 in   2 much   3 only   4 without
5 beyond   6 themselves 7 for   8 has

TEACHING IN PRACTICE: UNDERSTANDING CLOZE TEXTS

When you tackle Reading and Use of English, Part 2, always ask for ideas from your students about the content of the text before they do the task. This ensures that they understand as much as possible about the general meaning, which will help them with the task.

Student's Book pages 70–71

Listening multiple matching

1 Ask students to read the rubric, and elicit answers from the class. Encourage discussion.

2 Tell your students to read the quotation, and decide if the speaker approves or disapproves of space travel, and why.

Answers

2 disapproves (clues include the rhetorical question *So why pay …*, and the use of the word *extortionate*, which is strongly negative)

EXAM SPOTLIGHT

Read the Exam spotlight box with the class. It focuses on distractors, and the importance of listening to the whole extract and considering it carefully before choosing one of the options.

3 Allow students time to read the questions and complete their answers. Elicit answers, and give feedback. Students might be tempted to choose b in the first question, as the speaker's views are those that you might expect of a political activist. The fact that the speaker 'studies outer space for a living' is, on the other hand, unequivocal.

Answers

1 a   2 *anyone who studies outer space for a living as I do …*
3 b

4 ⊙ **26** Students now tackle the Listening Part 4 exam task. Allow them time to read the whole question before you play the recording. As follow-up, ask students to say which of the views about space travel they agree with, and to support their views with reasons and examples.

Answers

Task one: 1 G   2 H   3 C   4 D   5 A
Task two: 6 E   7 G   8 F   9 H   10 C

Listening ⊙ 26

Speaker 1: I've been fascinated by the universe and our place in it for as long as I can remember! As a property developer I built up a real empire here in sunny California, all the time keeping a close eye on developments in the space programme. The current race to create spaceflights for tourists is particularly exciting, but no sooner had NASA announced plans for a space station than I decided I had to have a piece of that pie. Space tourism is just moments away, so why not be the first to build an orbiting space hotel? Wild, huh!? We're almost there, though!

Speaker 2: To be honest, studying the space science modules in my physics course here at university has put me right off the idea of going into orbit in a spacecraft in this day and age. Not only are there risks involved in launching, but there's also the danger of space debris … surely that's more than enough to make me feel just fine looking at the stars with my feet placed firmly on the ground!

Speaker 3: Astronaut passengers will come to the spaceport three days prior to their flight for pre-flight training. This is to prepare them mentally and physically for the spaceflight experience, and enable astronauts to become acquainted with the spacecraft and their fellow passengers. As we speak, doctors and spaceflight specialists are developing the training programme, which will include g-force training.

Speaker 4: Space tourism, I ask you! No sooner do they make it to the moon than they start talking about commercialising space travel! Has anybody really stopped to consider the effects this is going to have on the environment? Not only on Earth, but in space, too! I recently interviewed an astro-environmentalist for an article I was writing, who stressed the need to avoid making the same mistakes in space as we have on Earth. What I want to know is, does anybody in authority really care about these issues, or are the potential profits to be made from commercial space travel too great?

Speaker 5: It's been my dream since I was small, really. I used to look up at the night sky and think about what it must be like to be up there, among the stars … And the money? Well, I know it's a lot, and I've heard all the ethical arguments about what better use it could be put to, and I agree with them all, but I think it'll be worth it. I've worked hard all my life, and it's my money! Rarely do people of my generation get the chance to fulfill such a dream. At my age, don't I have the right to have this once-in-a-lifetime experience?

Grammar inversion

5 Ask students to read both sentences, and elicit ideas from the class about the effect of inverting the sentence. Read the information in the box about using inversion, and decide which of the bullet points apply in this case. Give an example of each use of inversion.

Answers

The inverted sentence is more emphatic, and is more persuasive.

6 Make sure students are confident about how inversion works (the subject and verb are transposed), then ask them to complete the second sentence in each pair.

Answers

1 will this tough cleaning gel clean your kitchen surfaces, but it will also make your pans shine
2 had she opened the door than flames swept into the room
3 has anything like this happened in this town
4 must visitors take photographs inside the museum
5 will you have an opportunity to buy our product at this price

7 Students now look at the pairs of sentences and decide which is most appropriate for the situation, using the information about using inversion in the box on page 70. In feedback, explain that none of the sentences are grammatically wrong, but some of them use inversion when it is not natural to do so.

Answers

1 a (it's more emphatic and persuasive)
2 b (a small child is unlikely to use inversion, as it is too sophisticated)
3 a (a newsreader wants to gain the audience's attention, and so may use inversion for emphasis)
4 a is probably more likely, but an older and more formal person may use inversion

8 Ask your students to look at audioscript 26 on page 246 and underline examples of inversion. Then, ask them which speaker does not use inversion.

Answers

Speaker 1: no sooner had NASA announced plans for a space station than I decided I had to have a piece of that pie.
Speaker 2: Not only are there risks involved in launching, but there's also the danger of space debris …
Speaker 3: no inversion
Speaker 4: No sooner do they make it to the moon than they start talking about commercialising space travel.
Speaker 5: Rarely do people of my generation get the chance to fulfil such a dream.

9 Students do this in pairs. Tell them to look at the third speaker's speech, and make it more emphatic and persuasive. Point out that there is in fact only one point which can be realistically inverted. Inverted phrases should be used sparingly, so as to be more effective.

Possible answer

Three days prior to their flight, astronaut passengers will come to the spaceport for pre-flight training. This is not only to prepare them mentally and physically for the spaceflight experience, but also to enable them to become acquainted with the spacecraft and their fellow passengers. As we speak, doctors and spaceflight specialists are developing the training programme, which will include g-force training.

TEACHING IN PRACTICE: INVERSION IN WRITING

Make it clear to your students that whenever they wish to use inversion in a piece of persuasive writing, they should avoid using the structure more than once or twice.

You may like to prepare an example of the over-use of inversion in a text, and listen to comments from your students.

10 Students should do this exercise individually before you check their answers.

Answers
a Never before has   b No sooner had   c Under no circumstances must

11 Ask your students to read the statement. Elicit what the most important idea is that they should emphasise (the idea that this will be a first-time experience, so *never before ...*). Allow them time to rewrite the statement.

Answers
Never before has commercial space travel been available to the public, so book tickets for the first flight. This is a once-in-a-lifetime opportunity for anyone who is interested in space.

→ Grammar reference 7, page 213

→ Vocabulary organiser 7, exercise 5, page 168 (students' own answers)

Speaking discussing possible future developments

12 Invite students' reactions to each statement and allow for some disagreement. Don't let them go into too much detail, however, as they will be able to do this in exercise 2. While they speak, make a note of frequently used phrases, and repetition of language.

13 Tell your students to look at the Useful expressions box. Comment on any phrases you felt were used repetitively in the discussion in exercise 11 and ask students which phrases in the box could replace these. Students then discuss the statement in pairs, using phrases from the Useful language box. Monitor and give feedback.

See *Holiday dilemmas* photocopiable activity, pages 78–79.

Student's Book pages 72–73

Writing a proposal

Tell your students that they are going to look at how to write a proposal in this section. Make sure students understand the difference between a proposal and a report: while the format is similar (use of headings, etc.), a report focuses on the problems with the present situation, and usually makes recommendations, whereas a proposal often evaluates suggestions for improvement, and concludes which is the most practical.

1 Ask your students to read the exam task and make some notes.

Answers
Could include: suggestions for workshops in order to attract different age groups (give examples); suggestions for a variety of art media to be exhibited (photography, sculpture, textile design, graphic design, etc.). The writing should be formal in style.

2 Tell your students to read the two sample answers and compare them, considering style, register and effective use of the input material from the question. They should make notes in their notebooks individually. Then, elicit comments from the class as a whole.

Answers
Answer A answers the question, but the student lifts phrases from the input material at the beginning, and doesn't support her suggestions with reasons. She doesn't 'persuade' the reader in any way. Also, she mentions some negative aspects without softening them.
In answer B, the student uses more varied language, and supports her suggestions with positive reasons. Use of noun forms of words and inversion are effective in convincing the reader that her ideas are good ones.

PERSUASIVE LANGUAGE

Read the information in the box with the class and emphasise that many questions in the Writing paper will require students to use some element of persuasion. The following exercises focus on ways of making writing more persuasive.

3 Tell students to read sample answer B again and underline examples of language that the student uses to make her answer sound more convincing.

Possible answers
A good idea would be to offer *stimulating alternative* art forms. For example, *we could* hold a photographic exhibition, *then* one of sculpture, *followed* by fabric design *or possibly* graphic design. *Not only would* this cater for a *broader range of contemporary specialist tastes*, but the *variety* would also *arouse the interest* of the general public.
The costs to the gallery could be *kept to a minimum* by charging participants a nominal fee. The workshop feature could be *further developed* by the creation of an Art Club for young people. Through this, painting and photography competitions could be held, with sponsorship from local businesses.
Only by developing a broader range of exhibits, more *in line with contemporary interests*, can we make the gallery successful once more.

4 Tell students to read the sentences and compare them. Elicit which pair sounds more persuasive.

> **Answer**
>
> The second pair sound more persuasive. 2 a uses a noun phrase, and the strong adverb *dramatically*; 2 b uses inversion.

5 Ask them to read the rubric and phrases. They must try to improve sample answer A from page 72, using phrases from the box. Encourage them to make any other changes they think are necessary. This could be done in pairs.

6 Ask students to read the exam-style task. Elicit what the question is asking, and any key information in the input material. Make sure everyone is clear what they have to do, then set this task for homework.

Student's Book pages 74–75

Video our ATM is a goat

Aim: The main aim of the video is to raise awareness of different ways of life and to introduce and practise techniques for dealing with abstract topics.

Synopsis: The film follows two Kenyans who are visiting New York to run in the city's marathon. They are being shown round the city by Rene Lopez, a musician. They are amazed by many of the things they see, and by how different the way of life is to that in Kenya. The Ideas generator section looks at focusing your ideas to discuss abstract topics.

1 Generate interest in the video by looking at the photo. Elicit some of the differences between life in the boy's village, and the lives of the people in the class. Organise the class into two groups, and ask them to list ten things they might find unusual.

> **Possible answers**
>
> Areas of difference might include: food, dress, homes, living conditions, roads, transport, the weather, personal relations, dangers, animals, availability of water, etc.

2 Each student should work with a partner from the other group to exchange information.

3 Read the glossary and the title of the video. Encourage the students to predict what the video is going to be about. Students watch the video and check if any of the differences they came up with are dealt with.

4 Students watch the video again and tick the things they see happening.

> **Answers**
> 1 ✔
> 2 ✔
> 3 no – they walk
> 4 ✔
> 5 no – they take a goat
> 6 ✔
> 7 no – they're sitting, eating and chilling
> 8 ✔

> **Videoscript**
>
> Lemarti: After a long flight from Africa, we wanted to get out and stretch our legs. And Rene said, 'I'll show you around my village'.
>
> Rene: Follow my lead, follow my lead.
>
> Lemarti: Yes, boss!
>
> Lemarti: Village? This is not what I call a village.
>
> Rene: Check it out.
>
> Lemarti: Some people are living on top of that?
>
> Rene: Yeah, the apartment bit on top. That's the second floor, third floor, fourth floor. So we live on top of each other.
>
> Lemarti: Because there's no place to live, or what? Why do people go up there?
>
> Rene: There's no land so you have to live on top of each other. So you keep building and building and building, up, up, up, up.
>
> Lemarti: One very important thing we need to do first. If you want to walk on the street, you must have dollar.
>
> Rene: Here we go guys, ATM. This is where I get my money. Voilà.
>
> Boni: What's voilà? Have you taken someone else's money?
>
> Rene: There you go. I'm not taking it, this is my money.
>
> Boni: So you always put your money in here?
>
> Rene: It's from my bank account.
>
> Boni: […] and get your money here?
>
> Rene: Yes.
>
> Boni: Why do you put your money here?
>
> Lemarti: Where Boni and I come from, we trade things to get money. Our ATM it's a goat. We take the goat to the market, we sell it, we get money from it. No dollars coming from the wall. I think dollars talk in America very much, you know. You have no dollar, you have no voice.
>
> Rene: Yeah, I wish I could fully explain it to you, but I can't.
>
> Boni: That was easy money, easy!
>
> Lemarti: What's this place, Rene?
>
> Rene: This is Washington Square Park.
>
> Lemarti: We're walking to the park. It's a lot of people sitting around, eating, drinking, chilling. You know, people eat a lot here. People graze like cows man, you know. Non-stop; every corner you go, you see somebody sitting down, eating. Rene said 'Hey, let's grab something to eat, guys'.
>
> Rene: Alright, so we're going to order a hot dog.
>
> Boni: What kind of a dog's that ... that they sell?
>
> Rene: Hot dogs!
>
> Boni: Beef?
>
> Seller: Yes.
>
> Rene: Can we have one hot dog please, with mustard and ketchup on it.
>
> Boni: You can't even tell if this is meat or what.
>
> Lemarti: Rene, what's inside this hot dog? What's that, inside the hot dog?

Rene: It's a smushed up cow.

Lemarti: Boni just like, to the hot dog and says 'Oh yeah'. I'm going to take one home to show people what Boni ate.

Boni: Are you sure any of this is a cow? Is that New York style?

Rene: That's New York style. Let's hear you ...

5 Students suggest the answers they would give.

Possible answers

1 There isn't enough room for everyone to have his own house and garden, so people live on top of each other in high buildings in apartments.
2 They use an ATM to get money from their bank account. A bank account is where people keep their money.
3 Hot dogs contain minced-up meat inside a kind of skin. The food is very processed, it isn't very good for you.

6 Students interpret what Boni and Lemarti mean.

Possible answers

1 The way we get money is by selling things. If we sell a goat we can get money, that's our equivalent of an ATM.
2 If you don't have money people won't listen to you or care about what you think.
3 People eat all the time, whenever and wherever they want, instead of sitting down and having a meal together.

7 Students match the comments from exercise 6 to the possible consequences a–c.

Answers

1 c   2 b   3 a

IDEAS GENERATOR

Read through the Ideas generator box. In Part 4 of the Speaking test the examiners will be listening out for how well candidates can construct an argument. This box looks at a useful technique for building a discussion around a question by introducing one or more consequences and then adding a personal opinion.

8 Students work in groups and take it in turns to read the statements and add consequences. Demonstrate the activity with the first two statements.

9 Put the students in groups of three. Each student writes a further two questions related to the questions they are given. Examples for A, might be:

1 *Why do people eat so much processed food?*

2 *Do you think it's easier to live in a city or in the countryside?*

Students take turns to roleplay the interlocutor (asking the question they have written) and the candidates (answering the questions).

10 Students now analyse their roleplay in exercise 9 and discuss how they think they could improve their performance.

Vocabulary organiser 7, page 168

Answers

1
1 sprawl	2 overawed	3 bustling	4 surge
5 autonomy	6 trepidation	7 chains	8 haunt

2
a Positive description: amazing, appealing, breathless, cosy, grand, industrious, magical, passionate, remarkable, sparkling, unique
Negative description: crumbling, disgusting, dusty, eerie, horrible, run down, shoddy, sober

4
1 F (A road hog is a driver who drives selfishly and doesn't consider other drivers.)
2 T
3 F (We say a vehicle is roadworthy when it is in a good condition and can be driven.)
4 T
5 F (A roadshow is a touring TV or radio programme, which broadcasts from a different town each day or week.)
6 F (A road block is when the police stop cars at a certain point on the road in order to search them.)
7 T

Bank of English
Verb: travel by train, car or plane, travel light, travel widely
Noun: air travel, on their travels, rail travel, travel agent, travel rug, travel sickness, traveller's cheque, travel expenses, travelogue
Adjective: travelling musician, travelling salesman

Photocopiable activity instructions

Holiday dilemmas (pages 78–79)

Aim: to revise and consolidate grammar covered in units 1–7.

Instructions:

1 Students play in groups of four. Each group will need one copy of the game, one die and four tokens (one for each player, e.g. a coin or button).

2 Each student takes turns throwing the die. They should each throw the die once. The person with the highest number goes first, and moves their token the number of squares shown on the die.

3 They must follow the instructions on the square they land on. When they land on a square with a question, they must answer it. If they fail to answer the question successfully, they will miss their next turn.

4 The winner is the person in the class who reaches the 'FINISH' square first.

Holiday dilemmas

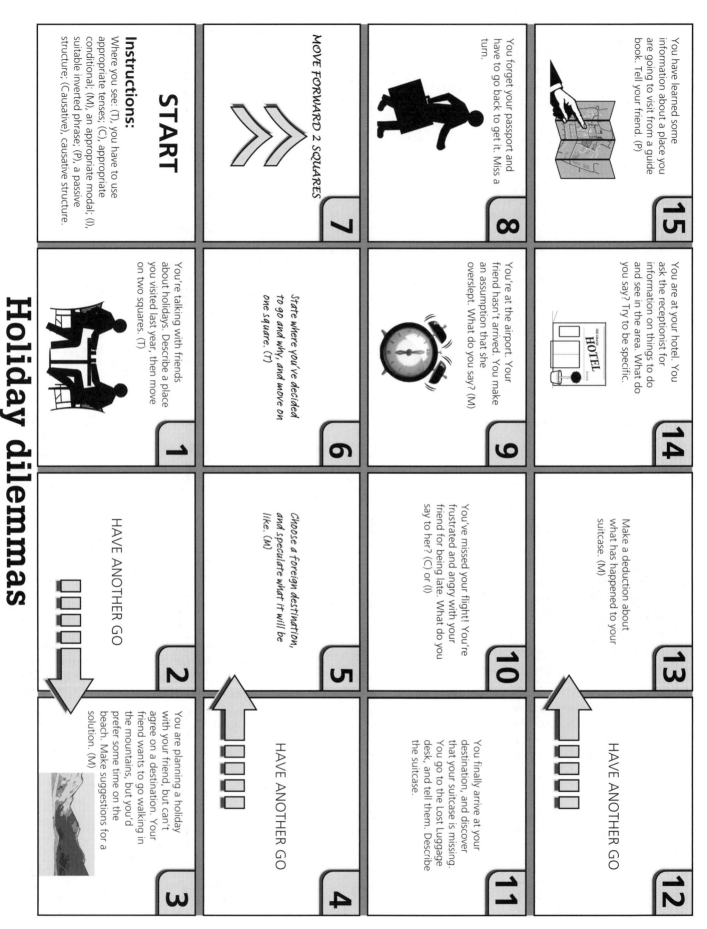

15

You have learned some information about a place you are going to visit from a guide book. Tell your friend. (P)

8

You forget your passport and have to go back to get it. Miss a turn.

7

MOVE FORWARD 2 SQUARES

START

Instructions:

Where you see: (T), you have to use appropriate tenses; (C), appropriate conditional; (M), an appropriate modal; (I), suitable inverted phrase; (P), a passive structure; (Causative), causative structure.

14

You are at your hotel! You ask the receptionist for information on things to do and see in the area. What do you say? Try to be specific.

9

You're at the airport. Your friend hasn't arrived. You make an assumption that she overslept. What do you say? (M)

6

State where you've decided to go and why, and move on one square. (T)

1

You're talking with friends about holidays. Describe a place you visited last year, then move on two squares. (T)

13

Make a deduction about what has happened to your suitcase. (M)

10

You've missed your flight! You're frustrated and angry with your friend for being late. What do you say to her? (C) or (I)

5

Choose a foreign destination, and speculate what it will be like. (M)

2

HAVE ANOTHER GO

12

HAVE ANOTHER GO

11

You finally arrive at your destination, and discover that your suitcase is missing. You go to the Lost Luggage desk, and tell them. Describe the suitcase.

4

HAVE ANOTHER GO

3

You are planning a holiday with your friend, but can't agree on a destination. Your friend wants to go walking in the mountains, but you'd prefer some time on the beach. Make suggestions for a solution. (M)

FINISH

30 — Home at last! Comment on your holiday, and make a decision about next year's holiday. (T)

29 — Your flight home has been cancelled! Go back to square 8. **8**

28 — You and your friend are shopping for gifts to take home. Your friend doesn't know what to buy for her mother. Make a suggestion. (M) or (C)

27 — You go out for the day alone, and have a good time. Describe your day to your friend. (T)

26 — You go out for the evening and get lost. Miss a turn

25 — The trip was a disappointment. Express your regret about going. (C) or (M)

24 — The driver fixes the problem! MOVE FORWARD 3 SQUARES

23 — You're going on an excursion into the mountains, and the bus breaks down! This is the first time you have experienced so many problems on holiday. Tell your friend this in an emphatic way. (I)

22 — It's raining! Miss a turn

21 — You suggest going to eat at a restaurant that specialises in a certain cuisine. Your friend has not tried such food before. Make predictions about what she can eat. (C) + (M)

20 — Go back to square 15. **15**

19 — You return to the hotel, and learn that your missing suitcase has been found. Make arrangements to collect it.

18 — You're visiting a historical site, when your friend's camera is stolen. Report this to the guide. (Causative).

17 — MOVE FORWARD 2 SQUARES

16 — You make plans for a day out. Tell the hotel receptionist about them. (T)

8 MAKING OUR MARK

Unit introduction

The topic of this unit is architecture and archaeology.

Since the dawn of civilisation, human beings have been making their mark on the landscape in more ways than one. This unit focuses on human-made monuments and buildings, artwork and architecture.

Warm-up activity

Ask your students to tell you what they think is the greatest mark ever made by human beings on this earth, e.g. a building, a monument, a piece of art. Write their suggestions on the board and discuss them.

Getting started

1   This activity aims to generate interest in the subject of landmarks, and to introduce vocabulary on the topic. Elicit a few ideas for world-famous landmarks from the class, then elicit what words from the box students might use to describe each one. Students can then continue the task in pairs.

→   Vocabulary organiser 8, exercise 1, page 169

Vocabulary organiser answers
1 massive   2 awe-inspiring   3 peculiar   4 imposing   5 unattractive

Reading understanding opinion

2   Students should number the criteria individually or in pairs. Check possible answers with the class.

Possible answer
The most important criteria for an eco-house are b, f and h.
Criteria i and j are important for safety, not for environmental reasons.
Criteria e is also important (the longer the house lasts, the less need there is to construct new buildings).
Finally, a, c, d, g may be important to the house owner / builder and need to be considered, but have less environmental significance.

3   Ask students to look at the picture, and elicit answers from the class. Write two lists on the board.

Possible answers
Advantages: cosy, cheap to build, good insulation, ecological
Disadvantages: unstable, fire-risk, not durable, etc.

4   ⊙ 27 Students should listen to the recording and note down the answers. Afterwards, check the answers against the lists you wrote on the board. You will probably note that many of the assumptions students had about the disadvantages of straw bales were in fact incorrect.

Answers
1 energy efficiency   2 sound proofing
3 fire resistance   4 environmental responsibility
5 natural materials   6 aesthetics
7 minimise wood consumption

Audioscript ⊙ 27
Here are seven great reasons why you should consider building your next house with straw bales.

Reason number one: Energy efficiency. A well-built straw bale home can save you up to 75% on heating and cooling costs. In fact, in most climates, we do not even install air conditioning units into our homes as the natural cooling cycles of the planet are enough to keep the house cool all summer long.

Reason number two: Sound proofing. Straw bale walls provide excellent sound insulation and are superior wall systems for home owners looking to block out the sounds of traffic or aircraft in urban environments.

Reason number three: Fire resistance. Straw bale homes have roughly three times the fire resistance of conventional homes. Thick, dense bales mean limited oxygen which, in turn, means no flames.

Reason number four: Environmental responsibility. Building with straw helps the planet in many ways. For example, straw is a waste product that is either burned or composted in standing water. By using the straw instead of eliminating it, we reduce either air pollution or water consumption, both of which impact the environment in general.

Reason number five: Natural materials. The use of straw as insulation means that the usual, standard insulation materials are removed from the home. Standard fibreglass insulation has formaldehyde in it, which is known to cause cancer. Bale walls also eliminate the use of plywood in the walls. Plywood contains unhealthy glues that can off-gas into the house over time.

Reason number six: Aesthetics. There is nothing as calming and beautiful as a straw bale wall in a home. Time and time again I walk people through homes and they are immediately struck by the beauty and the 'feeling' of the walls. I really can't explain this one, you'll just have to walk through your own to see what I mean.

Reason number seven: Minimise wood consumption. If built as a 'load bearing assembly', which can support a roof, the wood in the walls can be completely eliminated, except for around the windows. The harvesting of forests is a global concern and any reduction in the use of wood material is a good thing for the long-term health of the planet.

5 Read the box about understanding opinion with the class. Students should then read each paragraph carefully and answer the questions in their own words.

Answers
1 because builders are starting to realise that straw bale houses can have more advantages than other kinds of house
2 optimistic, joyful, motivated and it encourages women to join in
3 cost effectiveness and energy efficiency
4 houses with curved and circular shapes, thick walls and cosy interiors
5 You should be flexible, adaptable and patient. You should try to get a feel for it and not force it into precise measurements or calculations.
6 The chemicals and toxins in modern materials can have a detrimental effect on health.

6 Students should read the text again and answer the multiple-choice questions by reference to the text. Check answers with students and ask them to justify their answers.

Answers
1 D   2 B   3 A   4 B   5 C   6 D

→   Vocabulary organiser 8, exercise 2, page 169

Vocabulary organiser answers
1 innovative   2 sustainable   3 accessible   4 flexible
5 inspirational   6 empowering

Student's Book pages 78–79

Language development
phrases with *bring*

1 These questions aim to revise phrases and phrasal verbs with *bring*. Students should attempt exercise 1 individually to see how much they remember. Students should make a note of any new phrasal verbs and expressions in their vocabulary notebooks.

Answers
1 out   2 down   3 up   4 about   5 forward   6 on

2 These phrases with *bring* are more likely to be new to students. They should use the context to try to deduce the meaning of the phrases and match them to the definitions.

Answers
1 g   2 d   3 f   4 a   5 b   6 c   7 h   8 e

→   Vocabulary organiser 8, exercises 3 and 4, page 169

Vocabulary organiser answers
3
1 bring off   2 bring down   3 bring along
4 bring out   5 bring forward   6 bring back
7 bring about   8 bring up
4
1 down   2 home   3 herself   4 knees   5 rear   6 alive

Key word *that*

3 Read the information in the box with the class, then ask them to match the sentences in exercise 3 to the rules. Check answers and straighten out any problems.

Answers
a 4   b 2   c 5   d 1   e 3

4 Ask students to decide when *that* can be omitted from the sentence.

Answers
That can be omitted from sentences b + c.

5 The exercise can be done in pairs or small groups, or as a class activity.

Answers
It has been used 12 times in total:
1 6   2 0   3 2   4 4   5 0

Speaking reaching a decision through negotiation

REACHING A DECISION THROUGH NEGOTIATION

In Part 3 of the Speaking test, students are awarded marks for their ability to interact and negotiate with their partner to reach a decision.
This information box also focuses on the importance of persuading your partner using rational argument.

6 Ask students to read the options and choose the best response. Ask them to give reasons for their choices. In feedback, elicit students' reactions to the direct contradictions (*No* and *I don't think it is …*). Point out that in English these can seem rude and confrontational. The less aggressive ways of offering an alternative opinion are more likely to persuade someone.

Answers
1 b (a is too repetitive of what student A says)
2 a (b just disagrees without showing that the speaker is listening)
3 b (a is too short and doesn't demonstrate any fluency).

Speaking, Part 3

7 Students work in pairs to practise the exam task. Encourage them to use the expressions from exercise 6, or other polite ways of disagreeing. Listen to each pair as they do the task, and give feedback.

TEACHING IN PRACTICE: MIXING PAIRS

It would probably help your students here if you mixed pairs so that each student is working with a student they aren't so familiar with. Different students use different language, so when students are given the opportunity to work with a range of other students, it can help them pick up more expressions.

See *The Seven Wonders of the Ancient and Medieval World* photocopiable activity, page 92.

Listening *interpreting context*

EXAM SPOTLIGHT

Read the information in the box with the class. The following exercises should help students to pick up indirect clues in a dialogue in order to understand its context. This will help them answer multiple-choice questions that may ask for contextual information.

8 ⊙ 28 Play the recording. Students should jot down words or phrases that provide the answer.

Answers

a (*people actually live in your creations; make a real mark on the landscape, something that can probably be seen for miles around; to design structures that blend into the landscape, using natural materials and organic shapes*)

Audioscript ⊙ 28

Interviewer:	So what interests you most about your work?
Man:	Well, being able to create something that has real value is the main thing. I mean, it's great to be an artist or a sculptor and I'm certainly not belittling the value of fine art in society, but it's a totally different feeling knowing that what you create will have real practical value. I mean, people actually live in your creations! And of course, egotistically speaking, it's a chance to make a real mark on the landscape, something that can probably be seen for miles around.
Interviewer:	Sometimes that's not such a good thing though. There are some undeniable monstrosities in the landscape which somebody must have thought were beautiful.
Man:	Well, that's the second reason I love my work. My philosophy is to design structures that blend into the landscape, using natural materials and organic shapes. My clients come to me for that reason. I am confident that no one would call any of my designs an eye-sore and that gives me a real feeling of satisfaction.

9 Play the recording again and tell students to write down distractors.

Answers

Students might be tempted to choose b; the speaker talks about fine art, comparing it with his own work: *it's great to be an artist or a sculptor; the value of fine art in society*
Students might also be tempted to choose c; the speaker talks about *my philosophy* in connection with designing structures that blend into the landscape.

10 ⊙ 29 Tell students to use the same techniques to answer the six questions in this Listening Part 1 task. Play the recording twice, as in the exam.

Answers

1 A	2 C	3 B	4 A	5 C	6 A

Audioscript ⊙ 29

Extract 1

Interviewer:	So what interests you most about your work?
Man:	Well, being able to create something that has real value is the main thing. I mean, it's great to be an artist or a sculptor and I'm certainly not belittling the value of fine art in society, but it's a totally different feeling knowing that what you create will have real practical value. I mean, people actually live in your creations! And of course, egotistically speaking, it's a chance to make a real mark on the landscape, something that can probably be seen for miles around.
Interviewer:	Sometimes that's not such a good thing though. There are some undeniable monstrosities in the landscape which somebody must have thought were beautiful.
Man:	Well, that's the second reason I love my work. My philosophy is to design structures that blend into the landscape, using natural materials and organic shapes. My clients come to me for that reason. I am confident that no one would call any of my designs an eye-sore and that gives me a real feeling of satisfaction.

Extract 2

Woman 1:	When I first saw it I didn't realise quite how important it would turn out to be, although my first thought was that I was probably looking at something very old indeed.
Woman 2:	It must have been very exciting.
Woman 1:	I suppose it was, but I didn't know then that it would be a turning point for the project, and for me. I mean, the dig had been turning up very little, and our sponsors were threatening to pull our funds, so it was significant in more ways than one.
Woman 2:	When did you realise the significance of the find itself?
Woman 1:	Well, more or less at once. I called over Professor Hargreaves, and we carefully brushed out the piece in order to define it more clearly. It appeared to be man-made, but of course we couldn't date it until we submitted it for radio carbon testing, but from the level of the dig, we knew we must have been looking at something pre-Egyptian, possibly 10,000 years old.

Extract 3

Interviewer:	So it was ambition that drove you, from an early age?
Angel:	Yeah, I suppose you could say that. I knew I wanted to be famous when I was little. I used to tell all my parents' friends and say: 'I'm gonna be dead famous one day!'
Interviewer:	And what did they say?
Angel:	Well they laughed mostly. They thought I was being cute but that just made me more and more determined, see, so that's all I thought about all through school. I wrote my own songs and got a band together, even though my teachers kept telling me I'd never achieve anything the way I was going.
Interviewer:	And do you think that your fame will last? Are you more concerned about being the flavour of the month, or creating a legacy in music that has your name on it?
Angel:	Well, I've since realised that being famous isn't all roses. I mean, I love the media attention, and the money ain't bad either, but there comes a point where you think: 'OK, that's enough for today, can you leave me alone now!' and they don't. It just keeps going on and then you start to cherish your privacy and you put dark glasses and hats on and try to achieve anonymity like you had before – well, some of the time anyway.
Interviewer:	It must be a tough life!

Student's Book pages 80–81

Grammar relative pronouns / defining and non-defining relative clauses

1 & 2 Students complete exercises 1 and 2 individually. They should be familiar with these pronouns and be able to use them correctly. Check answers with the class.

Answers

1 1 whose	2 when	3 which	4 where	5 who
2 3				

→ Grammar reference 8.1, page 214

3 This exercise is more challenging for students. Suggest that they can refer to the Grammar reference if required. Point out that these phrases are more formal.

Answers

1 by which time	2 the person whom	3 as a result of which
4 in which	5 all of whom	6 neither of whom
7 some of which	8 both of whom	9 at which point

4 Students work individually or in pairs. Answers should be checked with the whole class and an opportunity given to all students to clarify any points of confusion.

Answers

1a: ND (the main clause refers to all Indians)
1b: D (the main clause refers only to the Indians who used to live there)
2a: ND (the name of the person, Petra, is given, this defines her, so the fact that she is the architect who built the house is extra information)
2b: D (the architect is not known, except as the person who built the house; this is the fact that defines her)
3a: D (only the trees that had been growing for over a century were cut down)
3b: ND (all the trees were cut down; their age is additional information)

→ Grammar reference 8.2, page 214

5 Elicit answers to the questions from the class, discuss any suggestions.

Answers

Commas are used around non-defining clauses to separate the additional information inserted into the main clause; the comma shows that this information is not essential to the meaning.
In defining clauses there are no commas because all the information is essential to the meaning of the clause.
In defining clauses, *that* can be used instead of *who* or *which*.

6 Students rewrite the sentences to give the two alternative meanings in the brackets. Do the first sentence with the whole class as an example.

Answers

1a The exhibits, which were very old, were in the Egypt section.
1b The exhibits that were very old were in the Egypt section.
2a The students that wanted some extra money got part-time jobs.
2b The students, who wanted some extra money, got part-time jobs.
3a The girls, one of whom was wearing a school uniform, were waiting for the bus.
3b The girls, who were waiting for the bus, were wearing school uniforms.
4a The house that has a beautiful garden is going to be knocked down.
4b The house, which has a beautiful garden, is going to be knocked down.

See *Party people* photocopiable activity, page 93.

reduced relative clauses

7 Read the rubric and exercise with the students. Elicit the changes that have been made.

Answers

1 'which are' has been removed
2 'which was' has been removed
3 'who walked' has become 'to walk'

8 Students rewrite the sentences using reduced relative clauses by making similar changes to those in exercise 7.

Answers

1 The tunnel, weakened by years of neglect, was no longer considered safe.
2 Children attending that school have all their lessons in French.
3 Gillian was the only person to volunteer to help organise the event.
4 Rebecca, embarrassed by what she had done, decided not to tell anyone.
5 Adrian, expecting to be paid that week, offered to buy drinks for everyone.

Use of English word building (noun groups)

9 Most students should be able to transform the words correctly in most cases, although there may be some words which confuse them. Ask them to transform as many words as they can. Afterwards go through the words one by one. Use the Teaching in practice tip below.

Answers

combination, cosmology, delivery, dependence / dependency, development, encouragement, inhabitant / inhabitation, naughtiness, obsession, persuasion, racism, redundancy, sensitivity, stupidity, tension, tiredness

TEACHING IN PRACTICE: NOTICING WORD PATTERNS

Ask a student to say the noun form of one of the words. Ask for a show of hands to see how many people agree. If the class agree unanimously, move on. If not, ask any students who disagree what they think the correct word is.

10 Elicit as much information as you can about the statues in the picture, or about Easter Island. If the class has never seen them before or knows nothing about Easter Island, elicit guesses and ideas from the class by asking questions, e.g. *Who do you think made them? Why did they make them?*

Ask the class to then quickly read the text to see if they had guessed any information correctly. This will also ensure that they read the text once through for understanding before attempting exercise 11.

BACKGROUND: EASTER ISLAND

Easter Island is a Polynesian island in the south-eastern Pacific Ocean. It is famous for its monumental statues, called *moai*, created by the Rapanui people. The history of Easter Island is rich and controversial. Its inhabitants have endured famines, epidemics, civil war, slave raids and colonialism, and the crash of their ecosystem.

11 Remind students that there may be more than one form of a word in a particular part of speech. They should be careful that they do not always automatically choose the first word they think of; they have to also make sure it is the correct word in the given context. Students should do the exercise individually. Check answers with the whole class.

Answers

1 inhabitants	2 Ecological	3 felled
4 cannibalism	5 enslaved	6 chillingly
7 isolation	8 eagerness	

→ Vocabulary organiser 8, exercise 5, page 169

Vocabulary organiser answers

1 destruction (damaging something so badly it can't be used or can't survive)
2 obsession (thinking about something all the time)
3 starvation (not having any food for a long period)
4 mythology (ancient stories, often invented to try to explain natural events)

12 Discuss the topic with the class. Point out that although the initial theory presented in the text claims that the people of Easter Island brought about their own destruction, it may in fact not be correct (and this is hinted at in the final sentence). Elicit further suggestions of what could have happened to them.

Afterwards ask students to read the questions for exercise 13 to see whether they reveal any further information.

13 ◉ 30 Students should do the listening task individually. Before you play the recording remind students to follow the steps given in previous units.

1 Read the questions to identify key words.
2 Identify the part of speech required in each gap.
3 Try to guess the possible meanings required to complete the sentences.

Answers

1 competed	2 evidence	3 Easter day (in 1722)
4 16 million	5 deforestation	6 rats
7 unreliable	8 invented	9 agricultural

Audioscript ◉ 30

Between 1200 and 1600 AD, the people of Easter Island built and erected around 400 enormous statues, or 'moai' as they are called, and another 400 were left unfinished in the quarries where they were made. Up to ten metres tall and weighing up to 75 tonnes, the enigmatic statues raise a host of questions – not least, why did the islanders build them, how did they move them and why were so many left unfinished? One theory is that different groups competed against each other, striving to build the most impressive moai.

Some researchers have suggested that this 'moai mania' was a disaster for the society. Yet others point to mounting evidence that prehistoric occupants made a success of life on the island and state that there is in fact painfully little archaeological evidence for the fundamental claims that underpin the self-destruction theory.

When the Dutch explorer Jacob Roggeveen 'discovered' the island on Easter day in 1722, he was stunned at the sight of monumental stone statues lined along the coast. He could see few trees, and he wondered how this apparently small, primitive society had transported and erected such monoliths without timber or ropes. Later on, pollen and soil analysis revealed that the island had once been home to flourishing palm forests with an estimated 16 million trees. Deforestation seems to have begun as soon as the settlers arrived around 1200, and was complete by about 1500. The reason why the islanders wiped out their forest has long nagged at researchers and is still open to dispute. Some palms may indeed have been cut down to assist in moving the statues, though, with their very soft interiors they would not have been ideal for the job. Other trees were used for firewood, and land was cleared for agriculture. Still, the blame

---

for the disappearance of the palms might not rest entirely with people. Recent genetic research suggests rats, which love to eat palm nuts, were introduced to the island in the canoes of the original colonisers.

Most of the evidence for starvation and cannibalism comes from oral histories, which are extremely contradictory and unreliable. Some researchers suspect that stories of cannibalism, in particular, could have been invented by missionaries. Very few of the remains of prehistoric islanders show any signs of personal violence. True, the 17th and 18th centuries saw an increase in artefacts identified by some as spearheads, but many believe the artefacts are agricultural implements.

The story of ecocide may usefully confirm our darkest fears about humanity but, for every society that self-destructs, there is another that does the right thing. It is far from clear that the Easter Islanders made their situation much worse for themselves, but only more evidence will resolve the issue.

Student's Book pages 82–83

Writing a review

1 Try to get a varied response from your students to this question, so after the first student has described a building, ask: *Who knows a building very different from that?*

Ask the class if they ever read reviews, and if so, what topics do they read about? e.g. music, films, TV programmes, books, hotels. Where do they read them? e.g. on the Internet, in magazines and newspapers. How much are they influenced by reviews that they read? Have they written any reviews themselves?

Read the information in the box about the purpose and structure of a review with the class.

2 Read the task with the class. Ask questions to make sure they have understood what this kind of writing requires. Elicit answers to the three questions. For question 3, tell students to spend a couple of minutes jotting down headings in their notebooks.

Answers
1 an interesting building
2 how old it is, what it looks like, why you find It interesting
3 an introduction, which may include where it is and how old it is; a paragraph on what it looks like; a paragraph on why it is interesting; possibly a concluding paragraph or recommendation.

3 Students read the model individually. Afterwards ask questions about the writer's description.

Answers
All the information is there. There is a separate paragraph on age because there is quite a lot of interesting information about that. There is a final paragraph drawing a conclusion.

4 Ask students to compare reviews with essays. Elicit the differences and similarities from the class.

Answer
A review presents a viewpoint but it is also descriptive and fairly factual, whereas an essay presents a more subjective argument.

5 Ask students to read the model again and underline the descriptive vocabulary. Write key words and phrases on the board if you like. Point out that they will have to brainstorm vocabulary for different tasks in exercise 6.

Answers
incredibly tall; very impressive; enormous temple; remarkable construction; unreal; fairy castle; astonishingly tall, conical towers; disappear into the skyline; a range of intricate sculptures of religious scenes and figures; absolutely spellbinding; internal columns; a geometrical design; a dazzling array of colours; unique; an astonishing experience

6 Students can do this exercise individually or in pairs. Elicit suggestions from the class.

7 Students use their dictionaries to complete the sentences. They can also find other meanings for each of the words listed (or other words) that can be used to mean 'house' in some way. Check answers with the class.

Answers
a housing	b dwellings	c habitat
d residence	e abode	f place

→ Vocabulary organiser 8, exercise 6, page 169

Vocabulary organiser answers
1 housing	2 residence	3 abode
4 dwelling	5 place	6 habitat

8 Students should plan their review in class. Check their plans and ideas of descriptive vocabulary. Students should then spend up to half an hour writing their review or should finish it for homework.

Student's Book pages 84–85

Review 2

Answers
1
1 confessed	2 digest	3 erected
4 sustain	5 run	6 enhance
7 consume	8 confide	9 convict
10 incite		

2
1 turning … down	2 bring about	3 looked up to
4 brought back	5 turned out	6 look into
7 turn in	8 bring up	

3

1 spill the beans	2 look the other way
3 go down that road	4 lay down her life
5 brought it home to me	6 on the road to recovery
7 bitten off more than you can chew	8 is above the law

4

1 B   2 A   3 D   4 B   5 C

5

1 deter from	2 accused of	3 turn off
4 charged with	5 resorted to	6 bringing forward

6

1 preconceptions	2 consumption	3 destruction
4 digestive	5 restoration	6 strengthen
7 maintenance	8 prescription / prescribed	

7

1 denied setting the house on
2 went on talking about
3 for Jasper's warning not to
4 no account must you
5 before have I seen such
6 neither of whom has / have

8

1 take	2 do	3 run
4 make	5 give	6 fall

Vocabulary organiser 8, page 169

Answers

1

1 massive	2 awe-inspiring	3 peculiar
4 imposing	5 unattractive	

2

1 innovative	2 sustainable	3 accessible
4 flexible	5 inspirational	6 empowering

3

1 bring off	2 bring down	3 bring along
4 bring out	5 bring forward	6 bring back
7 bring about	8 bring up	

4

1 down	2 home	3 herself
4 knees	5 rear	6 alive

5

1 destruction (damaging something so badly it can't be used or can't survive)
2 obsession (thinking about something all the time)
3 starvation (not having any food for a long period)
4 mythology (ancient stories, often invented to try to explain natural events)

6

1 housing	2 residence	3 abode
4 dwelling	5 place	6 habitat

Bank of English

a outhouse	b get on like a house on fire
c housekeeper	d Houses of Parliament
e housing benefit	

Photocopiable activity instructions

The Seven Wonders of the Ancient and Medieval World (page 87)

Aim: to practise using the skills of debate and argument.

Instructions:

1 Organise the class into pairs or groups of three and give each pair a copy of the photocopiable activity.

2 Explain that the Great Pyramid at Giza has been selected as number one in a list of surviving wonders from the ancient and medieval world.

3 Your students have to choose six more monuments from the list and put them in order of importance.

4 First each group works together for a few minutes to compile their lists and decide on reasons.

5 Each group has to argue why their list should be accepted.

Party people (page 88)

Aim: to practise using relative clauses.

Instructions:

1 Photocopy the first column of the activity once, cut out the statements and hand them out to the class so that everyone has at least one.

2 Photocopy the second column of the activity and give one copy to everyone in the group.

3 Tell everyone to stand up and 'mingle' in the middle of the room. Tell them that the information they have on their slips of paper says something about them. They must not show these slips to anyone.

4 The students should ask each other questions (e.g. *Did your dog just bite me? Do you have green hair?*) in order to find the names to complete their sheet.

5 The first person to complete all the names and sentences on their sheet is the winner. They should then read their sheets out to the class to check their information is correct. If they make a mistake they lose.

Answers

(Name) is the person **whose** dog just bit me.
1995 is the year **when** (name) **was born**.
(Name) is the person **who went to the same** school as me.
(Name) is the person **who speaks** five languages.
(Name) is the person **who is a year** older than me.
(Name) is the person **who has green** hair.
St. Mary's is the name of the hospital **where** (name) was born.
(Name) is the person **who has my** bag.
(Name) is the person **whose pen** you borrowed.
Texas is the name of the place **where** (name) **lives**.
August is the month (**which**) (name) likes best.
'Wobbles' is the name of the cat **which** belongs to (name).
(Name) is the person **who wants to go to** the moon.
Tigers are the animal **that** (name) **likes best**.
(Name) is the name of the person **whose** shoes I like.
Yesterday morning was the moment **when** (name) **realised he / she would be famous**.

The Seven Wonders of the Ancient and Medieval World

The Parthenon, Athens
- is a temple to the Greek goddess Athena
- was built in the 5th century BC on the Athenian Acropolis
- is the most important surviving building of Classical Greece
- its decorative sculptures are considered one of the high points of Greek art
- is regarded as an enduring symbol of ancient Greece and of Athenian democracy
- is one of the world's greatest cultural monuments.

The Great Wall of China
- is one of the most massive structures ever to have been built
- dates back to the 5th century BC
- was built over hundreds of years
- stretches over approximately 6,400 km in total
- it has been estimated that somewhere in the range of two to three million Chinese died as part of the centuries-long project of building the wall.

Maccu Picchu, Peru
- referred to as 'The Lost City of the Incas'
- is one of the most familiar symbols of the Inca Empire
- is a pre-Columbian Inca site
- is located 2,430 metres above sea level in Peru
- was built around the year 1460
- was said to have been forgotten for centuries when the site was rediscoverd in 1911
- is now an important tourist attraction.

The Colosseum, Rome
- is the largest elliptical amphitheatre ever built in the Roman Empire
- is one of the greatest works of Roman architecture and Roman engineering
- was built between 70 and 80 AD
- was originally capable of seating around 80,000 spectators
- was used for gladiatorial contests and public spectacles
- saw the death of about 500 000 people and over a million wild animals in the Colosseum games.

Haghia Sophia, Turkey
- was the largest cathedral ever built in the world for nearly a thousand years, until 1520
- was originally constructed as a Byzantine church between AD 532 and 537
- was in fact the third Church of the Holy Wisdom to occupy the site (the previous two had both been destroyed by riots).

The Leaning Tower of Pisa, Italy
- is a freestanding bell tower of the cathedral in the Italian city of Pisa
- is the third oldest building in Pisa
- began leaning to the southeast soon after the onset of construction in 1173 due to a poorly laid foundation
- presently leans to the southwest.

Stonehenge, England
- is one of the most famous prehistoric sites in the world
- is composed of earthworks surrounding a circular setting of large standing stones
- sits at the centre of the densest complex of Neolithic and Bronze Age monuments in England, including several hundred burial mounds
- dates back to around 3000 BC.

The Taj Mahal, India
- is a mausoleum built by an Emperor in memory of his favourite wife after she died in childbirth
- is considered the finest example of Mughal architecture, a style that combines elements from Persian, Ottoman, Indian and Islamic architectural styles.

The Great Sphinx of Giza, Egypt
- is a statue of a reclining lion with a human head that stands on the Giza Plateau on the west bank of the Nile, near modern-day Cairo, in Egypt
- is the largest monolith statue in the world, standing 73.5 m long, 6 m wide and 20 m high
- is the oldest known monumental sculpture, and is commonly believed to have been built by ancient Egyptians in the third millennium BC.

Petra, Jordon
- is an archaeological site in Jordan that is renowned for its rock-cut architecture.
- is one of the new wonders of the world
- was unknown to the Western world until 1812, when it was discovered by a Swiss explorer
- has been described by UNESCO as 'one of the most precious cultural properties of man's cultural heritage'
- was designated a World Heritage Site in 1985.

Party People

Your dog just bit someone.	_____ is the person _____ dog just bit me.
You were born in 1995.	1995 is the year _____.
You went to the same school as someone.	_____ is the person _____ school as me.
You speak five languages.	_____ is the person _____ _____ five languages.
You are a year older than someone.	_____ is the person _____ older than me.
You have green hair.	_____ is the person _____ hair.
You were born in St. Mary's Hospital.	St. Mary's is the name of the hospital _____.
You have someone's bag.	_____ is the person _____ _____ bag.
You loaned your pen to someone.	_____ is the person _____ you borrowed.
You live in Texas.	Texas is the name of the place _____.
August is your favourite month.	August is the month _____ _____ likes best.
Your cat's name is 'Wobbles'.	'Wobbles' is the name of the cat _____ belongs to _____.
You want to go to the moon.	_____ is the person _____ _____ the moon.
Your favourite animal is a tiger.	Tigers are the animal _____.
Someone likes your shoes.	_____ is the name of the person _____ shoes _____
Yesterday morning you realised you would be famous.	Yesterday morning was the moment _____.

Unit introduction

The topic of this unit is forms of art and design.

This unit tries to incorporate a range of art and design forms to accommodate students' varying tastes. The focus is largely on eliciting students' response to visual stimuli, so you may wish to capitalise on this by bringing in your own examples, or getting your students to bring in examples of their own work, or pieces that they like.

Warm-up activity

Before the lesson, write the following on the board:

a *Picasso, Van Gogh, Degas*
b *Le Corbusier, Henry Ford, Alessi*
c *T. S. Eliot, Shakespeare, Homer*
d *Mozart, Vivaldi, Beethoven*

Ask your students to find the connection between the people in each group. (Answers: a painters, b designers, c poets / writers, d composers)

Getting started

1 Elicit your students' comments on the work shown on page 86. Ask them to discuss the question with a partner, then take some feedback from the class.

Reading understanding tone and implication in a text

UNDERSTANDING TONE AND IMPLICATION

The explanation describes three ways in which authors can express their feelings about a subject without directly stating them. Read the information with the class.

2 Students should work individually to match the extracts to the three ways of expressing views in the box. Elicit answers.

Answers

A 2 (criticises the boots for not being stylish, then refutes the criticism by referring to their usefulness in a muddy field on a wet afternoon)
B 3
C 1 (negative vocabulary: *eyesore, blot*)

3 Ask students to answer the questions. Elicit answers and give feedback.

Answers

1 b   2 b   3 b

4 Ask the students to read the exam task, then read the texts and make notes about each one in relation to the questions. They should then use their notes to answer the questions.

Answers

1 A 'almost too tedious to write about'
   B 'Far from dull'
   C 'the subject matter is monotonous', 'Daniels's paintings ... have disappointingly little to say'
   D 'his most compelling to date', 'alluring surfaces'
   Answer: C (A and C find the paintings uninteresting.)
2 A 'irritatingly tiny'
   B 'very small, yet each one becomes a monument on the wall it occupies'
   C 'the tiny pieces ... seem shallow'
   D 'small, understated paintings'
   Answer: B (the paintings are striking although small)
3 A skill 'employed to such redundant ends'
   B 'highly intricate', 'a wonder of astounding colour and shape relationships'
   C 'this show proves Daniels's painterly ability and experimental creativity.' '... have disappointingly little to say'
   D 'the result is a rich blend'
   Answer: A (A and C believe Daniels has misused his abilities.)
4 A 'which raises the question of why Daniels is painting at all'
   B 'Each piece is a wonder of astounding colour and shape relationships', 'The colours seem to emerge from another, unknown dimension'
   C 'this show proves Daniels's painterly ability and experimental creativity'
   D 'Daniels knows how to work the brush'
   Answer: A (the only one suggesting that paint was the wrong medium to use)

→   Vocabulary organiser 9, exercises 1 and 2, page 170

Vocabulary organiser answers

1

1 alluring	2 angular	3 astounding
4 compelling	5 endless	6 extensive
7 frustrating	8 intricate	9 meandering
10 redundant	11 reflective	12 rich
13 shallow	14 tedious	15 understated

2

1 meandering	2 angular	3 understated
4 compelling	5 endless	6 tedious
7 frustrating	8 redundant	9 intricate
10 extensive		

Student's Book pages 88–89

Language development
compound words

1 Elicit the compound word formed by *paper* and a word from B (*paperclip*), then ask students to form further compound words. Elicit answers and read the information in the box about compound words.

> **Answers**
> paperclip, rooftop, windmill, desktop, fingerprint, fingernail, footprint

2 Ask students to complete the exercise. Check answers with the group.

> **Answers**
> 1 everyday   2 computer-controlled   3 all-purpose
> 4 time-wasting   5 stand-in

3 Students could do this individually or in pairs.

> **Answers**
> 1 footprints   2 stand-in   3 all-purpose
> 4 paperclip   5 fingernail   6 rooftops

evaluative adjectives and adverbs

4 Students should do this in pairs. Emphasise that they should look at how the words are used in the texts, as the overall context affects the meaning.

> **Answers**
> Text A: *tedious* and *misplaced* are negative; *alluring* is positive, but is used to contrast his photos, which adds to the overall negative evaluation.
> Text B: *dull* Is negative, but the whole phrase *far from dull* is very positive; *intricate, astounding, extensive* and *appealing* are positive.
> Text C: *shallow, monotonous* and *frustrating* are negative; *shiny* and *reflective* are neutral, but are used here to reinforce the impression of his work being *shallow*.
> Text D: *compelling, understated* and *rich* are positive; *crumpled* can be negative, but here it adds to the impression of his work being understated.

Key word *pay*

If students are struggling, elicit the meaning of phrases they do know, such as *pay attention to*, and *pay you a compliment*, and try to do the exercise with them through a process of elimination.

5 Ask students to read the rubric and sentences. Tell them that all the options can follow the verb *pay*, but only one fits the context in each case. Elicit answers.

> **Answers**
> 1 c   2 b   3 b

VOCABULARY: PHRASES WITH *PAY*

pay attention to: listen carefully to
pay homage to: show that you admire somebody or something
pay somebody a compliment: say something nice about a person's appearance or character
pay your respects to somebody: go and visit somebody in a formal manner, out of a sense of duty and politeness
pay somebody respect: show somebody consideration
pay the penalty for: experience something unpleasant as a result of a mistake you have made, or something wrong you have done
pay through the nose for: pay a higher price for something than it is really worth
pay tribute to: say something to show your respect for someone
pay your way: pay a share of the expenses of a group outing

6 Ask students to read the sentences. Elicit the meaning of the italicised phrases.

> **Answers**
> *pay you a visit:* come and see you
> *pay for itself:* earns or saves you the money you spent on it initially

→   Vocabulary organiser 9, exercise 3, page 170

> **Vocabulary organiser answers**
> 1 attention   2 a compliment   3 for itself
> 4 the penalty   5 my respects

Listening interview about an artist

7 Find out the students' views of the art in the photo, and ask them to explain what they like or don't like about it.

8 🔘 31 Ask the students to read the rubric. Play the recording. Elicit answers. If there is disagreement or confusion, play the recording again.

> **Answer**
> 2 (*glass background, window on the world, garish colours*)

> **Audioscript** 🔘 31
>
> Joe: Will ya look at this? The amount of work that's gone into it! It's amazing!
>
> Clare: Ummm ... But seriously, Joe, would you really want that hanging on your wall?
>
> Joe: Yeah, why not? So, OK, it's bulky, but it's powerful, and I love the symbolic effect of all those lyrics scrawled across the glass background. Set within the boat like that, it creates the effect of a window on the world as you travel on your voyage through life.
>
> Clare: Wow, Joe! That's a bit deep for you! Personally, I find the colours rather garish for my tastes.
>
> Joe: Well, ya see, Clare, I think they're meant to be. I mean, it's boat paint ... No, I really like it!

9 Read the information in the box with the class. Ask the students to read the rubric and the options. If necessary, play the recording again. If students have difficulty with this, analyse each option in turn and ask students to say why it is correct or incorrect (see the answer key below).

Answers

d (Joe says 'I love the symbolic effect')
a is incorrect: Clare does not sound positive or say anything positive about the piece.
b is incorrect: Clare thinks the colours are garish, but Joe does not disagree with her.
c is incorrect: Clare does not say anything about the work being *bulky*.

---

10 ⊙ 32 Ask the students to read the exam task. Explain any words they ask about. Play the recording. Pause, and play it again.

Answers

1 C	2 D	3 A	4 D	5 D	6 B

Audioscript ⊙ 32

Interviewer:	Now, Kapodistrias's kind of art is rather unusual, isn't it, so can you start by giving us a brief description of what he does?
George:	He does a lot of different things, really, because he loves experimenting with materials, and he's certainly innovative. He isn't just interested in the look of something, but in how it feels to the touch, if you know what I mean. So I suppose his work is a combination of three-dimensional painting and sculpture. He's been influenced by the work of Kostas Tsoklis, a popular Greek 3D artist, who he admires a great deal.
Interviewer:	Would you say Tsoklis was the reason Kapodistrias became interested in producing his own work?
George:	Tsoklis certainly influenced the direction in which his art developed. But in fact he's always had an interest. His father painted for a hobby, too – landscapes, mainly – and Kapodistrias talks about how as a boy, he went out on painting trips with his father, and sometimes he drew, as well. Then, at university, it was photography that intrigued him for a while, and he gradually moved on to painting watercolours, and then using acrylic. It was some time after his university days that he grew interested in working in three dimensions.
Interviewer:	What materials does he use?
George:	At first, he used cardboard, and then plaster. Here his professional work helped. As a dentist, he uses plaster, glues and materials for making dentures, wire for braces, and so on. So it seemed natural to experiment with such materials to develop his hobby. Now he's keen on polystyrene and fibreglass for their strength and durability. And because fibreglass is used in boat building, there's a link with a major theme in his art – the sea. He loves boats, and they appear in a number of his works.

Interviewer:	Isn't polystyrene a rather difficult substance to work with?
George:	Yes, and not very healthy, either! But it's versatile, and easy to mix with other materials to create different textures. Kapodistrias has an interesting approach to his work. He hasn't followed any art courses, and claims not to know much about particular techniques. He just, as he puts it, follows his heart in a painting. When he's creating a new piece, he feels he participates in it, but the materials gradually take on a life of their own, and seem to mould themselves. He finds that exciting – and many people would say the same about his work.
Interviewer:	He's produced a lot of work, yet he hasn't held an exhibition yet. Is there any particular reason?
George:	What Kapodistrias has said is that the symbolism in his work is increasingly reflective, and in a sense quite private. For instance, many of his backgrounds contain the lyrics from songs or poems that have a special meaning for him, one that isn't apparent to anyone looking at the painting. On top of that, he doesn't see himself in a professional light, and has never sold anything. It's hard to put a price on a work, since he spends months on each one. He's also rather shy of publicity.
Interviewer:	And finally, George, what do *you* think of Kapodistrias's work?
George:	He's not regarded as a major modern artist, admittedly, but I would stick my neck out and argue that he's underrated. His best work is expressive without spelling everything out. It encourages viewers to use their imagination. I find I can gaze at one of his works for a long time, and go into a reverie. I may not feel I understand the painting, but it certainly evokes ideas and feelings.
Interviewer:	George Buckingham, thank you very much for coming to talk to us today.
George:	Thank you.

Student's Book pages 90–91

Grammar changing sentence structure: change in emphasis, or different meaning?

1 Tell your students that you are going to look at how changing the word order in a sentence can affect its meaning. Ask them to read the sentence from the text and the two options. Elicit the meaning of the two sentences. Explain that *has yet to be* means the same as *has not yet been*, or *still has not been*.

Answer

Sentence 2 has the same meaning, 1 means the opposite.

---

2 Students work in pairs. Ask them to consider each pair of sentences carefully. Give feedback on each pair.

Answers

1 a I thought the poem wasn't written by Auden, and I was right.
   b I thought it was written by Auden, but I was wrong.
2 a He's still learning.
   b He's had his driving licence for two years.
3 a Sally (not someone else) borrowed the CD.
   b She borrowed a Shakira CD (not a different CD).
4 a There were several paintings, and Paul bought this one.
   b There was one painting, and Paul bought it.
5 a She used to paint the flowers and trees in a different way to the other students.
   b She had painted flowers and trees, whereas the others painted other things.

3 ⊙ 33 Ask your students to read through the rubric and sentences. Play the recording as the students read the sentences in the Student's Book. Elicit answers.

Answers

1 The second sentence is more emphatic, perhaps to show surprise or frustration.
2 The second sentence is more emphatic, perhaps to show slight impatience.
3 The second sentence is more persuasive and sympathetic.
4 The second sentence is more emphatic, and presses the point home.
5 The second sentence is more persuasive and calming.

4 ⊙ 34 Ask your students to read the sentence. Play the recording. Pause after the second sentence, and ask students how it differs from the first. Then pause after each subsequent one to elicit the change in meaning.

Answers

Van Gogh (not Picasso) cut off his ear.
He didn't hurt his ear, but cut it off.
He cut off his ear, not his hand.
The quarrel made him do it, not a letter.
Van Gogh quarrelled with Gauguin, not Monet.

Audioscript ⊙ 34

Vincent Van Gogh cut off his ear after a quarrel with his good friend Gauguin.

Vincent Van Gogh *cut off* his ear after a quarrel with his good friend Gauguin.

Vincent Van Gogh cut off his *ear* after a quarrel with his good friend Gauguin.

Vincent Van Gogh cut off his ear after *a quarrel* with his good friend Gauguin.

Vincent Van Gogh cut off his ear after a quarrel with his good friend *Gauguin.*

5 Students work in pairs. Play the recording in the same way again, this time allowing students to write down a suitable question to precede each answer.

Answers

Who cut off his ear after a quarrel with his good friend Gauguin?
What did Van Gogh do to his ear?
What did Van Gogh cut off?
Why did he cut off his ear?
Who did Van Gogh quarrel with before he cut off his ear?

→ Grammar reference 9, page 215

Use of English key word transformation

6 Read the information in the Exam spotlight box with the class. Students work in pairs. Ask the class for answers and give feedback.

Answers

1 Mary, it was Pete who
2 though it may be, we are / we're

7 Students should work individually. Ask them to read the exam task. Allow them eight minutes to complete the exercise. Check the answers and explain why any sentences are incorrect.

Answers

1 but what I don't like   2 to Claire, it was John
3 how she manages to stay calm   4 not me but the neighbours that
5 though / as it may, the match   6 whose paintings were of the sea

Speaking suggesting solutions, justifying ideas

8 Elicit students' views on the associations of black and white.

Possible answers

In many western societies black is associated with death and mourning, and white with purity and new beginnings (e.g. weddings, and religious ceremonies).

9 Students work individually. Ask them to read the rubric and the information in the box. This task is based on western perceptions of colour, but they may have different views. Elicit responses.

Possible answers

1 blue   2 red   3 black   4 yellow
5 orange   6 lavender   7 purple   8 green
9 grey   10 navy blue

10 Students work in pairs. Allow them time to discuss this.

11 Read out the rubric for this task, as students need to get used to hearing oral instructions. Then, tell them to read the emphatic phrases in the In other words box. Allow them about two minutes to perform the first part of the exam task.

Read the rubric for the second part of the task and give them one minute for this. Monitor and note examples of both good language and mistakes you hear. Give feedback to the class.

12 Ask students to work through this exercise in pairs.

Answers
1 It's a bright child's bedroom that will …
2 What's needed is strong colours to create …
3 What appeals to most people is a cool, …
4 What is needed is a photo of …
5 All that has to be done is keep it simple.
6 What will make people curious is one …
7 What's needed is colours which …
8 It's warm, inviting colours that will stimulate interest.

→ Vocabulary organiser 9, exercise 4, page 170

Vocabulary organiser answers
1 nostalgia	2 rebellious	3 deceit
4 transition	5 harmony	6 stability
7 joy	8 unique	9 balance
10 sophistication		

Student's Book pages 92–93

Writing supporting your ideas in an essay

1 Read the information in the Exam spotlight box with the class, then elicit students' opinions on the topic and encourage them to give reasons for their answers.

2 Ask your students to read the exam task. Make this active, by eliciting what the notes mean. For example, elicit that if paintings are *invaluable* they are important to society, not just worth a lot of money.

3 Look at the table and elicit more examples of 'key events' and other reasons why photography might be valued by society.

4 Ask students to read the rubric and paragraph, and underline the phrases as indicated.

Answers
The main reason for this is that…   Take the Olympic Games, for instance …

5 Ask students to reread the final sentence of the paragraph in 4 (*In many areas of life …*) and to consider its purpose. Elicit students' views on the sample.

Answer
It sums up the writer's views on photography – it is a main idea not a supporting point.

6 Ask students to complete the paragraph in pairs, using expressions from the In other words box.

Answers
1 for this reason
2 For example / For instance
3 Another reason why
4 such as

7 Ask students in pairs to make notes on the paragraph in 6. When they have finished, remind them that in the exam they only choose two of the three areas in the notes.

Answers
more challenging skill than photography; most people cannot produce a painting to hang in their home; rich history / treasures, e.g. Mona Lisa

8 Explain that the essay paragraphs in exercises 4 and 6 need an introduction and a conclusion. Discuss what these will include and then ask students to write these.

If there is time, elicit students' views on music (the third art in the exam task) and ask them to make notes, then write a paragraph on music.

9 Ask your students to read the exam question. Then discuss ideas about what students are required to write. Encourage students to brainstorm ideas. Set the writing task for homework.

Student's Book pages 94–95

Video Aboriginal rock art

Aim: The main aim of the video it to introduce us to Aboriginal art and its importance to the Aborigine people. The Ideas generator section focuses on decision making, a crucial skill for the second section of Part 3 in the Speaking paper.

Synopsis: This video is about Australian Aboriginal rock art and its importance in the culture of the Aborigine people. It follows anthropologist Adam McPhee as he flies over Arnhem Land, home to countless ceremonial sites which have been rediscovered, and their rock paintings. McPhee introduces us to a ceremonial site and shows us some rock paintings which are older than the pyramids. Margaret Catherine, an elderly Aborigine lady, explains the important of Aborigine art, its ancient myths, and the importance of the land in her culture.

1 Generate interest in the topic by asking students to look at the photo and say what they can see, and who they think made the artwork.

Possible answers
The painting shows a kangaroos and some plants; it seems to represent a person, with feet at bottom left and a head at top right; there is also a small child hanging upside down.

2 Put students into pairs. Tell them to read only the information in their paragraph, then answer their question, giving information from the paragraph to support their answers. If time allows, read through the two paragraphs asking more detailed questions and checking for pronunciation.

Answers

1 Art forms such as drawing, oral story-telling, song and dance are used in Aboriginal culture to pass on knowledge, cultural values and beliefs. There is a long tradition of this in the culture.
2 Either Queensland or Arnhem Land: in Queensland … human and animal forms; in Arnhem Land … complex and detailed figures

3 Read the words in the glossary and allow students a minute to read through the questions so they know what they have to listen out for. Play the video all the way through. Put students into pairs or groups to check their answers. Monitor what they say to get a general idea of how much they have understood.

Answers

1 ceremonial sites / rock paintings
2 Older than the pyramids / tens of thousands of years old / from before the last Ice Age / 40,000 years or more
3 It is very, very fine work.
4 images of the Dreaming
5 It is one of the most important stories; the Rainbow Serpent is the creator of everything.
6 The paintings have no meaning without the stories.

Videoscript

Narrator: Far in the Australian outback, in the Arnhem Land Plateau, ancient ceremonial sites offer an unprecedented glimpse into the fascinating culture of the Aborigines. Lost for generations, these sites were only recently found.

Wade Davis: So are there like dozens and dozens of sites out through here?

Adam McPhee: There are hundreds of sites, most of which they still haven't discovered.

Narrator: The ceremonial sites are home to rock paintings older than the pyramids. They are tens of thousands of years old, from before the last ice age. Adam McPhee, a local anthropologist, is our guide.

Adam McPhee: Talking about art that possibly goes back 40,000 years or more, probably some of the oldest art in the world. And the world doesn't know about it, that's the other thing.

Narrator: Aborigines settled in Australia about 55,000 years ago. Their ceremonies were performed here for millennia, all the way up to the 20th century. This was, in essence, a living museum.

Adam McPhee: This is an example of what I mean by a master artist. You can only imagine the detail that's missing here but this is very, very fine work. Very, very fine indeed.

Narrator: The drawings depict images of the Dreaming, a time when the world as we know it was created. Its rivers and mountains, human beings and the social order.

Adam McPhee: Come up here and have a look. There's a baby hanging on the breast here. Here are the feet, travel up the legs, the head.

Narrator: One of the most important stories of the Dreaming is that of the Rainbow Serpent, the creator of everything we see.

Wade Davis: What is the story of the Rainbow Serpent?

Margaret Catherine: It's really special, the Rainbow, and it stays underneath the water. It's their spirit that looks after the river and the country. If I die, my spirit will be there.

Narrator: These mythical stories are passed down, from generation to generation. And the drawings have no meaning without them. Together they create a link to the ancestors. And they are all part of the land.

Margaret Catherine: I feel really, really good when I come back to the land because I can always feel the presence of my great-great-grandfather. And he's there.

Narrator: Sadly there are fewer and fewer tribal elders like Margaret Catherine who speak the languages and know the ancient stories. For the aborigines, to tell the story of The Dreaming is to create the world anew. When the stories die, so do we.

Margaret Catherine: Don't forget your culture and live on with it forever in your heart and mind.

4 Play the video again and encourage students to expand on their previous answers.

5 Students complete the paragraph with the phrases from the box.

Answers

1 There are hundreds of   2 One of the most important
3 particularly   4 there are fewer and fewer
5 there is a danger that

6 Students discuss how knowledge and beliefs are passed on in their culture, and compare this with what happens in Aborigine culture. You could move on to ask about the importance of folk tales and the oral tradition in their culture. What myths and legends and traditional songs do they have?

Speaking Part 3 Collaborative task

IDEAS GENERATOR

The Ideas generator section looks at negotiation in Part 3 of the Speaking paper. Students should decide which adjectives best describe the three ideas for a present.
Possible answers
1 a, b   2 d   3 b, c

7 Students work in pairs and decide what would make the best wedding present from the choices presented in the Ideas generator box. Run through the useful expressions and elicit any other phrases that they might know for negotiating and discussing options.

8 This exercise provides further practice of collaborative decision making. Students choose one of the tasks to complete in groups of four.

9 Students perform the second task in pairs, as in the exam.

Vocabulary organiser 9, page 170

Photocopiable activity instructions

Creative compounds (page 96)

Aim: to practise a range of compound words.

Before-class preparation:

1 Photocopy sheets to a ratio of one for every three students.

2 Cut out the words, and place them in envelopes. If you wish to keep them for further use, you could stick the sheets to a piece of card before cutting them out, to reinforce them.

Instructions:

3 Students get into teams of three, and each team takes an envelope. They must keep these closed.

4 Explain that the envelopes contain words which can be used in various ways to make compound words.

5 Tell them they will have five or ten minutes to form as many compound words as possible.

6 Set the clock. Then tell the teams to open their envelopes and start.

7 Monitor from a distance. When the time is up, tell them all to stop.

8 Ask each team how many words they think they have found. Check the words from each team, and write them on the board.

Makeover advice (page 97)

Aims: to practise suggesting solutions and justifying ideas, vocabulary for colours and their emotional associations and uses, emphatic phrases.

Instructions:

1 Students work in groups of four. Photocopy one worksheet for every group. Cut out the four extracts and give one extract to each student in the group.

2 Students read the situation on the extract and work out what advice they would give the client, using the information about colours on page 91, or their own ideas.
   They can either make notes or write a full set of advice. Remind them to use the emphatic phrases from the Student's Book to be persuasive.

3 Each student takes turns to present their ideas to the rest of the group. They spend two minutes discussing the problem, with students suggesting alternative solutions. They then have one minute to decide on a final solution, before moving on to the next situation.

Alternative: give each student a full copy of the worksheet and ask them to prepare a solution for all four of the situations, before discussing possible solutions in their group.

Creative compounds

news	desk
paper	up
mill	**rise**
top	bring
make	**sun**
grade	load
down	over
m a n	**look**
power	mind
BLOW	absent
master	**POST**
clip	PIECE
wind	**roof**

Makeover advice

Cosy, romantic old cottage

Until I moved into our new house with my partner I'd always lived in modern, characterless boxes. I thought living in an old cottage would be romantic, but it has its problems. The ceilings are low and the windows are very small, so it's always dark. We have a particularly dark sitting room, which is cosy in the evenings when we have a log fire, but can be depressing during the day. We also have a study, which is a bit brighter, but is currently full of boxes of books. What can we do to make the house brighter and bring in more light? What sort of colours should we use? How can we make the best use of our space?

Practical family home

I've just moved into a new modern house with my husband and two children. The previous owners painted it in strong, rather garish colours which are hardly conducive to a relaxed atmosphere for us to enjoy our family time together. Our eldest daughter is seven and she hasn't been sleeping well since we moved. Her bedroom is painted bright red and I think she needs something more soothing. We desperately need to decorate at least the main rooms: our daughters' bedroom, the sitting room and the kitchen / dining room. All the rooms have big windows and lots of natural light. Can you suggest what colours we should use?

Contemporary design show home

I live in a modern house, which was built in the 1990's in a very innovative design by a well-known Dutch architect. It is all open-plan, so the downstairs is really one enormous room. The kitchen area has stainless steel appliances and a white and grey decor. The rest of the downstairs area is white, with mainly black furniture and some wood. I love the house, but after ten years I'm starting to find the stark colours quite cold and clinical; it can be quite depressing. I'd like to make the house feel more homely, and perhaps introduce some warmer colours. I have £10,000 in savings, which I would be happy to invest in some new furniture and accessories, but they would need to be in keeping with the modern design. My husband travelled a lot in Africa when he was young, and has an interesting collection of artefacts that we would like to display, including a series of wooden masks. How could we tie this in to the rest of the house?

Architect's office

As a self-employed architectural consultant it is important for me to work in attractive surroundings and to create a positive impression on any clients that might come to visit me. My office is in a converted industrial building and is a large space, divided into two areas; the office area has two desks and all my office equipment, and the other area is for meeting clients and has a large conference table and some comfortable seating. I have always preferred neutral colours and the whole office is currently painted a creamy beige colour. However, I feel ready for a change of colour scheme, something more inspiring and energising that will promote creative and practical activity. Could you give me any suggestions?

10 THE GOOD LIFE

Unit introduction

The topic of the unit is family values and ethical living. It focuses on ethical lifestyles, choices and dilemmas, and family values. These cover a variety of issues that are increasingly discussed in the media, as well as in social conversation or debate.

Warm-up activity

Ask your students to describe their ideal world. What would life be like in their utopia?

Getting started

1   This focuses on the topic of ethical choices and the decisions that we have to make in order to lead a good lifestyle. It introduces some of the topics that will come up in the unit. Discuss the questions as a whole class. Elicit from the students that in order to live an ethical lifestyle one needs to think about whether any people, animals or habitats were maltreated, abused, or destroyed in order to provide us with the things in our lives. Ask students to brainstorm where the clothes they are wearing and the food they ate for breakfast may have come from, etc. Ask them to think about what ethical or unethical processes may have been involved in their production, transport, sale, etc.

Extension

Suggest that your students check out the Freerice website at www.freerice.com to see how good their English vocabulary is. For every correct answer, the charity donates ten grains of rice through the United Nations to help end world hunger.

→   Vocabulary organiser 10, exercise 1, page 171

Vocabulary organiser answers

something that conforms to a set of principles or moral values (definition)
unethical (antonym)
ethics (n pl)
ethically (adv)

Reading gapped texts

BACKGROUND: LONG-DISTANCE FAMILIES

In the UK over the past few decades, increasing numbers of families have been living apart for all or part of the year, in order for one of the parents to pursue a career in another part of the country, or in another country altogether. This happened less often in the past because the woman didn't usually have a career of her own and so could follow her husband, whereas nowadays, the woman's career is often as highly valued as her husband's, if not more so.

VOCABULARY: TERMS TO PRE-TEACH

'Quality of life' refers to material things, wealth, etc. that can give you a better quality lifestyle (a nice house, two cars, foreign holidays, etc.).
'Quality time' refers to the time you spend doing something good (time spent with your children or partner doing something fun or constructive together).

2   Make sure your students understand the terms as defined above and ask them to give further examples of things that would constitute 'quality of life' or 'quality time'. Ask students to justify their answers. Students should conclude that a balance is required for a happy life, between money and material possessions in order to live comfortably, and time to spend with loved ones.

Ask students what kind of strains can be put on a family that prioritises 'quality of life'.

EXAM SPOTLIGHT

Read the information in the box. The purpose of this section is to help students gain a better understanding of the way most texts are structured, and a better understanding of what the text is saying on the whole. This will help them in Part 7 of the Reading and Use of English paper.

Check that students understand the box heading:
Text structure: the order of information in the text as a whole
Paragraph cohesion: how connections between paragraphs are made clear, e.g. through the use of linking words and phrases (*on the other hand; similarly; one example of this*)
Coherence: how the meaning of the text is conveyed, e.g. by having a generalisation followed by an example, or a positive opinion of something followed by a contrasting opinion, or a discussion followed by a summing up

Extension

Direct your students' attention towards the first paragraph of the text. Ask them what dilemma is being described.

Answer: that in order for your children to grow up in the country and live in a nice house, most people would have to work in the city.

3 Students read the table and do the task individually. This will help give them a general overview of the text. Elicit and check answers with the group in order to make sure everyone has identified the correct information. (Note that the information about the Veninger family is in paragraph G.)

Answers

1 Chitnis	2 Yardley	3 Veninger
1 Anthony and Jane	2 Jonathan and Jean	3 Laurie and Jim
1 three children	2 four children	3 daughters

4 Tell students to read the text and paragraphs again to find the information. When everyone has finished, check their answers.

Answers

Chitnis: they are coping but it is hard
Yardley: they got divorced
Veninger: they have coped but it has been difficult, and Jim is now returning home

TEACHING IN PRACTICE: UNDERSTANDING GAPPED TEXTS

You need to stress to your students the importance of reading the text as a whole, and not just focusing on each gap separately. They need to understand that getting an idea of the structure and understanding the development of the theme of the text are both important prerequisites to doing the task, and the best way to do this is by reading the whole text carefully in the first instance to understand it. Only then should students attempt to find the paragraphs that fit each gap. Students frequently make the wrong choices by selecting an option which fits the text before the gap, and neglecting to check that the text after the gap follows on smoothly.

Extension

If you feel that the students would benefit from gaining a closer understanding of the text before completing the exam task, provide them with the following questions.

1 Which days of the week is Anthony away from home?

2 Where does Anthony stay when he is in London?

3 Which factors help Jane to get through the week when her husband is away?

4 Why did Jean and the children not go to Germany with Jonathan?

5 Which factors does Jean feel contributed to the eventual break-up of her marriage?

6 What is it sometimes difficult to appreciate and why?

7 Why, according to the writer, is it 'ironic' that some families decide to spend part of their lives apart?

Extension answers

1 Tuesday till Thursday
2 He has a small flat.
3 They support each other, and Jane's parents live next door.
4 It would have been difficult to uproot their four children.
5 When Jonathan moved to Tokyo and only came home once every couple of months, he started to miss out on the everyday things.
6 The good things about one another, because you don't have enough time together.
7 It's ironic that they originally decide to spend part of their lives apart in order to give their children a better life, but instead they put an 'intolerable strain' on the family.

PARAGRAPH COHESION

Discuss the information in the box about techniques used by writers, and elicit further examples of each kind.

5 Students refer to missing paragraph A in the exam task in exercise 9 on page 97, and find the key words individually, then answer the questions. Check answers with the class and emphasise how useful this technique is for finding the correct gap for the missing paragraphs.

Answers

the years went by, Germany, four-kid, he, … (*he* must refer to Jonathan Yardley, because *Germany* and *four-kid* do not match any of the other people).

6 Students work individually or in pairs to underline the key information in the main article. Check answers with the whole class.

EXAM SPOTLIGHT

Read through the tip with the class. Emphasise that students should not simply accept that the last remaining paragraph is always the odd paragraph – they might have made a mistake with one of the others. They should apply the same techniques as they did to all the other paragraphs in order to ensure that it doesn't belong somewhere in the text after all. Stress that the information contained in the 'odd' paragraph will of course seem to fit in terms of theme, and may even be from another section of the original text itself, but there should not be any direct links to any of the gaps within the text.

7 & 8 Students complete the exercises individually or in pairs. Check answers with the whole class.

> ### Answers
> 7 Paragraph B refers to none of the three families. It mentions reasons why families may live apart. The general reference to the lifestyle choice *(why families live like this)* links in with the end of the second paragraph which signals a change from specific information about one family to a more general comment: *even they are finding long-distance family life tough going, and they're certainly not alone.*
> 8 Paragraph C mentions Anne Green. She has not been mentioned anywhere else. The paragraph gives information about long-term commuting and its effect on family life.

9 Students should now attempt the final task individually. They should spend no more than ten minutes doing this and they should be able to justify their answers.

> ### Answers
> 1 D (*Jane; from Tuesday to Thursday I'm in London:* this paragraph focuses on Anthony's views and follows on from *he doesn't like what that means*)
> 2 F (*Jane, Anthony:* focuses on Jane's views)
> 3 B (general comment on families follows on from *they are not alone*)
> 4 A (*somehow it all went wrong* links between *at first it was fine* in preceding paragraph and *it was the beginning of the end* in the following paragraph)
> 5 G (the following paragraph is clearly talking about a different family with two girls, as introduced in G)
> 6 E (Laurie links back to G)

→ Vocabulary organiser 10, exercise 2, page 171

> ### Vocabulary organiser answers
> 1 uproot   2 undermine   3 bachelor
> 4 frenetic   5 intolerable

Student's Book pages 98–99

Language development fixed phrases

1 Students should do the exercise individually or in pairs, or you can go through it with the whole class.

> ### Answers
> 1 e   2 a   3 c   4 h   5 d   6 b   7 g   8 f

→ Vocabulary organiser 10, exercise 3, page 171

> ### Vocabulary organiser answers
> 1 nitty gritty   2 rock the boat   3 take their toll on
> 4 tough going   5 stresses and strains   6 alarm bells started to sound
> 7 up sticks   8 The bottom line

Key word *pull*

> ### VOCABULARY: KEY WORD *PULL*
>
> When you pull something, you hold it firmly and use force in order to move it towards you or away from its previous position. *I helped pull him out of the water ...*
>
> When you pull an object from a bag, pocket, or cupboard, you put your hand in and bring the object out. *Jack pulled the slip of paper from his shirt pocket ...*
>
> When an animal pulls a cart they move it along behind them. *In early 20th-century rural Sussex, horses still pulled the plough ...*
>
> When a driver or vehicle pulls to a stop or a halt, the vehicle stops. *He pulled to a stop behind a pickup truck ...*
>
> In a race or contest, if you pull ahead of or pull away from an opponent, you gradually increase the amount by which you are ahead of them. *She pulled away, extending her lead to 15 seconds ...*
>
> If you pull something apart, you break or divide it into small pieces, often in order to put them back together again in a different way. *If I wanted to improve the car significantly I would have to pull it apart and start again.*
>
> If someone pulls a gun or a knife on someone else, they take out a gun or knife and threaten the other person with it. (INFORMAL) *They had a fight. One of them pulled a gun on the other ...*
>
> To pull crowds, viewers, or voters means to attract them. *The organisers have to employ performers to pull a crowd.*
>
> If you pull a muscle, you injure it by straining it. *Dave pulled a back muscle and could barely kick the ball ...*
>
> To pull a stunt or a trick on someone means to do something dramatic or silly in order to get their attention or trick them. *Everyone saw the stunt you pulled on me.*
>
> Pull is also a noun. *The feather must be removed with a straight, firm pull.*
>
> A pull is a strong physical force which causes things to move in a particular direction. *... the pull of gravity.*

2 Elicit answers from the students.

> ### Answers
> make something succeed, be successful at something

3 Students can use their dictionaries if necessary. They should also make a note of the definition of each phrasal verb in their vocabulary notebooks.

> ### Answers
> 1 pulled back   2 pulled down
> 3 pull (yourself) together   4 pull out of
> 5 pull over   6 pull through
> 7 pull up   8 pull off

4 Students should use their dictionaries to find the meanings of any phrases they don't know and complete the exercise. They should then add them to their vocabulary notebooks.

→ Vocabulary organiser 10, exercise 4, page 171

Answers	
1 pulled a muscle	2 pull out all the stops
3 pulled a face	4 pulling my leg
5 pull yourself together	6 pull strings
7 pulling your weight	8 pull a fast one on

Vocabulary organiser answers

1 pulling your leg	2 pulling his weight	3 pull off
4 pulled down	5 pulling a fast one on us	6 pull through
7 pulled strings	8 Pull over	

Listening (1) identifying feelings

5 This discussion activity should help students prepare for the listening task by focusing on the issue of sustainability, and introducing or revising some key language and ideas on the topic. Discuss the question with the class. Refer to the photo and ask the students what aspect of sustainable living it depicts.

TEACHING IN PRACTICE: LISTENING VOCABULARY

The following words and phrases all appear in the listening audioscript. Although it is not necessary for students to know the meaning of all words and phrases they hear in order to complete exam tasks, introducing such lexical items before they listen will help them to expand or consolidate their English vocabulary.

phrases: *jump on the bandwagon*
nouns: *detergent, water-butt, drainpipe, packaging, compost, fertiliser*
verbs: *patch, recycle, compost* (also a noun)
adjectives: *ecological, eccentric, organic*

EXAM SPOTLIGHT

Read the information with the students. Make sure they have understood the usefulness of this technique and then elicit any other words and phrases they know that might express surprise.

6 First students need to read and underline the key words. Then brainstorm words that could be associated with them on the board.

7 ⊙ 35 Students attempt both exam tasks individually. They should hear the recording twice. Afterwards, check answers with the group.

Answers				
1 E	2 F	3 A	4 G	5 B
6 E	7 H	8 C	9 B	10 F

Audioscript ⊙ 35

Speaker 1: Nowadays, everyone's suddenly jumping on the ecological bandwagon and talking about sustainable living. But really, my walking to the shops instead of driving is hardly going to make much difference, is it? I find it easy enough to do, but I suspect all it achieves is to make me feel virtuous. People think concern about the environment is something new, but when I was a child, we used to get told off if we left a light on when we went out of a room, and wearing your elder brother's or sister's handed down clothes to save money was just a fact of life. You didn't expect to have new clothes until you were an adult.

Speaker 2: I suppose most people have one thing that they really try hard with. I can remember my mum and dad being obsessed with water. They saved water from the kitchen for the pot plants, as long as it didn't have detergent in it. They also attached water-butts to the drainpipes around our house, to collect rainwater for the garden. That's had quite a powerful influence on me, because they still seem like natural things to do. I wish I could get the rest of my family to do the same, though – they just laugh at me, and refuse. Yet they're all very concerned about not wasting food. It's illogical, really!

Speaker 3: Where I live, the council can recycle certain materials, but in other districts they do far more. It's really annoying – I've contacted the council a couple of times about it, but they say they haven't got the facilities to recycle anything else. My target is to only buy things in packaging that can be reused, like cardboard, but it isn't easy. And of course we produce so much more waste these days. When I was young, we didn't have much money to spend, so a lot of my clothes were homemade. I remember my mother knitted me itchy pullovers that didn't fit. When they wore thin, they were patched, and patched again. It was pretty embarrassing, I can tell you!

Speaker 4: I travel by train rather than car, whenever possible, and I haven't flown for years. But it's surprising how many other people regard me as eccentric, which makes me feel uncomfortable. So to avoid awkward situations, I don't mention it – I say I don't *like* flying, or I prefer looking out of a train window. I wouldn't try to change people's minds. My concern about the environment came from my parents. I can remember everything organic from the kitchen got composted. It was the only household chore I enjoyed doing, taking potato peelings, egg shells, coffee grounds and so on out to the compost bin in the garden. It made excellent fertiliser for the plants.

Speaker 5: When I was a teenager, I wanted to start buying make-up, but my parents wouldn't let me. As a joke, my father said why didn't I make my own. I decided to take him seriously and rubbed beetroot juice into my lips to make them pink. I was very excited the first time I went out like that, and my friends thought I looked great! I do a lot more for the environment now, like cycling instead of driving a car. But it has an impact on my children. They'd love to go ice skating, but the only way to get to the nearest skating rink is by car, so it's impossible.

8 Discuss the topic with the class. Refer back to the opening discussion at the beginning of this section and ask students to talk about any new things they have learnt, or ask them to suggest any new ways they can think of to conserve natural resources.

Student's Book pages 100–101

Grammar direct and reported speech

1 After students have identified the direct speech in the article, elicit ideas about the effect that direct speech has on a piece of writing.

> **Answer**
>
> The direct speech in the article makes some points more immediate and engaging. It helps the reader to relate more clearly with the speaker. It makes the tone less formal and is generally more lively and engaging than reported speech.

DIRECT SPEECH TO REPORTED SPEECH

Ask the students to read through the information or read it with them. Ask them why they think it is useful to be able to change direct speech into reported speech. This technique is useful in conversational English, and also when paraphrasing dialogue in written work.

2 Students underline the changes. Check with the class.

> **Answers**
>
> *I can > he could; my company's > his company's; I'm in London > he was in London*
> Rules: tense changes, subject / object pronoun changes

3 Students should do this exercise individually before coming together as a group to share answers.

> **Answers**
>
> a Anthony said that he had a small flat in London, but it wasn't home.
> b Jean said it had been a good career move for him, but they had known uprooting their four children would be impossible.
> c Laurie said that Jim taking a job abroad had been right at the time, but the girls had never got entirely used to it.

→ Grammar reference 10.1, page 216

REPORTED SPEECH TO DIRECT SPEECH

Read the information in the box with the students. Explain that it may also be necessary to transform reported speech into direct speech in the exam, and that the opposite rules will apply.

4 Students underline and explain the changes to the sentence.

> **Answers**
>
> The sentence reverses the changes normally used to make reported speech: *he → I; he had been offered → 'I have been offered'*; name (Jean) used to clarify who he is speaking to.

5 Students do the exercise individually. Check answers with the class.

> **Answers**
>
> 1 I had a good time in Spain and I can't wait to go back next summer.
> 2 I went to the concert last night and I'm feeling rather tired.
> 3 I'm not coming because I hate the theatre.

TEACHING IN PRACTICE: REPORTING VERBS

Say the following sentence to the class in an aggressive and angry manner:
> *I don't like this soup – it's cold!*
Ask the class what you are doing. Elicit that you are complaining. Give a few more examples:
It wasn't me that broke the window, honest! (denying)
I know what – I'm going to call my grandmother! (deciding)

6 Students complete the exercise individually. Check answers with the class.

> **Answers**
>
> | | | |
> |---|---|---|
> | 1 admitted | 2 propose | 3 demanded |
> | 4 swore | 5 begged | 6 suggested |

→ Grammar reference 10.2, pages 216

7 Students should attempt this exam task individually. Do not allow more than five minutes for the task as students should now be used to doing this kind of task under pressure.

> **Answers**
>
> 1 denied having anything to do with
> 2 insisted on inviting me
> 3 predicted that it would snow
> 4 apologised for what he had said
> 5 recommended that we (should) try
> 6 objected to me / my getting a

See *Reporting the news* photocopiable activity, page 108.

Speaking organising a larger unit of discourse

EXAM SPOTLIGHT

Read through the information with the class. Ask the students to summarise what they are expected to do in this part of the Speaking test.

8 Do this task with the class. Look at the pictures and ask students to decide which two they think are the most interesting. Ask them why. They do not have to agree – each student should be able to justify the reasons for their choice. Ask which pictures seem to have more things to talk about. Point out that the picture that students like the most may not always be the one that they can say the most things about, and so they should think carefully before deciding which pictures to discuss.

9 Put students into pairs or open pairs: Student A and Student B. Listen as a class to one pair answering the first task, (Student A comparing the pictures and answering the question on the page, Student B answering the follow-up question asked by the interlocutor, given in the speech bubble on page 101). Ask the class to comment. Elicit suggestions and encourage other pairs to attempt the task. When you are satisfied that everyone is performing all the functions of the task correctly (comparing, describing, expressing opinions, explaining, speculating), tell them to swap roles and carry out task B.

Use of English multiple-choice cloze

10 This exercise should heighten students' awareness of the meanings and / or usage of certain words, and subtle differences in usage between several words with a similar meaning. Ask students to do the exercise individually or in pairs, then check the answers. Point out that many of these words form collocations or fixed expressions. The extension task can be used to consolidate students' understanding of the key phrases.

Answers

1 B   2 A   3 D   4 B   5 C

Extension

Elicit expressions from exercise 10 that mean the following, and suggest students write them in their vocabulary books:

1 to not be sensitive to or care about what people say or think
2 there's no point in doing something

3 a considerable amount of money
4 to have a strong regional or foreign accent / way of pronouncing words
5 so much

Answers to extension task

1 to have a thick skin / to be thick-skinned
2 It's no good ... (followed by -ing form)
3 a small fortune
4 to speak with / have a thick accent
5 to such a degree

11 Ask students to complete this Part 1 exam task. Remind them to consider all four options carefully, even when they feel confident that they know the correct answer. Elicit answers.

Answers

1 C   2 A   3 D   4 B   5 A   6 A   7 B   8 C

→   Vocabulary organiser 10, exercise 5, page 171

Vocabulary organiser answers

1 heavy	2 depths	3 value
4 solid	5 contract	6 packet

Student's Book pages 102–103

Listening (2) note-taking

BACKGROUND: THE FREECYCLE NETWORK

The Freecycle Network (often abbreviated TFN or just known as Freecycle) is a non-profit organisation that aims to divert reusable goods from landfill. It provides a worldwide online registry, and co-ordinates the creation of local groups and forums for individuals and non-profit organisations to offer and receive free items for reuse or recycling. The organisation began in Arizona, USA, and has since spread to over 85 countries, with thousands of local groups and millions of members.

1 Discuss the topic with the class. If they haven't heard of freecycling before, elicit what other word it reminds them of (recycling) and ask them where or what you might recycle for free.

2 ◉ 36 Tell students that they are going to listen to three people talking about freecycling and mentioning items they have either acquired, given away, or come across themselves. Explain that their task is to make notes in the box while they listen (or in their notebooks if there isn't room in the box). Point out that this is not an exam task but that it will give them extra practice in listening for specific information.

Answers

Dave acquired: a bathroom cabinet, a set of bookshelves, a laundry basket, kitchen utensils and crockery, a huge shelving unit, a sofa, a sewing machine

Dave gave away: an old chair, some speakers and Helen's old curling tongs.

Dave's other items: would like a garden table and chairs

Julia acquired: shower doors, a sewing machine, a farm gate, a china umbrella stand

Julia gave away: a broken lawnmower

Julia's other items: ancient office furniture, windfallen apples, spare firewood

Anna acquired: a vacuum cleaner

Anna gave away: excess chicks, two cockerels, egg for sale signs written on slate

Anna's other items: sofas, TVs, computers, cots, dogs, geese, a sow and her piglets and sheep

Audioscript ◉ 36

Dave: We love *Freecycle*. My girlfriend Helen enforces a policy of household recycling as much as possible and it was her idea to join, because we were about to move in together and had a lot of stuff lying around that was doubled up. We've also used the site to help furnish our new flat. We had absolutely no furniture so it was a big challenge for us. But our *Freecycle* group seemed to offer everything we needed, from three-piece suites to the kitchen sink. After bagging some great stuff in the first few weeks, we were completely hooked. We managed to wangle a bathroom cabinet, a set of bookshelves, a laundry basket and loads of kitchen utensils and crockery. Helen seemed to have more success at claiming things than I did – maybe it was the female touch or maybe it was the sheer speed of her email responses, I don't know.

I have shifted, among other things, an old chair, some speakers, and Helen's old curling tongs. It is so much more rewarding to have people pick up the goods from you than just putting things in the bin.

The pinnacle of our *Freecycle* success has got to be claiming a huge shelving unit and a lovely sofa. Helen then requested a sewing machine, which she used to make a cover for the new sofa. We have been able to put other people's unwanted (but perfectly good) furniture to new use. It has also made the cost of decorating an entire flat far easier to stomach. I am now offering a lot more stuff on the site. I'm well and truly converted, and use it more than Helen! I check the site all the time for new offers – come summer, I'd love a garden table and chairs.

Julia: I found out about *Freecycle* when my colleague posted up loads of our ancient office furniture that would have been dumped otherwise. I've been hooked since.

When I drive past the dump, the amount of wonderful stuff I see that's going to waste seems criminal. I'm tempted to give out flyers for *Freecycle* when I go past, to tell people they don't have to throw good things away. There are three main benefits to *Freecycle*. First: people can get things for free. I've got a massive list of things I'm really happy with: shower doors, a sewing machine, a farm gate, a china umbrella stand. I've actually taken more than I've been able to give. Second: people usually post up stuff that they think isn't worth selling, which makes *Freecycle* good for avoiding landfill. Third: people come and collect what you've advertised, so it's very convenient for you. I once offered a broken lawnmower, which somebody snapped up!

Freecycle in Oxford has quite strict guidelines, because everything on the forum should be stuff that could end up on the dump otherwise. People accept the rules, but they also love the community feel of the group, so in order to avoid clogging up the *Freecycle* forum, a subgroup has been set up called the Oxford Freecycle Café. The Café is more chatty and people offer all kinds of things on it, such as wind-fallen apples or spare firewood. It really shows the demand for free community networks.

Anna: My partner and I moved to a smallholding here just over a year ago with the aim of setting up a more sustainable lifestyle. We provide for ourselves by growing produce, raising and eating our own poultry and meat and using our own fuel. We found out about our local *Freecycle* group from an article in our daily newspaper (recycled for composting and firelighting), and its philosophy seemed to go hand-in-hand with our own, so we thought there would be no better way of offloading some of the excess chicks we had at the time. We instantly got involved with this wonderful system of free exchange, and have since taken many items that have been incredibly useful. Since we started out we have found homes for two cockerels, and we took someone's vacuum cleaner which is now in my son's flat, and we have given away some lovely 'eggs for sale' signs written on slate.

One of the great things about *Freecycle* is that you can choose whom to give things to. You are encouraged to give items to charities if they request it, but otherwise choosing a recipient is entirely up to you and no explanations are necessary. In our *Freecycle* group, there are the usual postings for items like sofas, TVs, computers and cots, all of which are extremely useful to members, but there are also postings which probably would not be found in groups in cities; requests to re-house dogs, geese, a sow and her piglets and sheep. These latter items reflect the fact that here *Freecycle* has become a real aid to those of us who value the idea of sustainability while being part of the farming community.

3 Discuss the advantages quickly with the class. This will lead you into the writing section that follows.

See *Scruples questionnaire* photocopiable activity, page 107.

Writing a proposal

4 Read the rubric with the students and ask them to underline the key words in the exam question. This will give them the headings.

Possible answers

Unnecessary waste, repair, redistribution

5 Allow students a few minutes to read the proposal and write in the headings. Check the answers with the class.

Possible answers

1 Excess / Unnecessary waste	2 Find repair agents
3 Sell reusable goods	4 Conclusion

6 Go through the functions in the box with the class. Make sure they understand what each one means and elicit examples of each. Students decide which functions are required in the writing task. You should get your students used to recognising the different functions required in each task whenever they attempt one. They should also familiarise themselves with the structures and vocabulary relevant to the required functions.

Answer

outlining and suggesting; the example proposal also explains / describes possible solutions, hypothesises possible situations, persuades using rhetorical questions, expresses opinions

USING REGISTER

Read the information in the box with the students and make sure they understand what *register* is. In order to know what register to use, tell your students that they will need to think carefully about who the target reader is for each task. Ask:

Is the target reader someone from your school, college or place of work?

Do you need to present difficult information politely (as in a complaint) or are you trying to persuade somebody to do something for you?

Is the target reader somebody you know or someone unknown to you?

Is the target reader a close friend, family member or someone in a position of authority?

Point out that students must adopt the appropriate style and tone for the reader, but at all times it is important to have a balance between the function(s) required by the task and the relationship with the target reader.

Note: Cambridge Assessment advises that students look at past papers and note the vocabulary and structures needed for each Part 2 choice to help them decide which one can best demonstrate their language skills and knowledge.

7 Ask students to look at the proposal in pairs and answer the questions. Elicit ideas from the class. Point out that proposals can be informal (though this is fairly uncommon), formal, or neutral, depending on who the intended audience is.

Answers

In this case the audience is the newspaper editor, but it is also being written for the readers of the paper (if the proposal is printed), i.e. people from the community, in particular people who have things to give away or who don't have much money to spend on new clothes, furniture, etc. So the register is more likely to be neutral, rather than formal, but there may be a mix of elements.

The example proposal is generally quite formal / neutral, but the third paragraph has a more informal register that does not fit with the rest of the proposal or the target audience. So it is not consistent.

8 Students decide which sentence in each set (a, b or c) is formal, neutral or informal. They can do this in pairs or individually. Go through their choices and ask them to justify their reasons.

Answers

1 a formal	b neutral	c informal
2 a neutral	b informal	c formal
3 a informal	b formal	c neutral

9 Ask students to underline vocabulary and structural elements in exercise 8 that indicate the style or register of the sentences. Discuss the questions with the students.

Answers

The most formal sentences are the longest, and they often use the passive. Informal sentences often use slang or colloquial expressions, extreme language (*fantastic*) and also informal punctuation (dashes rather than commas or colons).

Informal style is generally unsuitable for a proposal.

10 Students rewrite the third paragraph individually or work in pairs. Offer help where necessary. As well as the words in the box, ask students to use other language from this section.

Possible answer

Another solution is to set up a shop next to the rubbish tip where we discard unwanted items such as furniture. I propose that the newspaper approaches the local council and asks them to handle this. Then, rather than throwing things away or recycling them, some could be sold on to people who need them. In this way, anyone who cannot afford new items may be able to have second-hand ones that only need minor repairs.

11 Students need to spend some time on this and think of their own ideas. They can work alone or in pairs, or it could be done as a class activity.

12 Students write their proposal. As they will have done all the preparation, 15 minutes will probably be enough for most students to complete the task.

Vocabulary organiser 10, page 171

Answers

1
something that conforms to a set of principles or moral values (adj)
unethical (antonym)
ethics (n pl)
ethically (adv)

2
1 uproot	2 undermine
3 bachelor	4 frenetic
5 intolerable	

3
1 nitty gritty	2 rock the boat
3 take their toll on	4 tough going
5 stresses and strains	6 alarm bells started to sound
7 up sticks	8 The bottom line

4
1 pulling your leg	2 pulling his weight
3 pull off	4 pulled down
5 pulling a fast one on us	6 pull through
7 pulled strings	8 Pull over

5
1 heavy	2 depths
3 value	4 solid
5 contract	6 packet

Bank of English
1 conscience	2 dilemma
3 ethics	4 morals
5 scruples	

Photocopiable activity instructions

Scruples questionnaire (page 107)

Aim: to practise discussing ethical issues; to help students discuss their choices and give reasons for what they say.

Instructions:

1 Write the following on the board:

1 point = no scruples or ethics whatsoever; no.1 ('me') is the only person who matters!

2 points = got a bit of a conscience, but won't make a big personal sacrifice if it complicates life.

3 points = morally conscientious and very PC (politically correct)

2 Copy the questionnaire once and cut out the dilemmas. Give each student one dilemma. If there are more students than dilemmas then you can repeat some or make up a few more.

3 Each student reads out their dilemma and then names three other people in the group to say what they would do in the situation.

4 Everybody in the group (except the speakers) awards a mark of 1–3 to each speaker's answers based on the formula you've written on the board.

5 Go round the room several times, reading the same questions but choosing different people to answer so that everyone has had a chance to answer at least twice.

6 At the end add up the scores: the person with the highest score wins.

Reporting the news (page 108)

Aim: to help students practise using reported speech when talking about past events.

Instructions:

1 Organise the class into groups of six and allocate roles (a reporter, a police officer, and the four roles on the cards).

2 Photocopy the activity and cut out the newspaper clipping and the character notes.

3 Give one newspaper clipping to each group and tell them to pass it round so everyone reads it. Meanwhile, give each student their own character notes.

4 Students can either stand or swap places for each interview. Alternatively, line up a set of desks with chairs on each side. First, the police officer interviews the two suspects, one at a time, by asking them direct questions. Meanwhile the reporter interviews the two eye-witnesses by asking direct questions.

5 Afterwards, the two suspects, the two eyewitnesses and the police officer and reporter report back to one another on what they were asked and what they said.

6 Finally each person writes up or verbally reports on what they found out.

Scruples Questionnaire

What would you do?

An old lady needs help crossing the road, but you are late for an important interview. If you help her across, you know you'll miss your bus and it's an hour until the next one. Your potential employer has told you that punctuality is a very important quality!

You have just got married and your partner has announced he or she wants you to give up your career (which you love) to become a full-time parent / housekeeper. You don't want to upset him / her because you can see it is important to them.

You've just found a very cheap piece of land to buy to build a house on, but discover that there is a campaign to turn it into a wildlife sanctuary for endangered animals and plants. You know you won't be able to find such a bargain again and land prices are going up all the time.

You've just found out that the hamburger you are about to eat was made from a factory farmed cow that was slaughtered inhumanely. Trouble is, you're starving, and there's nothing else to eat!

You've just found out that the company you work for has business dealings with 'sweat shops' (clothes manufacturers that use illegal child labour) in the Far East. At the same time, you've just been offered the promotion you've been waiting years for.

You've invited some friends round for dinner. One of them doesn't eat pork for religious reasons but you had forgotten this. Unfortunately, you've used bacon fat as an ingredient in the main course.

A girl in the office where you work is getting upset because her boss keeps making lewd comments whenever he sees her. Last time someone said something in her defence, they got the sack.

Your brother has asked you to keep a secret and you have given him your word. Then he tells you that he's been invited to a party with some friends and they've decided they are going to take drugs for the first time to see what it's like.

You've just found out from your parents in trust that your cousin is adopted but he / she doesn't know this. Your cousin confides in you about everything and has told you that he / she suspects the truth about being adopted and has asked you what you think. You do not want to lie to anyone but you also feel it is not your place to tell the truth.

While on holiday in Africa you spend a lot of money on a beautiful necklace which you intend to give to your mother for her birthday, However, after arriving back in your home country, you notice that the necklace is made of ivory, and your mother strongly believes it is wrong to kill animals for the sake of vanity.

You've just been offered a large sum of money to set up the charity organisation you've always dreamed of, helping disabled children. However, you have reason to suspect that the money has come from someone who has dealings with the illegal sale of arms and ammunitions.

Your fiancé's parents have invited you round to their house for dinner. When you arrive there you find that most of the furniture has been made from tropical Amazonian hardwoods, there are the skins of endangered dead animals on the floor, and rare stuffed animals in glass cases. They ask you what you think of their house.

Reporting the news

Suspect still at large!

Mr Simon Smith, aged 101, was found dead in his home this morning by his housekeeper, Mrs Wiggins. The police are looking into the matter and have not yet ruled out foul play. It appears that the last person to have seen Mr Smith alive, was …

Eyewitness 1
Miss Crimson

Miss Crimson is a neighbour who lives opposite Mr Smith. She is 66 and a retired schoolteacher. She lives alone and spends a lot of time at home. Miss Crimson gives the following information in her statement.

- She left her house at 10.30 pm.
- It was dark.
- She saw a man come out of No. 12.
- She didn't see his face.
- She thought he had blond hair.
- He was quite tall.
- She didn't hear anything strange.

Suspect 2
The nephew, Alfred White

Alfred White is 20 and works as a builder. He is medium height and has dark hair. He is fond of his great-uncle and often comes to visit him and do jobs around the house for him. Alfred gives the following information in his statement.

- He came to see his great-uncle at 9 pm and stayed for about an hour and a half.
- The nurse seemed to be in a bad mood with him because he wouldn't take his pills.
- Alfred left the room for 10 minutes to make some tea.
- When he came back the nurse had gone and his uncle was asleep.

Eyewitness 2
Professor Purple

Professor Purple is a scientist who works at the university. He is 55 and he lives in the next road to Mr Smith. He doesn't know Mr Smith very well. Professor Purple gives the following information in his statement.

- He was crossing the road at 10.35 pm.
- He heard a loud bang.
- He saw two people running away from No. 12.
- They looked like kids.
- One of them might have been carrying a gun, but he can't be sure.

Suspect 1
The nurse, Sarah Black

Sarah Black is the nurse who comes in every day to look after Mr Smith and make sure he has taken his medicine. She is 30 and has known Mr Smith for two years. Sarah gives the following information in her statement.

- She left Mr Smith at 10.20 pm.
- Mr Smith's nephew was still there.
- Mr Smith was in bed asleep.
- He had always been very kind to her.
- He had taken his medicine at the proper time.
- He seemed in good spirits.

11 MAKING ENDS MEET

Unit introduction

The topics of the unit are making a living in a foreign country and credit-card fraud. The unit aims to look at money and its uses, to discuss the various ways in which people make a living (and whether this makes them happy or not), as well as the topical subject of credit-card fraud.

Warm-up activity

If you have any foreign currency coins at home, bring them to the class to show your students. Alternatively, you could search on the Internet for images of the currencies mentioned below, and print them off to show students.

Write the following on the board:

A 1 yen 2 dinar 3 lek 4 ruble 5 krone
6 lev 7 peso 8 taka 9 renminbi 10 pula

B a Bulgaria b China c Belarus d Botswana
e Japan f Algeria g Albania h Denmark
i Chile j Bangladesh

Place students in teams and ask them to match the currencies with the country in which they are used. Set a time limit, or state that the first team to find all the correct matches are the winners.

Answers				
1 e	2 f	3 g	4 c	5 h
6 a	7 i	8 j	9 b	10 d

Getting started

1 Ask your students to read the quotations, and elicit their responses. Once they have discussed each one in turn, ask them to look at the pictures on the page, then ask them about the meaning of the unit title.

Reading interpreting literature

2 Students read the question. Gather ideas about why people move to another country to live and work. Then discuss what the potential difficulties are.

Possible answers
problems with getting your qualifications recognised by the country; employers not wanting to employ foreigners; adapting to ways of working, customs and way of life of the country; climate; language / local dialect or accent; being accepted

3 Tell students to read the extract and decide whether the statements are true or false. Discuss their reasons for choosing these answers together.

Answers				
1 F	2 F	3 T	4 F	5 T

4 Elicit any unfamiliar words before students do the task. Allow them no more than ten minutes to complete the task. Elicit answers and ask students to justify their choices.

Answers					
1 A	2 B	3 B	4 C	5 D	6 A

TEACHING IN PRACTICE: SPECULATING ABOUT A READING TEXT

When reading an extract from a novel or short story, it is a good idea to encourage students to speculate about what has happened before in the story, and what will happen next. This gives them useful oral practice in using language for speculating and may also encourage them to seek out the novel and read it.

5 Elicit ideas about what might happen next in the story. Encourage the use of *may*, *might* and *could* for speculation. Now you may wish to provide your students with the background information on *Brick Lane*.

BACKGROUND: *BRICK LANE* BY MONICA ALI

Brick Lane is the story of Nazneen, a young Bangladeshi woman given in an arranged marriage to Chanu Ahmed, a man almost twice her age. Chanu takes her to London, where he has lived and worked for almost 20 years. Nazneen not only has to learn to live with Chanu, but she has to survive in a whole new culture as well.

In the small Bangladeshi estate community in London, Nazneen meets other Bangladeshi people who cope with their own struggles. Some of them struggle against the traditions they left behind, while others struggle against the new traditions that their English-born children are exposed to. Then Chanu is made redundant, and Nazneen has to find work to support the family. This extract describes the start of her working life in London.

Extension

For further language work on the text, ask students to find words or phrase in the article that mean the following:

1 smiled broadly
2 express something uncertainly
3 briefly
4 a type of large bag
5 simple, basic
6 an item of clothing
7 performed a ritual to get rid of
8 make something easier
9 to make something vanish

Answers to extension task

1 beamed	2 venture	3 fleetingly	4 holdall
5 rudimentary	6 garment	7 exorcised	8 facilitate
9 dispel			

→ Vocabulary organiser 11, exercise 1, page 172

Vocabulary organiser answers

1 ventured   2 totted up   3 troublesome   4 dispel   5 feverishly

Student's Book pages 106–107

Language development idiomatic phrases with *out*

1 Ask your students to read the rubric and the two quotations from the text. Elicit the meaning of the underlined phrases.

Answers

a *work out:* calculate, solve a problem
b *count out:* check the number that you are giving

2 Students work in pairs. Ask them to decide which phrase is needed to complete each sentence. Discuss their answer choices together.

Answers

1 out of the question	2 out of the blue
3 out of your mind	4 out of respect
5 out of this world	6 out of it
7 out of order	8 out of luck

→ Vocabulary organiser 11, exercise 2, page 172

Vocabulary organiser answers

1 T	2 F	3 F	4 T	5 F	6 F

Key word *money*

3 Students work in pairs to decide which of the verbs in the box can be followed by *money*. In feedback, check any of the words they don't know the meaning of (e.g. *launder money* = to put money gained from crime into legal business in order to make it 'clean'; *raise money* = to collect money, usually for a charity).

Answers

borrow, charge, earn, inherit, launder, lend, lose, make, owe, pay, raise, refund, save, spend, waste

4 Students work in pairs. Ask them to read each sentence carefully, and use the context to work out the meaning of the italicised phrase.

Answers

1 a   2 a   3 b

5 Students work in pairs. They won't know all of the definitions, so elicit the ones they do know first. They should be able to work out the meaning of the others, or they can use a dictionary to find them. Check the answers with the class.

Answers

1 d	2 e	3 f	4 b	5 a	6 c

→ Vocabulary organiser 11, exercise 3, page 172

Vocabulary organiser answers

1 have money to burn
2 gave him a good run for his money
3 put your money where your mouth is
4 put my money on
5 is pumping money into

6 Ask students to quickly read through the text and say what it is about (credit-card fraud). Allow them ten minutes to complete the task. Ask them to compare their answers with a partner, then check the answers with the class.

Answers

1 penniless	2 financial	3 fraudulent	4 insecure
5 transactions	6 careless	7 suspicion(s)	8 conspiracy

Extension

Ask students if they know of any similar stories. If they show interest, tell them to search the Internet for newspaper articles about credit-card fraud. They can use these to increase their vocabulary on the topic.

Listening sentence completion

7 Ask the students to read the sentences and decide which views they agree with. Ask them to compare the use of credit cards with that of cash.

8 Ask students to read the information in the Spotlight box, then speculate about what kind of information they expect each gap to contain.

Answers

1 a sum of money   2 a year
3 and 4 elements of household expenditure, such as energy, rent, housing, leisure, food, etc.

---

9 ◉ 37 Play the recording twice. Elicit answers and give feedback.

Answers

a £483.60   b 2009   c transport   d recreation and culture

Audioscript ◉ 37

As you may know, there's an international classification system for household spending, called the Classification of Individual Consumption by Purpose. If we look at the figures for household expenditure in the UK in 2011, average weekly expenditure was £483.60, a rise of £10 from 2010's £473.60. Total expenditure generally increases from year to year, partly because of inflation and partly because incomes tend to rise. However, the 2009 figure of £455 was in fact *lower* than in 2008.

If we now break down that total into categories, the highest area of spending in 2011 was transport, which accounted for £65.70 a week. Most of that was related to purchasing and running cars and other vehicles, with only £10.20 a week being spent on public transport.

Slightly less – £63.90, in fact – was spent on recreation and culture, which was the second largest category. Just under £19 of that was spent on package holidays – mostly holidays abroad – while the remaining £45.10 went on computers, TVs and other leisure activities.

---

10 Students read the rubric and sentences for exercise 11, which is an exam-style task. Elicit predictions about what the missing words and phrases might be.

TEACHING IN PRACTICE: MAINTAINING GOOD HABITS

At this stage in the course, some of the stronger students may feel that the introductory prediction tasks are unnecessary. Weaker students, however, often feel intimidated by listening tasks, and will still welcome the support. Training them to predict what they are going to hear every time they are faced with a listening task helps them to feel more confident, and so is valuable even at this later stage in the course.

---

11 ◉ 38 Play the recording twice and allow students time to complete their answers. Check the answers with the class, referring students to the audioscript on page 249 if they are still unsure.

Answers

1 gift economy	2 1300 BC	3 real estate
4 transferring money	5 city(-)states	6 (merchant's) voyage
7 fairs	8 negotiations	

Audioscript ◉ 38

The credit card is a 20th century invention, but the concept of credit goes back over 3,000 years. Basically, it means providing somebody with money or goods, and trusting them to repay or return those resources at some later date.

It's sometimes said that before the emergence of money, the earliest farming communities exchanged goods or services in a barter system. It now seems more likely that a form of credit called a 'gift economy' was in operation, where people helped others without receiving anything in exchange. Instead, there was an expectation that if they later needed help, they would get it.

The earliest records of a form of credit date back to around 1300 BC, among the Babylonians and Assyrians of present-day Iraq. And by 1000 BC, the Babylonians had devised a system of credit that simplified payments in trade between distant places. A merchant who bought from one supplier might be asked to pay a third party who had given the supplier credit.

In ancient Egypt, grain functioned as both food and money, and was stored in granaries, whose administration was effectively a government bank. This became a trade credit system, with payments transferred between accounts without money changing hands. Egyptians also sold real estate with payment being made in instalments.

The vast area of the Roman Empire 2,000 years ago, encouraged widespread trading and the use of credit, particularly among traders on the shores of the Mediterranean. Then, as the empire declined, and transferring money became both dangerous and difficult, credit was widely used to get round the problems.

During the Middle Ages, from about 500 to 1500 AD, credit was essential to the trading activities of the prosperous Italian city-states. Lending and borrowing, as well as buying and selling on credit, became commonplace among all social classes, from peasants to nobles.

In a common form of investment and credit, especially in Italy, a capitalist might help to finance a merchant's trading expedition, and share the risk. If the voyage was a success, the creditor recovered his investment plus a large bonus; however, if the ship was lost, the creditor could lose his entire investment.

Trading centres of the Middle Ages held fairs at regular intervals, and here another form of credit developed. A merchant who was short of cash could secure goods on credit by writing a letter promising to pay on a certain date. Before repaying the money, he had time either to sell the goods he'd brought with him, or to take home and sell the goods that he'd purchased on credit.

The first English settlers in North America, in the early 17th century, used credit to finance their voyage. Before they set sail, negotiations to raise the funds they needed lasted for three years. A wealthy London merchant organised a group of investors to finance the trip. Although these investors were supposed to be repaid in seven years, it was 25 years before they received their money in full!

Now I'll go on ...

Student's Book pages 108–109

Grammar modal auxiliaries (2)

1 Students match the sentences to the functions individually or in pairs. Discuss the answers as a class.

> **Answers**
>
> 1 a   2 d   3 c   4 e   5 b

2 Read through the information in the boxes for each modal type and discuss any questions or queries students have. Students work individually to complete the three mini-dialogues.

> **Answers**
>
> 1 'll / will, will be / may be, may / might as well
> 2 would, might as well, won't, could have
> 3 won't, would, could, will / may

→ Grammar reference 11, page 217

3 Allow approximately five minutes for this exercise. Elicit answers and give feedback.

> **Answers**
>
> 1 you may / might as well
> 2 'll become a nanny and
> 3 could / should / might have offered to pay
> 4 it would be difficult to persuade
> 5 would stop playing basketball
> 6 could at least have done

See *Monopoly token personality quiz* photocopiable activity, page 117.

Use of English multiple-choice cloze

4 Read the information in the box with the class and explain that the sentences before and after the gapped sentence may include important information. Ask students to read the sentences carefully before deciding which option is correct.

> **Answers**
>
> 1 c   2 d

5 Tell students to read the text through quickly and say what it is about. Elicit views from the class on the board game, Monopoly, which is the topic of the text. Ask them to read the question options and give them ten minutes to complete the exercise. Elicit students' answers and explanations.

> **Answers**
>
> 1 D   2 C   3 C   4 D   5 B   6 A   7 B   8 C

6 This is a speculative question. We might speculate that someone who is good at the game might make an astute business person, or be good in the property market! Or that someone who is very cautious might make a good scientific researcher. Welcome students' ideas, and generate discussion.

Speaking disagreeing with someone else's opinion

7 🔘 39 Ask the students to read the rubric, and the In other words box. Play the recording. Allow students time to tick phrases. Then play the recording again to allow them to check what they've ticked.

> **Answers**
>
> I think it depends on …
> Yes, but if …, what then?
> I'm afraid I don't agree with you.
> That becomes a problem if …
> I cannot say the same for me …

> **Audioscript** 🔘 **39**
>
> | | |
> |---|---|
> | Interlocutor: | Some people say that having any job is better than no job at all. What do you think? |
> | Fernando: | Well, I think it depends on the kind of job we're talking about, and the kind of person you are. A university graduate, for instance, would not want to clean the streets for a living! I mean, he'd expect something better than that! |
> | Katrina: | Yes, but if there was no other job available, what then? Would you rather be unemployed? |
> | Fernando: | I think I would try to create a job for myself. Now, with the Internet, an imaginative person can find a way to earn a living. |
> | Katrina: | I'm afraid I don't agree with you. Perhaps you can do that, but it's not always so easy. For me, I would find it frustrating to be unemployed, so I think I would get a job cleaning rather than not work at all. I hate sitting around doing nothing. |
> | Fernando: | I think there are certain jobs I would find it embarrassing to do, so I cannot say the same for me. Also, if you are looking for a specific career, you need to be available for interviews, etc. So, remaining unemployed until you find what you are looking for is not always bad. |
> | Katrina: | Maybe, but that becomes a problem when you are out of work for … six months! I think a potential employer will be more impressed by someone who shows a general willingness to work. |
> | Fernando: | Yes, but … ! |
> | Interlocutor: | Thank you. That is the end of the test. |

8 Students work in pairs. Ask them to read the question. They should aim to use some of the useful phrases, particularly if they disagree with their partner's view. Monitor, and note down phrases you wish to draw attention to, then give feedback.

Student's Book pages 110–111

Writing a report – being concise

1 Find out your students' views on the photographs, and how they like to shop. Explain that this is relevant to the sample writing topic.

2 Elicit what the task is asking them to do. Then ask how long their answer to this question should be.

> **Answers**
>
> You must examine the customers' comments on the store, outline the situation in a report, and make recommendations for improvements. The answer must be 220–260 words long.

3 Students read the sample answer individually. Elicit that it is actually a fairly good answer in itself, but it needs to be shorter (it is 345 words long), and the repetition needs to be removed.

> **EXAM SPOTLIGHT**
>
> Read the information in the box. Emphasise that although it might seem a good thing to write a lot, students can lose marks if they don't follow the instructions and keep within the word limit.

4 Students work in pairs. Elicit answers and give feedback. If necessary, provide them with the suggested answer.

> **Possible answer**
>
> This report aims to provide an overall view of the current situation in the store, based on comments made by customers, and to make suggestions for improving sales in certain departments.

5 Students work in pairs, and discuss what needs to be kept in the sample answer, and what can be deleted, or reduced in length. After a few minutes, elicit their ideas.

> **Answers**
>
> Good points: the answer is well organised into paragraphs with headings, and answers the question.
> Important points to keep: ladies' and men's clothing: plenty of choice and spacious changing rooms; stationery: successful layout and items easily accessible; furniture: little choice and old-fashioned; children's clothing: not enough choice for boys and prices too high.
> conclusion: need to invest in developing the furniture department (modernising it); more choice needed for boys' clothing, and more reasonable prices.

6 Students work in pairs, with one doing the writing. Remind them to read the In other words feature. Tell them to reduce the sample answer in length, so that it falls within the required word limit. Explain that they will need to change the sentence structure in places, and join points together. See the suggested answer for ideas.

> **Possible answer**
>
> Aims
> This report aims to provide an overall view of the current situation in the store, based on comments made by customers, and to make suggestions for improving sales in certain departments.
> Successful departments
> The ladies' and men's clothing department is experiencing a boom in sales at present and some customers went so far as to say they bought all their clothes here. This can be attributed to the fact that customers can try on the wide range of clothing available in spacious changing rooms. Similarly, the practical layout of the stationery department provides customers with easy access to all products.
> Problem areas
> In contrast, sales in the furniture and children's clothing departments have dropped considerably in the last year or so. Complaints have been made that the current range of furniture available is rather limited and old-fashioned in style. In the children's clothing department, concern was expressed over the lack of clothing items in stock for boys, and prices were thought to be too high.
> Recommendations
> It is clear from the comments that considerable investment should be put into expanding and modernising the furniture department to incorporate a wider range of styles, while a greater range of boys' clothing should be made available, at more reasonable prices. If all this can be achieved, then sales will almost certainly improve in these departments, and the store in general will benefit.

7 Ask your students to read the rubric and exam question. Brainstorm ideas as to what is needed in the answer. Then, students write the task.

See *Fiction or fact?* photocopiable activity, page 116.

Student's Book pages 112–113

Video rainy day flea market

Aim: The video contrasts the fortunes of two sellers at a flea market and shows the importance of a positive attitude. The Ideas generator section helps students formulate and balance different points of view.

Synopsis: This video follows the fortunes of two sellers, Natalia and Jill at an outside flea market. Both are given tips on how to draw customers in and get the best price for their wares by Jimmy, an experienced seller. The video contrasts the different attitudes of the two women. Natalia is depressed by the rain and doesn't take Jimmy's advice. By contrast, Jill has a far more positive attitude and manages to make a number of sales.

1 Students look at the photograph and choose the best description.

> **Answer**
>
> 2

2 Students discuss whether they ever go to flea markets. You can ask if they are good at finding bargains, and whether they are any good at haggling (negotiating the best price). Discuss the kind of items that can be found. Check the meanings of the words.

VOCABULARY: FLEA MARKET

cast offs: old clothes that you don't wear any more
curios: strange and unusual items
junk: discarded items of little value
ornaments: items used for decoration in the house, e.g. statues, vases, objets d'art
vintage goods: old goods of good quality

3 Students watch the video and answer the questions.

Answers

1 The weather makes Natalia depressed, but Jill doesn't care. Some of the buyers leave (in droves).
2 Jimmy is annoyed and frustrated that she ignored his advice. He thinks she made a big mistake by not bringing in the chairs.
3 Jill is enthusiastic and optimistic.
4 Jill made more money, Natalia only made enough for her mother to pay for a cab to the airport.

Videoscript

Natalia: I have no idea how we're going to sell all this stuff and make our goal.

Natalia's mother: But we still have time. It's so cold now.

Natalia: Hello.

Jimmy: How's it going?

Natalia: I'm cold.

Natalia's mother: Tired.

Natalia: Getting tired.

Jimmy: Where's the chairs?

Natalia: The chairs?

Jimmy: Yeah, the ch …

Natalia: I decided to keep them at home.

Jimmy: Oh, I mean, I knew you weren't going to sell them, but you didn't even want to bring them?

Natalia: No, no.

Jimmy: OK.

Natalia: I … yeah, I wasn't ready to let them go.

Jimmy: I told Natalia to bring the folding chairs, the big brass ones. You know, even if she didn't want to sell them, they bring people into the booth. You know, they see it, they're drawn to it, they come in, you sell them something else. She should've brought the chairs; she should've listened. Big mistake.

Natalia: First it was really, really cold and now, in the last five minutes, it's starting to rain badly and I can see people are leaving. I feel pretty bad. So far, we've just made money for my mum to take a cab to the airport and back. We'll see, I guess it's just my luck.

Jill: I could not care less about the rain because people are still coming here in droves.

Jill's friend: Jill, I think, is doing a lot better since we started early this morning. There were a couple of missteps, I think, when she was just so eager to make a sale, and Jimmy's really kind of helped her figure out, you know, how to get more for what she's trying to sell. And so, so far we're doing really good.

Male buyer: Do you know who this is? That's Fred Packer. He did Mavis advertisements in 1920 and *Ladies Home Journals*.

Jill: Oh, OK.

Male buyer: He did women similar to this.

Jill: As you can see, it's in excellent condition.

Male buyer: Yeah, I can see what it is, yeah. How much are you asking?

Jill: It's authentic, it's in the original frame and it's in great condition, which is why I'm asking $100.

Male buyer: OK.

Jill: Please, take a look. Yeah.

Male buyer: Yeah. No problem. I have the larger print, the one that's 15 x 30. So I'm looking for the medium. OK, I'll do it.

Jill: Fabulous! Fantastic, thank you. OK.

Male buyer: Thank you. I like Fred Packer, I like the deco. I have the large print and I was always looking for the medium one. So, now I've found the medium one. It's the hunt. I can say that's what I like the best. Once you find it, move on to something else.

Jill's friend: High five!

Jill: This is great.

Jimmy: So Jill learned another valuable lesson and that is, she's learning to keep her mouth shut, she's letting the buyers do the talking. Sometimes it's best to let somebody educate you. Even if they buy it or not, you'll learn more about it than you knew when you brought it.

Jill: It is raining money. Like raindrops from heaven! As is my money! Love it! Yes!

4 Students watch the video again and match the names to the quotations.

Answers

1 Natalia	2 Natalia
3 Jimmy	4 Jimmy
5 Natalia	6 Natalia
7 Jill	8 Jill
9 Jimmy	10 Jill

5 Students work in pairs and discuss the questions.

Answers

1 She didn't bring them because she didn't want to sell them.
2 Jimmy thought she should have brought them anyway. It would have attracted buyers to her stall who might have bought something else.
3 Students' own answers.

6 Students roleplay Natalia and Jill, making sure they use their prompts. If you wish, feed in expressions for congratulating and sympathising such as *Well done! Bad luck! Lucky you! Some people have all the luck! Better luck next time!*

This Ideas generator section encourages students to look at different sides of a situation. In Part 4 of the Speaking test, the discussion will quickly run out if the candidates agree on everything! The object is for candidates to have a discussion and to show the interlocutor and examiner what they are capable of. This means they need to be flexible enough to think of counter arguments.

7 Decide whether the comments support or contradict the proposition.

Answers
agree: 1, 3, 4
disagree: 2, 5, 6

8 Students discuss the statement following the flow chart in the Ideas generator box.

9 Students review the useful expressions and repeat the activity in exercise 8.

10 Students think of pros and cons for each of the statements, then discuss them in pairs, with one student agreeing with the statement and the other disagreeing.

11 Students reflect on their performance and how they could improve it.

Vocabulary organiser 11, page 172

Answers

1
1 ventured   2 totted up   3 troublesome   4 dispel   5 feverishly

2
1 T   2 F   3 F   4 T   5 F   6 F

3
1 have money to burn
2 gave him a good run for his money
3 put your money where your mouth is
4 put my money on
5 is pumping money into

Bank of English
1 d   2 c   3 g   4 e   5 b
6 a   7 h   8 f   9 j   10 i

Photocopiable activity instructions

Fiction or fact? (page 116)

Aim: to provide students with practice in dealing both with different types of reading texts, by comparing journalistic and literary styles of writing, and also in producing these two styles of writing.

Instructions:

1 Place your students in pairs for the first part of this activity. Photocopy one page per student.

2 Ask your students to read the two extracts, A and B. Tell them they are based on the same story, but one is an extract from a newspaper article, and one is a narrative account. This should be fairly obvious to them.

3 They should note down the differences in style between the two pieces of writing and the difference in approach to the story.

4 Elicit observations, and encourage class discussion.

5 Ask students to look at the cartoon strip.

6 Tell them to write the new story shown in the cartoon as a newspaper article, and then as a narrative account. This could be set as individual homework. Tell them the pieces of writing do not need to be long, but it is important to use the correct style of writing.

Monopoly token personality quiz (page 117)

Aim: to give students further practice in speculating and making predictions, using modal structures.

Instructions:

1 Place your students in pairs. Give each student a photocopy of the page.

2 The students choose the token they would most like to play with, and tell their partner about their choice.

3 Each student then makes predictions about the kind of person their partner is going to be, and speculates what kind of job they might choose in the future.

4 Elicit answers from the class as a whole, and find out your students' opinions of the predictions made.

Fiction or fact?

A A 61-year-old woman took the popular game of Monopoly a step further in Denmark last week, when she managed to persuade a bank to exchange 2000 kronor's worth of Swedish Monopoly money for real Danish money. However, she got too greedy, and foolishly returned to the same bank the following day with even more Monopoly money. This time, the bank tellers were ready for her, and she landed on the 'go to jail' square.

B She glanced at the clock. One o'clock. The bank was busy, filled with impatient office workers anxious to get back to work. She hesitated. Could she really pull it off? It was a crazy idea. But she needed the money. It was now or never. She stood in the queue behind a particularly exasperated-looking man. It was a good choice. When his turn came, he managed to intimidate the young cashier to such an extent that she was quite flustered by the time Maggie reached her. Feigning a relaxed manner she didn't feel, she casually pushed the wad of Monopoly notes towards the girl with a sympathetic smile. It worked. Instead of examining the money, the girl looked at her, relieved to see a friendly face.

The glass mousetrap

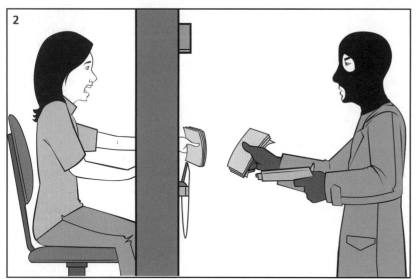

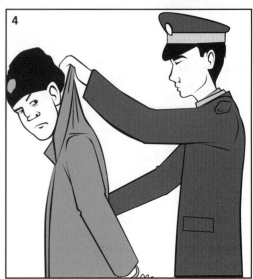

Monopoly Token Personality Quiz

Some psychologists suggest that the Monopoly token you choose to play with says something about the kind of player you are. Of the traditional tokens shown in the pictures below, choose the one you would like to play with. Tell your partner, who will then read what it says about the token, and speculate and make predictions about your life.

Monopoly Token Personality Quiz

CANNON

Constantly aiming to be a big noise in the property world, you see yourself as a player of the highest calibre. Your business dealings are conducted with almost military precision – you guard against the unknown and place as much emphasis on defensive strategy as you do on tactical attack. Ultimately you're far more interested in boom than bust. What better token than the cannon to get you there?

SHOE

You've trodden your way round the classic Monopoly board so many times you could find your way in the dark. Still, there's no substitute for experience and the wisdom that comes from hours of game play makes you a canny contestant indeed. Your scruffy appearance masks a player whose property dealing is methodical and focused.

DOG

The tenacity and courage of the terrier is a fine metaphor for your playing style, and that's reason enough to choose the dog. Though you're almost certainly an animal lover, when playing Monopoly, you are anything but man's best friend. Opponents had better be on their guard because once you're off your leash you'll be hard to catch!

BATTLESHIP

An aggressive contestant, you see every game as all-out war. Inevitably, your playing style will always make waves – you're intent on building a property empire and no one's going to stop you. But will your course to victory be an epic battle or plain sailing? We'll see.

HORSE

Fancying yourself as hot favourite to win any contest, you are naturally inclined to choose the horse even though you know there will be a number of hurdles on the way to victory. Any one of these could upset your chances, but your cool head allows you to stay focused on the ultimate goal and, providing you don't let go of the reins, you should end up with your nose in front.

RACING CAR

An extremely confident sort, you only know one way to play Monopoly – fast! You drive hard deals in all your property negotiations and, try as they might, your fellow players struggle to keep up. You just can't wait to build up your property stable, and you'll spend what you have to, to own it all. The only question is, do you have the skills to stay on track?

WHEELBARROW

Perhaps in anticipation of winning barrow-loads of money off your fellow players you choose the wheelbarrow. With a firm grip on the handles you're unlikely to let commercial opportunities pass you by. Manoeuvrable, spacious, and designed to cope with bumps along the way, the course you steer is inexorably towards owning it all.

IRON

It's not so much that you want to completely flatten your opponents – though of course that is what you'll need to do, to own it all. It's more that you're habitually neat and tidy in all your dealings, and that you like things to go smoothly. For you, the only thing that rightfully belongs on a board is an iron.

TOP HAT

There's no mistaking your aspirations. Your ambition is simple – to own it all. Your taste for the finer things in life can lead to a preoccupation with the more valuable properties on the board and you are unlikely to be satisfied until they are fully developed. You resent paying your fines and taxes, but are magnanimous in handing over rent and birthday presents.

THIMBLE

Cautious by nature, you prefer not to risk spending your money too quickly. You're only too aware that a slip up in your money management could lead to painful ruination. Then again, you're aware of the need to speculate to accumulate. Ultimately, buying well within your means, your prudence is your greatest playing strength.

12 BEHIND THE SILVER SCREEN

Unit introduction

The topic of this unit is film, scripts and Hollywood. Almost everyone loves watching films and many people are interested in the lives of actors and TV celebrities. Talking about films is something that many of us enjoy. In this unit, we focus on Hollywood and reviews of mainstream popular films, while allowing the opportunity to digress into more specialised areas.

Warm-up activity

Tell the class to imagine that they are going to live on a desert island for a year, though miraculously this island has a fully functioning TV / DVD room! They are allowed to choose ten films to take with them to the island. Tell each student to note down their three favourite films. Students take turns naming films, one at a time, and saying why they like each one. Write the names of the films on the board. Afterwards take votes from the class for each film. The activity finishes when you have a list of ten films on the board that everyone agrees on. Be careful not to spend too long on this part though!

Getting started

1 This section is meant as a bit of fun, and it's a good way to introduce key words and prepare students for the subject matter of this unit. Go through the questions with the class and elicit responses. Write any new vocabulary on the board so that students can copy it into their vocabulary notebooks.

Answers		
1 a thriller	2 a documentary	3 the cast
4 the score	5 a musical	6 computer graphics (CGI)

2 Students can number and discuss the options in pairs at first, or just do it as a class activity to save time. Ask students to give reasons for their choices.

   → Vocabulary organiser 12, exercise 1, page 173

Vocabulary organiser answers				
1 b	2 a	3 c	4 b	5 a

Reading understanding humour, irony and sarcasm

UNDERSTANDING HUMOUR, IRONY AND SARCASM

Read through the information with the class. Ask someone to tell you why the words 'understand' and 'appreciate' are in inverted commas. Elicit that neither word is being used in its most literal sense.
Tell the class that one of the hardest things to understand in any foreign language is humour. This is because most of the time humour is either based on language or culture and it can be very hard to translate. Ask students if they know any funny films, TV programmes, stories, etc. in English, and if possible encourage a discussion comparing the humour of those items with humour in the students' own language(s).
The purpose of this section is to help students identify humour, irony or sarcasm in a text, as it is not always obvious to them whether a writer is being serious or not, and this may affect the correct answer in the tasks.

3 Point out that this particular reviewer tends to write humorous reviews about the films he dislikes, using quite a lot of irony and sarcasm. He doesn't do this so much with the films he likes.

Answers				
1 B, C	2 B, C	3 A, D, E	4 B, C	5 Students' own answers

TEACHING IN PRACTICE: SKIMMING AND SCANNING

There are two basic ways students can approach Part 8 of the Reading and Use of English Paper.
1 Read the whole text once all the way through. Then look at each question or sentence in turn, trying to find the text it relates to. This will mean skim reading each text again.
2 Read the whole text once all the way through. Then go back and read each separate part of the text one at a time. Then try to find the questions that refer to it.
A third technique could be a combination of both methods above, which ensures that if you missed something one way, you are more likely to find the correct answer the second way. A good tip is to underline the parts of the text where you find the answers.

4 Students should work individually as this is an exam-style task. Give them ten minutes, but allow a bit more time if they find it difficult. Before they start, go through the techniques for skimming and scanning mentioned above. Tell students they should experiment with both techniques in order to find out which one works best with the text in question, as the best technique can depend on the complexity of the text.

> **Answers**
> | | | | | |
> |---|---|---|---|---|
> | 1 D | 2 E | 3 B | 4 A | 5 C |
> | 6 A | 7 C | 8 B | 9 E | 10 D |

Degree of difficulty

Increase the level: Allow no more than 5–10 minutes for exercise 4. Do not pre-teach any vocabulary or go through the texts until after the students have answered the questions. Elicit justifications and text references for each answer.

Decrease the level: Go through the texts first with the students. Pre-teach key vocabulary, and perhaps go through exercises 5 and 6 before students attempt exercise 4. Ask students to paraphrase each paragraph in their own words. Allow approximately 15–20 minutes for students to complete the task and answer the questions.

Consider pre-teaching the following vocabulary (in the order they appear in the text):

cynical, plead, resistance fighter, gallant, spine-tingling, redundant, enamoured (of), macho, caulk, moonstruck, goofy, hopscotch, showreel, euphoric, implausible, shot, render up, melancholy, triumphantly, whingeing, fatigue, IQ, outpace, gags, mantle, absurdity, send up, quips, gadgets, preposterous.

→ Vocabulary organiser 12, exercise 2, page 173

> **Vocabulary organiser answers**
> | | | |
> |---|---|---|
> | 1 cynical | 2 gallant | 3 redundant |
> | 4 enamoured | 5 euphoric | 6 melancholy |
> | 7 implausible | 8 gargantuan | 9 inspired |
> | 10 preposterous | | |

5 Ask the class the question. The point is to introduce the film reviewer's particular style of describing certain aspects of a film, using interesting and often extreme adjectives to convey his impressions accurately. This leads on to exercise 6.

> **Answers**
> *Wooden* suggest that it is without life or emotion, the word is often used to describe poor acting that is unconvincing. *Deathly* also suggests lifelessness, but is more extreme.

6 Students can attempt the exercise alone or in pairs. Check the answers with the class.

> **Answers**
> | | | |
> |---|---|---|
> | 1 big-hearted | 2 cracking | 3 thrilling |
> | 4 spine-tingling | 5 pounding | 6 razor-sharp |
> | 7 inspired | 8 preposterous | |

Student's Book pages 116–117

Language development
modifying and intensifying adjectives

1 Students can work in pairs or individually. Elicit the context for each pair of words and get students to say what they describe. Ask them to explain why they think the writer chose these words.

> **Answers**
> 1 the hopscotch dance that the character does (it makes the character seem childish and silly, and it is embarrassing to watch)
> 2 Rocky's attempt to get the world heavyweight boxing title (at his age)
> 3 the script / the film
> 4 the new James Bond film (part of the charm of the film is that it is sometimes ridiculous; it is still enjoyable)

EMPHASISING ADJECTIVES

Go through the information with the class. Elicit that when used as modifiers, most adverbs such as *extremely, terribly, incredibly*, etc., fail to carry their literal meaning and instead are just a stronger form of *very*. (For example, if you say something was *terribly funny*, you don't mean that it was funny in a terrible way, you mean it was very funny.)

2 Students can work individually or in pairs. Elicit responses and go through the answers with the class. The answers given here are the most obvious and likely choices for the sentences, though other combinations would be possible.

> **Answers**
> | | | |
> |---|---|---|
> | 1 delightfully | 2 tediously | 3 ridiculously |
> | 4 strangely | 5 genuinely | 6 back-achingly |

3 Read the sentences with the class and elicit responses. Check that students understand the difference between gradable and ungradable adjectives (*ungradable* adjectives are extreme and therefore cannot be 'graded' by words like *very*).

Answers

a *brilliant* is a non-gradable adjective, so should be intensified with *extremely* or a similar adverb.
b *good* is a gradable adjective, so should be graded with *very* or a similar adverb.

4 Students can work in pairs or individually. Check answers with the class.

Answers

annoying, exciting, interesting, scary, funny, dull, good

5 Students can work in pairs or individually. Check answers with the class.

Answers

Can be used with non-gradable adjectives: *absolutely, completely, incredibly, quite, rather, really, totally*
Can be used with gradable and non-gradable adjectives: *awfully, extremely, quite, rather, really*

6 Students may have come across some of these collocations before, or may have a passive knowledge of some of them. To help them, read the first question with each option and ask the class to raise their hands after the option that they think doesn't sound right.

Answers

1 angered	2 embarrassed	3 ill	4 different
5 kidnapped	6 amused	7 cold	8 nice

7 Arrange students in pairs or open pairs, or if you prefer, hold a whole-class discussion. The aim is to let students practise using some of the adverb + adjective combinations they have just learnt to discuss their own views about films, etc. in speech. If students are not forthcoming with their own ideas, prompt them with questions, e.g. *Do you think musicals are boring or entertaining?*

→ Vocabulary organiser 12, exercise 3, page 124

Vocabulary organiser answers

1 highly amusing	2 bitterly disappointed
3 most kind	4 deeply offended
5 seriously injured	6 perfectly simple

Key word *quite*

USE OF *QUITE*

Explain that the word *quite* is different from many of the other quantifiers in that it can have a number of meanings depending on how it is used. Read through the list with the students.

8 🔊 40 Play the recording and tell students to match the sentences to the points in the box.

Answers

a 6	b 5	c 1	d 3	e 4	f 2

TEACHING IN PRACTICE: EMPHASIS ON *QUITE*

Point out that with the word *quite*, the spoken stress in the sentence reveals a lot about the meaning. For example read the following sentence in two different ways and ask students to tell you what you mean in each case:
I went to see the new James Bond film at the weekend. It was quite good. (Strong emphasis on *quite*, meaning it was moderately good, or OK, but not very good.)
I went to see the new James Bond film at the weekend. It was quite good. (Emphasis carries on to the adjective, meaning that it was actually better than you'd expected it to be.)

Listening understanding purpose and function

9 Ask students to read the comments. For each point, ask the students if they agree or disagree, and why.

10 Read the information about understanding purpose and function in the box with the class. Give students several minutes to read questions 1–6 carefully. Tell them to underline key words and then to match the options a, b or c with each extract. Elicit answers and ask students to justify their reasons.

Answers

a extract 3	b extract 1	c extract 2

11 🔊 41 Play the recording and ask students to choose the answers. Check the answers with the class.

Answers

1 C	2 B	3 B	4 C	5 A	6 C

Audioscript 🔘 41

Extract 1

Interviewer: So Richard, tell us about what got you started as an independent filmmaker.

Richard: From an early age I was obsessive about film, about directing and cinematography but it never occurred to me that I could do it myself until one day I picked up my dad's 8 mm camera and started recording family life. I used to watch films all the time too. My local video shop had a section of 'unclassifiable' films that didn't belong in any section, and these were all my favourite films. They were totally unique, they made up their own rules and they always left me feeling as if something inside me had changed. These films proved that the medium of film had the power to change someone's perception of the world, and that just made me more determined.

Interviewer: And yet you claim that you don't make 'arty' films.

Richard: While I knew I wanted to work in this genre, I also knew how easy it was for experimental films to turn into pretentious rubbish. I wanted to express my message through film, using abstraction and music, but not some over-the-top art piece. I'm just not interested in art films where I watch ten minutes and know what's going to happen in the next hour.

Extract 2

Woman: I went to see the latest *Narnia* film last night. Have you seen it?

Man: No, I haven't. What was it like?

Woman: It's got great special effects and everything, but you know how sometimes an adaptation brings a book to life, and you think 'this is exactly right'? Well this one couldn't have been more different from my childhood memory of it. I sat there getting more and more annoyed! But that reminded me of why I loved the book in the first place, so as soon as I got home, I went and dug out my old copy and started reading it again.

Man: And did you enjoy it?

Woman: I certainly did.

Man: I just don't think I'll ever be satisfied by an adaptation. I'm sure they're made with the best intentions, but every time I read good reviews and go and see one, I'm disappointed. With books I grew up with, I feel I inhabit them – every character and every scene means something very specific to me, and I don't want the film to interfere with that.

Woman: Mm.

Man: Obviously there's an audience for these films, though, and if they introduce the book to some people who don't know it, that can't be bad.

Woman: Absolutely.

Extract 3

Woman 1: I think it's depressing that women film directors are in such a tiny minority. There are some that *have* done well commercially, like Jane Campion with her film *The Piano*, or Gurinder Chadha's *Bend It Like Beckham*, and Nora Ephron – she had several big successes, like *Sleepless In Seattle*. But, really, how many films can you actually think of that were directed by women? I'm sure that if this imbalance were to occur in any other profession, there'd be a major outcry. Why is it that film-making continues to be the most unbalanced career in the arts?

Woman 2: Well, obviously there are the difficulties of working in a male-dominated industry. Women need role-models – like the two women you just mentioned. And if they're raising children, they may not be able to make the most of the opportunities that present themselves. And there's no easy solution to that. But the truth is that, whether you're male or female, it's really hard to make films. Creativity is stifled because film-makers have to spend far too much time fundraising. And women are not generally used to asking for money – it seems to come more easily to men.

12 Discuss the topic with the class.

Student's Book pages 118–119

Grammar participle clauses

1 Ask students to read through and match the examples to the explanations. Ask students to identify the participle clause in each sentence. Then read the information in the box with the class.

Answers		
1 c	2 a	3 b

2 Elicit explanations from individual students about what changes have been made to the sentences.

Answers

The pronoun and verb is replaced by a participle. A past participle can replace *because* / *since* / *as* + pronoun + noun.

→ Grammar Reference 12, page 217

3 Students rewrite the sentences using a participle clause.

Answers

1 Not knowing what else to do …
2 The sea being so warm, they decided …
3 Having been told off, we stopped talking.
4 Having told Annette …
5 Looking for a film to watch, Jackson …
6 Having fallen in love with him …

Degree of difficulty ▐▬▬▬▬▬▌

Increase the level: If students have a good grasp of the grammar they should complete exercise 3 individually. Ask them to add one example sentence of their own using each of the structures.

Decrease the level: Students can work in pairs. You can also provide them with extra help, such as the first word of the first sentence, etc.

4 Students could do this exercise as a whole class, individually or in pairs, as you see fit. Tell students to read through the whole text before they make any changes.

Answers

Lara Croft, recognised as one of the world's most dynamic action
heroines …
Facing …
Demonstrating her physical prowess and revealing her courage as never
before, Lara proves …
Knowing that Pandora's box is concealed there, she must protect the
secret …
the most unspeakable evil ever known.

PARTICIPLES AS ADJECTIVES

Read through the information with the students. Make sure
they understand the difference here between a 'general quality'
(something that is true all the time) and a 'current event'
(something that is just happening now).

5 Elicit the correct answer and ask students to identify
a 'general quality' (*annoying* in sentence 1) and a
'current event' (*annoying* in sentence 2).

Answer
Sentence 1

6 Elicit the correct answers.

Answer
Sentence 2

PARTICIPLES WITH OBJECTS

Read through the information with the students. Point out that the
example comes from the review of *Casino Royale* on page 117.

7 Students rewrite the sentence using a participle
adjective.

Answer
were organically-grown vegetables

8 Students complete the exercise individually.

Answers
a tiring journey
b concerned should come to the meeting
c are French-speaking Swiss people
d faded colours
e barking dogs were getting on my nerves
f retired teacher
g Only balcony seats were left
h grown-up children

→   Vocabulary organiser 12, exercise 4, page 124

Vocabulary organiser answers
1 handmade clothes   2 amusing book
3 genetically-modified fruit   4 a water-resistant watch
5 floating debris on the river

See *'Ellie' Award Ceremony* photocopiable activity,
page 127.

Speaking exchanging ideas
(Parts 3 and 4)

EXCHANGING IDEAS

Make sure students understand what *interact* means and ask them how
they can effectively interact with their partner in the Speaking test.
* They should sometimes initiate by expressing their opinion and
   sometimes respond by agreeing or disagreeing with their partner
   and giving reasons.
* They should make sure that they clearly and logically link their
   response to what their partner has said.
* They should maintain and develop the discussion and negotiate
   towards an outcome.
Explain that Part 3 is a good opportunity for the assessor to
evaluate candidates' interactive communication. However, point out
that throughout the whole Speaking test, the assessor is allocating
marks for all the assessment criteria: grammar and vocabulary,
discourse management (ability to produce extended stretches
of language, to make contributions relevant and to organise
discourse clearly, to use a range of linkers and discourse markers),
pronunciation and interactive communication.

9 Students form pairs or groups of three. Tell them to
look at the task on page 236 and answer the question
by discussing and evaluating the different options. Go
round the class and monitor, and make notes of useful
phrases and vocabulary you hear.

After two minutes' discussion, ask the students to
choose which aspect of the film industry would be
the most difficult. Allow one minute. Afterwards you
can ask one or two pairs to demonstrate the complete
Part 3 in front of the class.

10 Explain that the discussion points in this exercise are
typical Part 4 questions. Remind students that there
are no right or wrong answers, so they should express
their views clearly and fully. Depending on the size of
your class, you can deal with this in one of two ways.
a Read out the questions one at a time and ask specific
   students to answer each time; try to make sure that
   everyone gets an equal chance to speak.

b put students into pairs or groups of three and ask
   them to discuss the questions while you monitor.

Use of English open cloze

11 Students should be able to do this exercise individually but if you think they need extra help let them work in pairs or tell them to use dictionaries. Alternatively, spend a bit of time revising different parts of speech and going through some of the examples.

Answers

1 preposition	2 adverb	3 particle
4 verb	5 modal	6 relative pronoun
7 quantifier	8 conjunction	9 pronoun
10 article		

TEACHING IN PRACTICE: READING THE TITLES

The texts in Parts 1, 2 and 3 of the Reading and Use of English Paper all have titles. Encourage your students to pay attention to each title as it will indicate the main theme of the text.

12 Students should do the exam task individually. Allow approximately ten minutes for this. Elicit answers and give feedback.

Answers

1 do	2 in	3 apart	4 despite
5 without	6 one	7 at	8 of

→ Vocabulary organiser 12, exercise 5, page 173 (students' own answers)

Student's Book pages 120–121

Writing a film review

1 ⊙ 42 The films that are described are chosen for being fairly well-known Hollywood films, but it is unlikely that all your students will have seen all of them. Some students may not have seen any of these films, and some students may only have seen some of them. Stress that this doesn't matter – the exercise is to help them focus on the information given. Tell them to make a few notes based on what each speaker says, and then discuss what they imagine the film to be like.

Answers

1 *Pirates of the Caribbean: Curse of the Black Pearl*
2 *Shrek*
3 *The Blues Brothers*
4 *Titanic*
5 *The Sixth Sense*

Audioscript ⊙ 42

Speaker 1: Well it's about a pirate, Jack Sparrow, played by Johnnie Depp, who used to be captain of a ship called The Black Pearl, but now that ship's been commandeered by a zombie pirate called Captain Barbosa. He has been cursed with living death until he can find the living heir of old 'Bootstrap' Bill Turner, who is actually played by Orlando Bloom and, to that end he has kidnapped the beautiful Elizabeth Swann …

Speaker 2: It's an animated film about an ogre who lives in a swamp. Coming home one day he finds that all these fairytale characters have moved in, which he is not very happy about, to say the least. Accompanied by a talking donkey that irritates him greatly, he sets off on a fairytale adventure of his own, and comes face-to-face with dragons, princesses and even happy endings …

Speaker 3: It's a musical actually, and it's about two brothers, Jake and Elwood, who are on a mission from God to save a convent orphanage from closure. In order to legitimately raise the money they need, they have to put their old blues band back together, no mean feat in itself, despite the fact that the police and all their old enemies are all in hot pursuit. What I love is the wonderful performances by John Lee Hooker, James Brown, Aretha Franklin, Ray Charles, to name but a few …

Speaker 4: The film is based on an actual historical event of course, but the main story is a romance, told in flashback by the old woman, Rose, remembering Jack, whom she met on board the ship for the first time. He is a penniless artist who won his ticket to America in a game of cards; she is an attractive young lady engaged to marry a wealthy aristocrat to pay off her family's debts …

Speaker 5: I love this film – even though it's quite spooky really. I think the actor who plays the scared little boy with psychic abilities is excellent, and Bruce Willis is great as the failed child psychologist who wants to make sure he gets it right second time around. You really need to see it twice because only then do you really appreciate all the details leading to the final twist.

2 Read the exam task with the class. Find out how many students have seen a film recently at the cinema and how many have seen a film recently on TV or on DVD. If any students haven't seen a film recently, suggest that they can write about any film they've seen, or they can invent one.

Answers

college magazine, review, outlining the plot, giving their opinions: acting, directing, other elements

3 Read the planning stages and tips with the class, giving students time to follow each of the points and write some notes. If time is limited here you can speed up this section by eliciting suggestions from students and writing a class answer on the board.

4 Point out that most reviews avoid using personal feelings too often as this makes the review seem too subjective, whereas most reviews tend to aim to be objective.

Possible answers

1 The dull script failed to bring life to the story.
2 The actors' wooden performances were unconvincing.
3 The story was interesting but could have been developed further.

---

5 Read the example sentences with the class and elicit what is wrong with them. Point out that at their level of English, students should not be using descriptions like *very nice*. Elicit suggestions for better descriptive vocabulary.

Possible answers

1 awe-inspiring / stunning
2 absolutely excellent / particularly talented
3 extremely dull / tedious
4 atrocious / appalling / terrible

→ Vocabulary organiser 12, exercise 6, page 173

Vocabulary organiser answers

1 acting   2 characters   3 story   4 plot   5 casting

---

6 Read the words the box with the class and ask them which elements they would plan to include in their review. Students then read the review of *The Illusionist* and tick the elements in the box that have been mentioned. Students can compare this with what they would have included.

Answers

acting, directing, genre, plot, reviewer's opinion, script

TEACHING IN PRACTICE: READING REVIEWS

Encourage your students to read as wide a range of reviews as possible, not just for films, but for all kinds of things, including holidays or travel locations, books, television programmes, consumer goods, computer equipment, etc. They need to be taught the use of appropriate adjectives, and how to describe and explain. They also need to know how to give an opinion, positive or negative, and make a recommendation.

---

7 Remind students of the Grammar section and refer back to it if necessary. Students then work individually or in pairs, rewriting the underlined phrases as required.

Answers

charismatically played
Discovering he has a talent for magic, he soon …
being the son of …
Having changed his name, he is known as …
Needing an assistant …
Prince Leopold, played very convincingly …
a short story written by …

EXAM SPOTLIGHT

Read through the information with the class. Answer any questions.

8 Students write down their ideas.

Extension

Students could prepare plans for any of these as they did in exercise 3.

9 Students can either answer the new exam question, or write a full review using notes they wrote in exercise 3. If answering the new question, they could prepare using the notes in exercise 3 (points 1–4), and just adapting the relevant details.

See *Film characters* photocopiable activity, page 126.

Student's Book pages 122–123

Review 3

1
1 tediously dull   2 ridiculously small
3 deeply offended   4 most kind
5 bitterly disappointed   6 fully aware
7 thoroughly / most annoying   8 greatly mistaken
9 deliciously mouthwatering   10 perfectly reasonable
2
1 tough going   2 out of luck   3 taken its toll
4 nitty gritty   5 out of order   6 out of the question
7 rock the boat   8 bottom line   9 out of your mind
10 out of the blue
3
1 awareness   2 activists   3 materialistic
4 unethical   5 sustainable   6 unfashionable
7 penniless   8 unwanted
4
1 you should do is go out and meet people more
2 wanting to disturb them, I left without saying goodbye
3 he managed to work it out that way, I don't know
4 you need is a break from the computer
5 was the weather that they decided to light a fire
6 dreamed of going to Alaska all her life, Grace was extremely excited
7 he gets his bad temper from, I don't know
8 to become an Olympic swimmer, Hannah trained very hard
9 having seen Mike and Helen for several years, we had a lot to talk about
10 though this car is, it is very reliable

5

1 might have got	2 can't have got
3 would have phoned	4 won't / may not have
5 would be	6 may / might as well go
7 'll be	8 might / could have called
9 would have done	10 could order

6
1 apologised for missing / having missed
2 denied putting / having put
3 threatened to kill
4 accused her of lying / having lied
5 recommended the Indian restaurant on the corner to him
6 admitted to taking / having taken
7 predicted that
8 warned us not to go / against going

7
1 might have apologised to her for
2 insisted on seeing the manager
3 having been delayed
4 did not / didn't cancel dinner as
5 not knowing where
6 someone would tell Nick to

Vocabulary organiser 12, page 173

Answers

1

1 b	2 a	3 c	4 b	5 a

2

1 cynical	2 gallant	3 redundant
4 enamoured	5 euphoric	6 melancholy
7 implausible	8 gargantuan	9 inspired
10 preposterous		

3

1 highly amusing	2 bitterly disappointed	3 most kind
4 deeply offended	5 seriously injured	6 perfectly simple

4

1 handmade clothes	2 amusing book
3 genetically-modified fruit	4 a water-resistant watch
5 floating debris on the river	

5
Students' own answers

6

1 acting	2 characters	3 story	4 plot	5 casting

Bank of English
1 humorist, humorous, humorously, humourless, humourlessly, humourlessness, humoristic
2 dehydrated

Photocopiable activity instructions

Film characters (page 126)

Aim: to help students practise articulating their ideas, working in pairs, and summarising narratives.

Instructions:

1 Tell the class that when deciding which films to make, movie studios have to choose between literally thousands of film scripts every year. Because they can't read every single script, producers often make their choice based on the best 'spiel' they receive (or plot summary).

2 Students form pairs or groups of three. Photocopy and hand out the film characters worksheet.

3 Each pair / group has five to ten minutes to think up an idea for a film which they have to present to the class. They must choose six of the characters on the worksheet and include them in the story; everything else is up to them. Tell them to be as wacky and imaginative as they can, but the basic story should make some kind of sense and have a clear beginning, middle and an end.

4 When they have finished they have to present their outline to the class. Their 'spiel' should last no more than 60 seconds and should be as visually descriptive as possible.

5 The class votes for the best story idea.

'Ellie' Award Ceremony (page 127)

Aim: to practise using participle clauses.

Instructions:

1 Photocopy the worksheet and hand out to students. (Students can either work individually or in pairs).

2 Tell your students that they have attended the 64th annual Ellie Award Ceremony as reporters for the entertainments section of the local newspaper which they work for. The worksheet contains their own handwritten notes based on the events of the evening.

3 Students have to rewrite each award box as only one sentence. Each sentence should begin with a present or past participle. They should use further participles wherever they can. Do the first box as an example, or write it on the board so students are clear what they need to do:
The Moment of Truth, forecast as the winner by the bookies months ago, and clearly deserving the award, walked off with the 'Ellie' for best film.

Film characters

Harry Potter

- **Harry Potter,** the teenage student of magic at Hogwarts School of Witchcraft and Wizardry

- **Hermione Granger,** friend of Harry Potter, intelligent, studious and efficient

- **Voldemort,** evil wizard and Harry Potter's arch-enemy

Lord of the Rings

- **Gollum,** the underground creature who spends his life finding and pursuing his lost ring ('my precious')

- **Gandalf the Grey,** the wizard

- *Shelob,* the giant spider who lives within the mountain passes leading to Mordor

Star Wars

- **Darth Vader,** the evil servant of the Galactic Empire

- **Princess Leia,** a beautiful and strong-minded young woman and an excellent warrior

Spider-Man

- **Spider-Man,** the comic book superhero with incredible powers to climb buildings and swing from surfaces using spider-web shooters

Alice in Wonderland

- **Alice,** the young girl who falls down a rabbit hole

- **The Mad Hatter,** played by Johnny Depp in the 2010 film

Raiders of the Lost Ark

- **Indiana Jones,** the action hero and professor of archaeology

Jurassic Park

- *Tyrannosaurus Rex* dinosaur

Skyfall and Casino Royale

- **James Bond,** the British secret agent

Toy Story

- **Sheriff Woody,** the cowboy doll who is Andy's favourite and likes to take charge of the other characters

- **Jessie,** the yodelling cowgirl who is always cheerful and optimistic

Lara Croft: Tomb raider

- **Lara Croft,** the intelligent and dynamic archaeologist and adventurer who battles with villains and solves mysteries

'Ellie' Award Ceremony

Best film

The film had been forecast as the winner by the bookies months ago. It came as no surprise that *The Moment of Truth,* walked off with the 'Ellie' for best film. It clearly deserved the 'Ellie'.

Best supporting actor

Everyone was surprised. James Robbins picked up the 'Ellie' for best supporting actor. He had been a clear outsider.

Best cinematography

Ice World was filmed almost entirely on location in Antarctica. It was hardly surprising that it received the award for best cinematography. It earned the award for those amazing rolling vistas of sparkling ice and snow.

Best director

Caroline Meers didn't believe she would win the 'Ellie' for best director. She hadn't prepared a speech. She nervously stumbled through a long list of thank yous.

Best supporting actress

Gloria Goldberg was wearing a red satin dress by Versace. She knew how to pose for the photographers. She won the 'Ellie' for best supporting actress.

Best documentary

Peter Williams clutched his 'Ellie' tightly. He gave a heart warming speech. He talked about his inspiration to make the film. The film focuses on the plight of the polar bears.

Best actor

Ronald Smith had been nominated for an 'Ellie' three times previously. He had never won one. It was about time he did. He got the award for best actor.

Best original screenplay

Jannis Patridopoulos had worked for over four years on the script. He was clearly overwhelmed that he had been awarded the 'Ellie' for best original screenplay.

Best visual effects

Gillian and Rosemary Craig confessed that ambition had been driving them to make this moment come true. They said they had lived without sleep for almost six months while they worked on the computer graphics for this film.

Best actress

19 year old Sylvia Watson was the youngest actress ever to be nominated. She burst into tears when she picked up her 'Ellie' for best actress. It made it difficult to hear her speech.

Best animated film

The director, producers and animators all crowded onto the stage. They all took turns saying how grateful they were. They received the 'Ellie' for best animated film.

Best make-up / Costume

The Moment of Truth producers were grateful to accept their 'Ellies' for best costume and best make-up. These were the fifth and sixth awards they swept up for the evening.

13 GETTING THE MESSAGE ACROSS

Unit introduction

The topic of the unit is sending messages, talking to aliens, communicating ideas. It looks at various ways in which we communicate, not only with other people, but with animals as well. We also take a look at the human attempt to communicate with beings beyond this planet, in an attempt to stretch beyond our own boundaries of experience.

Warm-up activity

1 Try to communicate with your students in a different language, or using mime only. If you know anything about Esperanza, you may want to try introducing yourself using this language. Alternatively, use a language that you know but which is unfamiliar to your students. You could use visual prompts and gestures to help you, but do not use English or your students' native language.

2 Students work in pairs. One of them is an alien who is visiting the town. It doesn't speak any human languages. Each pair in turn should try to introduce themselves to each other and the alien should ask for some information. This is intended to be fun, so don't worry about pointing out mistakes.

Getting started

Aim: to get students thinking about various different ways in which we communicate, to generate the use of 'communicating' language which will be useful for tasks in the unit.

1 Elicit the meaning of the unit title (communicating any sort of idea, including educating people or selling a product). Encourage students to talk about the different ways in which we communicate messages such as information, ideas, thoughts, needs and desires. Students work in pairs to categorise the words in the box. Elicit answers they are confident of. Then, if necessary, provide them with definitions for the more difficult items (see Vocabulary box below).

> **Answers**
> **Ideas:** broadcast, clarify, convey, exchange, instil, publish
> **Information:** broadcast, exchange, publicise, publish, send, share, reveal
> **Messages:** convey, exchange, send, transmit
> **Knowledge:** convey, exchange, impart, publish, reveal, share

VOCABULARY: COMMUNICATION

To *convey* information or feelings means to cause them to be known or understood by someone (= *communicate*)
In every one of her pictures she conveys a sense of immediacy.
If you *impart* information to people, you tell it to them. (FORMAL)
I am about to impart knowledge to you that you will never forget.
If you *instil* an idea or feeling in someone, especially over a period of time, you make them think it or feel it.
They hope that their work will instil a sense of responsibility in children.

2 Students work in pairs, or individually. Make sure they are aware that there is more than one possibility in some sentences.

> **Possible answers**
> | | | | |
> |---|---|---|---|
> | 1 clarify / explain | 2 send / transmit | 3 convey | 4 impart |
> | 5 instil | 6 share | 7 publishing | 8 broadcast |

→ Vocabulary organiser 13, exercise 1, page 136

> **Vocabulary organiser answers**
> | | | | |
> |---|---|---|---|
> | 1 broadcast | 2 reveal | 3 published | 4 publicise |
> | 5 exchange / share | 6 instil | 7 impart | 8 explained |

See *Reading skills* photocopiable activity, pages 135–136.

Reading understanding text structure

EXAM SPOTLIGHT

Discuss different types of factual text with the class: a newspaper article reports an event, while a journal or magazine may provide a general article on a particular subject. Read the information in the box about different types of text structure.

3 Ask students to choose the best structure (a or b) for the texts described.

> **Answers**
> 1 b   2 a

4 Students predict what they are going to read about from the title of the extract. Discuss their ideas.

> **Possible answers**
>
> communicating with aliens / the question of life on other planets / films about making contact with aliens

5 Students do this individually. Ask them to read through the text quickly first, to see if their predictions were right, then do the task. Ask students to give reasons for their choices.

> **Answers**
>
> 1 E   2 A   3 B   4 G   5 C   6 D

→ Vocabulary organiser 13, exercise 2, page 136

> **Vocabulary organiser answers**
>
> 1 sophisticated   2 decades   3 haziest
> 4 trenches   5 initiate

Extension

If your students appear interested in the subject, you could direct them to websites such as the SETI institute website. The article in the unit was published in 2005. You could ask your students to find a more recent one related to this subject. Suggest they search for articles in magazines like *New Scientist* and *Forbes*. Invite discussion on how they think we should try to communicate with extraterrestrial beings.

Student's Book pages 126–127

Language development nouns followed by particles

1 This exercise should develop students' awareness of the particles which follow specific nouns, and the fact that some nouns can be followed by more than one particle. Students find the sentences in the text and complete them with the correct particle.

> **Answers**
>
> 1 of   2 about   3 in   4 to

2 Explain that some of the nouns in this exercise can be followed by more than one particle, depending on the context of the sentence. They must decide which one is suitable in each case. Elicit answers, and discuss which items can be followed by other particles, and give examples of each. In feedback, make sure you look at the alternatives in the box.

> **Answers**
>
> 1 d   2 a   3 b   4 c   5 d   6 c   7 c   8 b

> **ALTERNATIVE PARTICLES**
>
> *In dispute* **over** something, but you can be *in dispute* **with** someone.
> Someone *is an authority* **on** *a subject*, but someone *has authority* **over** other people.
> You *have*, or *are in contact* **with** someone, but we say *there has been contact* **between** *humans and extraterrestrials*.

→ Vocabulary organiser 13, exercise 3, page 174

> **Vocabulary organiser answers**
>
> Nouns followed by
> *of:* effect, matter, product, question, result, threat
> *for:* admiration, argument, respect, search
> *to:* access, alternative, approach, connection, solution, threat
> *on:* authority, effect
> *over:* authority, dispute
> *with:* argument, connection, communication, contact

Key word *set*

3 Students can work in pairs, or individually. Explain any unknown phrases.

> **Answers**
>
> Only two NOT possible: a desire, money

4 The list of phrases here contains items which give the idea of 'preparing' something, rather than starting it. Once students have completed the exercise, you may wish to elicit this slight difference in meaning in, for example: *set the table, set a date, set a bone, set a trap.*

> **Answers**
>
> 1 i   2 d   3 b   4 j   5 h
> 6 c   7 f   8 a   9 g   10 e

> **TEACHING IN PRACTICE: DEVELOPING WHAT IS DONE IN CLASS**
>
> As always, the list of items contained in this section is not exhaustive. Word games such as jigsaw games and word partner games can provide useful practice in both practising items from this page, and introducing additional items.

→ Vocabulary organiser 13, exercise 4, page 174

> **Vocabulary organiser answers**
>
> 1 arrange a day when something will happen
> 2 do something for the first time, and provide a valuable example for others to follow
> 3 behave in a way that can be followed as a model by other people
> 4 start a new fashion
> 5 make something happen, start a chain of events
> 6 start writing
> 7 achieve something that has not been achieved before
> 8 to start a journey (in a boat)

5 Elicit the answers, and emphasise the importance of knowing and using the correct particles, the correct structures after verbs, etc., particularly for this part of the exam.

Answers

1 in dispute over	2 convey an impression of
3 is set on going	4 the general public to access
5 clarified his idea by	6 were (all) set to go on

Grammar (1) text references (*this, that, it, such, these, those*)

6 Read the information about reference words with the class, then do the first item with the class as a whole, as an example. Students can complete the activity in pairs or individually. Go through the answers, and explain any points which cause confusion.

Answers

1 the messages
2 using mathematical patterns
3 life on earth as portrayed through the Internet
4 aliens

7 Elicit the meaning and use of *such* here. If necessary, give a further example to illustrate its use.

Answer

Such refers to ideas like that of studying communication in animals in order to understand our own ability to speak.

→ Grammar reference 13, page 218

8 Ask students to read through the text quickly and say what it is about. If you are in a coastal area, where it is likely that some of your students may have had contact with dolphins, elicit their stories and generate discussion. Point out that it is not an exam task, as all the answers are reference words. Allow students to complete the task. Check the answers.

Answers

1 Such	2 this	3 These	4 they
5 This	6 them	7 this	8 that / this
9 that	10 that		

9 Based on the level of knowledge and interest among your students, develop this question into a discussion.

Student's Book pages 128–129

Use of English word formation (1)

SUFFIXES

Read the information with the class and elicit a few suffixes, e.g. *-tion, -less, -ful.*

EXAM SPOTLIGHT

Explain that these guidelines show how complex the structures and patterns of English can be. Perhaps give students a list of adjectives ending in *-ible* or *-able*, and ask them to match each one with the rules a–h. Encourage students to add further examples.

1 Ask students in pairs to write both positive and negative adjectives in *-ible* or *-able*.

Answer

(un)answerable, changeable, (in)conceivable, (in)dispensable, (in)exhaustible, (un)noticeable, (un)pronounceable, regrettable, (un)reliable, irrepressible, unstoppable, terrible, transferable, (in)variable, (in)visible

2 Point out that the changes include changes of consonant and the loss of vowels (amongst other things). Ask students in pairs to write the adjectives.

Answer

(in)comprehensible, indestructible, (in)divisible, negotiable, (im)perceptible, irreparable

Speaking sustaining interaction

3 ⊙ 43 Tell your students to look at the task on page 237. Play the recording. Elicit students' comments on how the two candidates interact.

Answer

Their interaction is very limited (details in 4).

Audioscript ⊙ 43

Female interlocutor:	Now, I'd like you to talk about something together for about two minutes. Here are some different methods of advertising a product or service. Talk to each other about how effective these different methods might be for advertising a new language school.

Carlos:	Yes ... Well, I think the billboard is a very effective way of advertising, as it can be seen by everyone in the area. Also, people are not so angry at seeing billboards, whereas they get annoyed when people push leaflets under their door. Do you agree, Magda?
Magda:	Yes, you're right. They don't like leaflets ... erm ... not at all ...
Carlos:	Er ... I know I usually throw leaflets away without looking at them! But I think it depends on what product you want to advertise. Leaflets might be a good idea for a new language school, because you can include information on courses, and photos of the classrooms and facilities in the school ... and a bold advert in the local newspaper is a good idea, as most people read the newspaper, and so they will see it. But I still think the billboard is the best idea, don't you?
Magda:	Yes, I agree with you. It will be seen by the largest number of people, and so will be most effective ... erm ... That's all.

SUSTAINING INTERACTION

Read the information in the box and remind your students of the importance of interacting with their partner in Part 3 of the Speaking test. Emphasise the importance of the two following points in this part:
a You mustn't monopolise the conversation, but should encourage your partner to speak as well.
b Do not simply repeat what your partner says; build on what they say.

4 After reading the information in the box and dealing with any questions raised, ask your students to discuss how Carlos and Magda could improve their interaction. Take feedback from the class. Emphasise that candidates need to both initiate and respond. Magda should learn to develop her contributions, for example, by relating her opinions to her personal experience. But Carlos should also be aware of how long he is speaking without his partner saying anything. He should ask his partner if she agrees / disagrees or what her opinion is. Sometimes if candidates disagree, it's easier for them to extend their discussion and it becomes more lively.

Possible answers
Carlos could have asked Magda what she thought of billboards before going on to talk about leaflets.
Magda should have agreed or disagreed with Carlos' point about billboards, giving reasons for her opinion.
Magda should have then initiated a discussion about leaflets and then asked Carlos what his opinion is.
Carlos speaks for too long without encouraging Magda to respond.

5 Students carry out the task in pairs. Monitor them and note any useful phrases.

Listening communicating with a purpose

6 Read the Exam spotlight box, then ask students to do exercise 6 in pairs.

Answers
1 b	2 h	3 f	4 a	5 c	6 e	7 d	8 g

7 ⊙ 44 Ask students to read the exam tasks, and elicit any unknown words. Play the recording twice before getting answers and giving feedback.

Answers
1 D	2 B	3 E	4 F	5 C
6 B	7 G	8 A	9 C	10 E

Audioscript ⊙ 44

Speaker 1: Communication seems to be absolutely non-stop these days. You can even receive emails and text messages in the middle of the night. But though the quantity is increasing, quality seems to be going downhill. At least we were more careful when we used a pen or typewriter for letters, because changing anything could look a mess, so they were much more accurate. It was while I was discussing this with a friend that we came up with the idea of setting up a training firm. We know there's a demand for training in all types of communication skills, so potentially it could be very profitable. And we've both got a lot of relevant experience.

Speaker 2: What I find fascinating is how delicate a tool language is. You can express tiny nuances of meaning through the choice of words, or, in speech, your intonation, or by putting in a pause. It's such a pleasure to listen to someone who has really good communication skills – some stand-up comics, for example, and one or two people I've heard giving presentations. I've decided to develop this interest of mine further by writing a series of children's books. This will involve quite a lot of work. First I'll enrol on a creative writing course, and improve what I've already produced, and during the course I intend to contact several publishers, to find out how best to get my work published.

Speaker 3: The organisation I belong to monitors the press, TV and radio, and our aim is to challenge anything that we consider harmful to children. And believe me, there's a great deal that worries us, particularly some of the things that are shown as acceptable behaviour for children. We want to make journalists think carefully about the potential effects of what they write on young readers. Now, we're all volunteers, so our work is unpaid. However, we have numerous expenses, not least of which is the cost of postage on letters. So I'm here today to ask for your financial assistance. Even a small contribution from each of you would be greatly appreciated, and will be put to good use.

Speaker 4: We've had a lot of feedback from the public pointing out mistakes in the information sheets and leaflets we produce. Most of them contain grammatical mistakes or spelling errors, or don't make the meaning clear. And there's really no excuse. It harms the image of the whole organisation, and anyway, what's the point of having information sheets that aren't fit for purpose? So could each of you try to set aside some time to look through the materials you've produced yourself, and classify them as being fine as they are, needing some quick and easy improvement, or requiring a major rewrite? It would certainly help us to improve our materials.

Speaker 5:	We have quite a few communication difficulties at work, with clashes between people that can get out of control. One of the other managers, Stephen, is very good at handling that sort of thing. When it happens, he chats to each person individually, to find out how they see what's going on, and usually he can defuse the situation before it gets too serious. And I try to learn from him. So I really don't think there's any need to worry about Stephen's style of management. He always encourages people to make up their own minds, and to play an active role in the running of the department. I think that's far more effective than giving orders to everyone.

8 Students work in four groups. Allocate one discussion point to each group. Allow them to discuss it for a few minutes, and monitor their discussions. Then, elicit a summary of what each group said, and give feedback on the language they used.

Student's Book pages 130–131

Grammar (2) *it / there* as introductory pronouns

1 Elicit students' ideas about each pair of sentences. Answers may vary.

> **Answers**
> 1   a   this is a comment on the weather at the moment.
>   b   this would be more likely to talk about general weather in a particular place.
> 2   a   a general comment about the distance between two places
>   b   more specific and personal, describing the distance the speakers have to go
> 3   a   They need to do their homework now.
>   b   It is possible to do both things.

2 Ask students to read the information in the boxes. Answer any queries, then ask students to complete exercise 2. To help them with the task, suggest they find all the sentences beginning with *It* first, (which match with rules 1–4), then match the remaining sentences with rules 5–8. Check the answers with the class.

> **Answers**
> a 3   b 2   c 7   d 4   e 8   f 1   g 5   h 6

3 This could be done orally, to consolidate exercise 2, or ask students to complete the sentences individually.

> **Answers**
> 1 it   2 There   3 There, it
> 4 there, It   5 It, there   6 There, it

Writing a proposal

4 Ask students to read the rubric and task. Check that they understand what the question is asking them to do.

5 Ask students to discuss this briefly in pairs, and elicit their answers.

> **Answer**
> The answer should be neutral / formal as it is directed at an organisation.

6 Students work in pairs or small groups and discuss which points should be included in the answer. Elicit ideas, and allow some discussion, if disagreement arises.

> **Answers**
> Only points 4 and 7 are specified in the exam task.

7 Tell students to underline the relevant points covered in the sample answer. Explain that the individual words in bold are for exercise 5 in the Vocabulary organiser, so students can ignore them for the moment. Check answers, and discuss any discrepancies with students' own views. Explain why the other points are not relevant to the task.

> **Answers**
> 2, 4, 7, 9

8 Ask students to find the answers individually. Elicit their answers.

> **Answer**
> 1 in response to (your appeal)
> 2 I would like to put forward (the idea)
> 3 In my view
> 4 on two levels
> 5 I feel certain that

9 Students work in pairs, or individually. They should replace the underlined verbs in the sample proposal using the words from the box, but may also need to make slight changes to the verb forms. As they do this, they should explain why their substitutions are more correct or precise choices.

> **Answer**
> has – plays, has – holds, join – participate, is – resembles, hits – beats, gets to – reaches, makes – produces, know – get to hear, pushing – publicising

10 Students work in pairs or as a class for the brainstorming task. Elicit ideas, and give feedback.

11 Students write their proposal individually.

Student's Book pages 132–133

Video the Braille Hubble

Aim: The main aim of the video and Ideas generator is to stimulate students' ideas on this exam topic and help them to talk with confidence about forms of communication.

Synopsis: This video is about an extraordinary project which allows visually and hearing impaired people to learn about the discoveries made by the Hubble space telescope.

Some of the photographs taken by Hubble have been put into a book with an accompanying overlay in braille. This means blind people can understand the images through touch alone. The video shows us blind children at a special school testing and evaluating the prototype braille project. Their feedback is used to produce an improved version. The Ideas generator section focuses on making relevant contributions and responses in Part 3 of the Speaking test.

1 Generate interest in the topic by asking students to look at the photo and say what they think it shows. Ask them if anyone knows anything about the Hubble telescope. (The Hubble telescope is in space, which means that it can take much clearer images than a telescope situated on the earth.) Students read the short text and replace the words in bold with those in the box.

Answer

1 orbits	2 extremely	3 images
4 data	5 the general public	6 spectacular

2 Students think about some of the possible issues in a school for deaf and blind children and add their ideas to the mind map.

3 Students speculate how they might teach visually or hearing impaired people about space. Elicit some ideas. Students may mention braille, but may find it hard to see how this can be translated into interpreting an image, rather than a word.

4 Read through the glossary and allow students a minute to read the questions so that they know what they are listening and looking out for. Play the video all the way through.

Answer

1 b   2 a

Videoscript

Narrator: From the endless reaches of space, images that delight the eye are admired in a most unlikely place – the Colorado School for the Deaf and Blind.

Female student 1: Are these stars?

Narrator: Where students have the universe at their fingertips.

Nimer Jaber: I've got Jupiter.

Male student 1: That one shows the arms of the galaxy.

Male student 2: Let's see, I see those moons and I see, like, those stars.

Narrator: Images taken by the Hubble Space Telescope have found their way into a classroom for students with different levels of vision loss. These are the critics who were chosen to review a new book that displays some of the most spectacular space images ever produced.

Male student 1: Now it says red for sulphur, green for hydrogen and blue for oxygen. But the problem with that is that I can't tell the different coloured gases, these lines are all the same.

Narrator: The book is called *Touch the Universe, a NASA Braille Book of Astronomy*. Each photo comes with a transparent plastic sheet overlay, covered with raised dots and ridges, giving visually impaired readers a feel for the limitless reaches of space.

Nimer Jaber: I've always wondered about space. You know, what it feels like, you know, how big it really was.

Noreen Grice: I mean, you can't just reach out and touch the stars, nobody can. But we can bring it to people's fingertips, we can bring images that people might have only imagined. And we can bring it close to them so people can understand what these objects are in the universe and I think better understand their place within the universe.

Narrator: When asked to feel test prototypes of the book, the students were happy just to be involved. Then they realised that their opinions would shape the way the book was presented to people who were blind around the world.

Ben Wentworth: Then they started tearing the images up.

Narrator: Part of the problem with early versions of the plastic overlays is that they had touch-points for everything in the photograph. Fingers got lost in the galaxy of dots and ridges. Later versions of the book provided more room to manoeuvre.

Nimer Jaber: It has great pictures. I can, you know, you could feel them better, you could, you know, you know what their shapes are.

Narrator: Revisions were duly noted.

Noreen Grice: Alright, I can make that change in the plate.

Male student 1: Yeah, that's all the really suggestions I have.

Noreen Grice: OK.

Narrator: Exactly what these students see in their mind's eye remains a mystery for sighted people.

Female student 1: This one reminds me of onion rings.

Narrator: Still, it's clear that with each raised ridge and dot, an image of space that makes sense reveals itself.

Female student 2: That's pretty cool.

Ben Wentworth: To get the kids to say 'Oh, that's what you're seeing', and I … that's what's so unique about the Hubble book.

Narrator: The images provided by the Hubble Space Telescope continue to astonish and amaze, and provide a window on the wonders of space, no matter how you see them.

5 Students talk about what surprised them. For instance, they might be amazed at how children can pick out different shapes just through using their fingertips. They can also identify colours, although for totally blind children this is just an abstract concept.

6 Students watch the video again and answer the questions. You may wish to pause the video at relevant points.

Answer

1 stars, galaxies, moons
2 It has raised dots and ridges to help the visually impaired interpret the images.
3 The author will listen to their feedback and make changes to the book.
4 The plastic sheets had too much information: *touch points for everything in the photograph*.

IDEAS GENERATOR

Read the Ideas generator box with the students. Remind them that in the exam the examiners will be listening out for contributions and responses that are relevant and follow on from each other. Students decide which response would be most suitable.

Answer

B3 sounds the best response. The speaker responds politely in a way that shows he/she is listening, *Yes, I think that's it*. The second sentence then moves the conversation on to talk about the students' attitudes about the project: *And clearly these students are really motivated to be involved in this*. In B1 and B2, the speaker just answers the original question in a slightly different way rather than responding to the suggestion of speaker A.

7 Students exchange their ideas as though they were in Part 3 of the Speaking test.

8 Students look at the Useful language box and decide which expressions suggest agreement or disagreement. It is worth pointing out that *yes, but…* is a polite way of acknowledging what the other person has said before going on to modify or disagree with it. Elicit other ways they may know of acknowledging the other person's point of view, e.g. *I hear what you're saying …*

Answers

These expressions suggest disagreement:
Yes, I think that's right. But …
You're right. On the other hand …
I see what you mean. But …

9 Students practise using the expressions in the box.

10 This activity provides intensive practice of responding and developing arguments. Monitor the students and check that they are using the expressions from the box.

11 Students reflect on their performance.

Vocabulary organiser 13, page 174

Answers

1

1 broadcast	2 reveal	3 published	4 publicise
5 exchange / share	6 instil	7 impart	8 explained

2

1 sophisticated	2 decades	3 haziest
4 trenches	5 initiate	

3

Nouns followed by
of: effect, matter, product, question, result, threat
for: admiration, argument, respect, search
to: access, alternative, approach, connection, solution, threat
on: authority, effect
over: authority, dispute
with: argument, connection, communication, contact

4

1 arrange a day when something will happen
2 do something for the first time, and provide a valuable example for others to follow
3 behave in a way that can be followed as a model by other people
4 start a new fashion
5 make something happen, start a chain of events
6 start writing
7 achieve something that has not been achieved before
8 to start a journey (in a boat)

Bank of English

1 collaborated	2 conversed	3 co-operate
4 communicate	5 contacted	

Photocopiable activity instructions

Reading skills worksheets (pages 135–136)

Aim: the reading task in the unit is quite demanding, so this worksheet could be used as an aid to preparing the students.

Instructions:

1 Prepare a copy of worksheet 1 for each student, and worksheet 2 for every two students.

2 Hand out copies of worksheet 1 only. Students should initially work individually on questions 1, 2 and 3.

3 Students work in pairs. Each pair compare their answers to questions 1, 2 and 3, and then work together on question 4. Tell them they need to give reasons for their choices.

Answer

1 1 scientific article	2 general magazine article		3 news article
2 1 iii	2 i	3 ii	
3 1 C	2 A	3 B	
4 2 A	3 B	1 C	

Reading Skills worksheet 1

1   Read paragraphs 1–3 below, and decide which type of article they come from. This will help you understand what kind of information is likely to follow.

2   Decide which of the following types of information you would expect to follow each paragraph. Underline the key words and phrases which help you reach your decision.

    i   background information

    ii   an opposing point of view

    iii a supporting point for clarification

        1   The advantage exists because of the nature of electromagnetic waves. Although electromagnetic radiation can travel very fast (about 6.7 million miles per hour), it disperses and weakens across space. That's why a flashlight beam only shines brightly enough to see over short distances, and why a parent has to shout more loudly at her child, the further away the child is.

        2   Rose and co-author Gregory Wright, a physicist at Antiope Associates in Fair Haven, N.J., published that surprising conclusion in the journal *Nature* in 2004. But they did not set out to make the headlines on the best way to contact 'E.T.'.

        3   The idea of sending physical objects into space is nothing new. When NASA's Pioneer 10 spacecrafts went plunging into space in 1977, they carried twin 12-inch disks bearing words, music and images selected by a team of scientists to represent life on Earth. Now at the edge of the solar system, the Pioneer 10 craft may represent the best approach, says Rose.

3   Match each paragraph (1–3 above) with one of the subsequent paragraphs A, B, or C below.

    A   Rose's research began with a grant from the National Science Foundation to study how to make wireless communications on Earth more efficient. The project's goal, he explains, was to figure out how to 'get the most amount of information across for the least amount of energy'. While investigating that subject, it occurred to him that this work might have implications for interstellar communications as well.

    B   Like much good news, however, this discovery comes with a catch: A physical package could not travel as fast as radio or light waves. At a reasonable speed, Rose estimates a package could take 20 million years to reach distant stars. That's but a blip in time, given the galaxy's 10 billion-year history, but it doesn't inspire hope for the kind of 'contact' made famous by Jodie Foster in the movie of the same name.

    C   In other words, the farther a light beam travels, the more it spreads out. Any message encoded by it will have likewise faded in the voyage. The same is true for radio waves: for a message to retain its meaning over a long distance, it must be beamed out with high energy. A message inscribed on an object, on the other hand, remains as legible when it reaches its destination as on the day it was sent, no matter how far it has gone.

4   Now look at the whole text. The three paragraph pairs above (1–3 and A–C) have been removed. Decide which pair goes into each gap.

© 2015 National Geographic Learning, a part of Cengage Learning

Getting a message across the universe: would E.T. send a letter?

10th March 2013

The prospect of communicating with intelligent life beyond Earth has long captured human imagination. For decades, scientists have been sending hopeful messages in the form of radio signals into space and patiently scanning the skies for signs that someone, somewhere, is doing the same.

So far, that search has been fruitless. But we might be wise to look as well as listen, says Christopher Rose, a physicist and professor of electrical engineering at New Jersey's Rutgers University. By his calculations, it's vastly more efficient to send large messages across space not in the form of radio waves or beams of light, but in physical packages. That's right: If we want to send a note to outer space, Rose says, we should consider sending a message in a bottle.

Likewise, we should anticipate messages that might arrive here as physical artefacts – embedded in a meteorite, perhaps, or falling to Earth after hurtling across the cosmos on a comet's tail.

[…]

[…]

In wireless communications, transmitting information with radio waves makes sense because speed is a critical consideration. But in some instances – such as when two people are just around the corner from each other – it's more efficient, from an energy conservation perspective, to simply deliver a letter than to use radio waves or some other form of electromagnetic energy.

'That was the jumping off point,' says Rose. 'I thought, "Huh, there's a fundamental issue here. When is it better for me to hand over the information than to radiate it?" And that was the kernel of the idea.'

Rose calculated how much energy would be required to ship a message 1,000 light years into space. A package travelling a million kilometres an hour (about 670,000 miles per hour) would need a million years to reach its destination. A radio transmission would get there in only a fraction of that time – an obvious advantage when the sender can't tolerate a delay, as in the case of cell phone conversations on Earth.

But when timing is irrelevant, Rose found that sending a physical message makes more sense.

[…]

[…]

What's more, once a physical message arrives at a given destination, it stays there. A radio signal must be intercepted at the moment it passes by in order to be 'received'.

While it would take a serious amount of protection – thousands of pounds of lead, in Rose's estimation – to prevent damage by cosmic waves in transit, the energy required to package information and hurtle it across space would be far less than that required to beam out high-powered electromagnetic signals on a regular basis. The further a message must go, and the longer the message is, the greater the advantage of sending that message in a physical form.

The advantage is strong enough, Rose says, to compensate for the fact that thousands, or even hundreds of thousands, of messages might need to be sent to cover the range of potential star systems that could potentially pick up a single radio signal.

If, for instance, we wanted to send a very large message – say, all of the information inside the Library of Congress – to a star 10,000 light years away, it would be a hundred billion times more efficient to encode it in silicon chips than it would be to radiate the same amount of information from the world's largest radio telescope.

[…]

[…]

For simple messages meant to convey only 'I am here', Rose says radio waves are still more efficient. And because radio waves travel so quickly, they offer the possibility of two-way communication. So the efforts of researchers looking for signals with giant radio telescopes – like those at the California-based SETI Institute – are worthwhile, he says.

Still, says Rose, there's something to be said for sending a message out for 'posterity', and for devising ways to look for physical messages that other life forms may have shipped across space, hoping to find us.

Rose's *Nature* paper was the first quantitative comparison of the costs of the different ways of delivering information across space. Since then, Rose has been working on the next logical question: If sending a physical message is the most efficient way to communicate, in what form might these message arrive, and how should we look for them?

He stops short of guesswork, though, preferring not to speculate about what an extraterrestrial life form might say or why it might want to communicate with people in the first place. For Rose, it's not about psychology or science fiction: 'It's just the physics, ma'am'.

14 GAIA'S LEGACY

Unit introduction

The topic of the unit is the history of the Earth, life on Earth and Gaia theory.

This unit will look at the history of the Earth and bring our own existence into perspective. In it we will discuss 'Gaia theory' and its implications for life on Earth, examine the biodiversity of life on Earth and consider the consequences of an expanding human population.

Warm-up activity

Warm up the class by asking them to brainstorm a list of questions about the Earth. Don't worry if you don't know the answers yourself; treat it as an exercise in discovery. Ask: *Where is the Earth in our solar system? How old is the Earth? How was the Earth formed? How fast does the Earth spin around the sun?*

Afterwards get students to read out their questions. Anyone else can attempt to answer them.

Getting started

1 **⊙ 45** This exercise offers students practice in listening to a long text with lot of detailed information. They should just write down the number that represents the million of years since each event happened. Play the recording twice. Check answers with the class.

Answers

1 700	2 570	3 500	4 470	5 380	6 350	7 300
8 250	9 200	10 150	11 50	12 3	13 3	

Audioscript ⊙ 45

The earliest multi-celled animals might have been sponges, which although they look like plants are actually animals. They most likely appeared around 700 million years ago. Invertebrates, which are the first animals that could get around, such as flatworms and jellyfish, are believed to have evolved around 570 million years ago. And then, about 500 million years ago, vertebrates, the group which includes fish and other animals with a backbone, suddenly appeared.

About 470 million years ago, the first plants began to grow out of the water, and this is when life on land established itself. Insects originally appeared on land about 380 million years ago and were followed, relatively soon after that, by the first amphibians, which surfaced from the water to become land animals approximately 350 million years ago. Essentially, they were fish that evolved lungs to breathe air. They employed their fins to crawl from one pond to another and these gradually became legs. The next group to emerge, about 300 million years ago, were the reptiles.

For the next 50 million years, life on Earth prospered – but about 250 million years ago, the Earth experienced a period of mass extinction, which meant that many species disappeared. Around this time, one group of reptiles, called 'dinosaurs', started to dominate all others. Their name means 'terrible lizard'. They were the commonest vertebrates and they controlled the Earth for the next 150 million years.

Throughout this time, a new type of animal began to evolve. These animals were the mammals. They gave birth to live young, which they nourished with milk from their bodies, and they first appeared about 200 million years ago.

The closest living family to the dinosaurs is believed to be birds. The first known bird, Archaeopteryx, appeared about 150 million years ago. It existed for around 70 million years, before becoming extinct, and was replaced by the group which includes modern birds, believed to have appeared around 60 million years ago, at the same time that the dinosaurs became extinct.

The group of mammals to which humans belong – the primates – emerged from an ancestral group of animals that ate mainly insects, around 50 million years ago. But it wasn't until about three million years ago – about the time the last ice age started – that intelligent apes, with the ability to walk on their back legs, appeared in southern Africa. Simultaneously, their brains evolved and they learnt to make and use tools. Although called *Homo habilis*, meaning 'handy man', these creatures were more like apes than men. About two million years ago, *Homo habilis* evolved into the first people called *Homo erectus*. Their bodies were like ours, but their faces were still ape-like. They evolved in Africa and spread as far as South-East Asia. Modern people (*Homo sapiens*) appear to have evolved in Africa about 100,000 years ago (although the date is far from certain).

See *Odd animal out!* photocopiable activity, page 143.

Reading multiple-choice questions

2 Elicit answers to the question. Some students may well answer 'no', in which case ask them to guess, based on the content of the page. If no guesses are forthcoming, move on to exercise 3.

3 Ask students to skim read the text to find out who or what 'Gaia' is and to write a sentence in their own words. This will help them practise their skimming technique. Allow them three minutes only.

Answer

Gaia is the name that James Lovelock gave the planet Earth as a self-evolving and self-regulating system that adjusts itself to support life.

MATCHING GIST TO DETAIL

Read the information with the class. Explain that different words can be used in the options to convey the same meaning as sections of the text, or different meanings can be conveyed by using similar words, thereby creating confusing distractors.

4 Ask students to do the exercise and explain the reasons for their answers. This can be done individually, in pairs or all together in class.

Answer

D (could adjust itself to support life)

5 Students should attempt the task individually. They can now read the text carefully and should follow the techniques outlined so far. They should spend no longer than ten minutes on it.

Answers

| 1 B | 2 C | 3 A | 4 A | 5 D | 6 B |

→ Vocabulary organiser 14, exercises 1 and 2, page 175

Vocabulary organiser answers

1
1 salinity	2 metabolism	3 phenomenon
4 entity	5 biosphere	6 diversity
7 void	8 myriad	9 equilibrium

2
1 profound	2 attain	3 postulated
4 imprecise	5 provoked	6 optimum
7 sustain	8 allotted	

Student's Book pages 136–137

Language development idioms from nature

TEACHING IN PRACTICE: PICTURES AND IDIOMS

A good way to help students remember idioms is by association with images. Ask students to think of an appropriate visual image to describe each idiom. If they are good at drawing they could draw a picture, or they could take images from magazines.

1 Students complete the exercise individually or in pairs. Allow a few minutes for this, and let them use dictionaries if you like.

Answers

| 1 a | 2 b | 3 a | 4 a | 5 a | 6 a | 7 b | 8 a |

ADJECTIVES FOLLOWED BY PARTICLES

Read through the explanation with students and remind them that correctly used particles can sometimes make the difference between a good English speaker and an average one! It is therefore important to learn adjectives with the particle they use, preferably in the context of a sentence. As an illustration of this point, ask them to find the words *analogous* and *reliant* in the reading text, and say what particle is used with each (*analogous to* and *reliant on*).

2 Most students will know the correct particle to follow each adjective, but focusing on the gap in context will help to reinforce good habits. Remind them that it is a good idea to note down any new word pairs in their notebook if they are not familiar with them. You could extend the task by asking students to suggest other adjectives that are used with each particle.

Answers

| 1 of | 2 about | 3 with | 4 at | 5 to |
| 6 by | 7 for | 8 in | 9 from | 10 on |

→ Vocabulary organiser 14, exercise 3, page 175

Vocabulary organiser answers

| 1 of | 2 about | 3 with | 4 at | 5 to |
| 6 by | 7 for | 8 in | 9 from | 10 on |

Key word earth

3 Students can work individually or in pairs. Allow them to use dictionaries if necessary. Check answers with the group and elicit example sentences for each phrase.

Answers

| 1 d | 2 g | 3 b | 4 e | 5 f |
| 6 h | 7 i | 8 c | 9 j | 10 a |

→ Vocabulary organiser, Bank of English, page 175

Vocabulary organiser answers

1 biosphere	2 geography	3 biology
4 geology	5 biographer	6 geometry
7 biodiversity	8 biodegradable	9 geophysicist
10 geopolitical		

Grammar unreal tenses

4 This exercise will help students focus on the structure with *as if*. Elicit answers from the students and ask why they chose their answers.

Answer

b

UNREAL PAST

Elicit examples of past tense structures that are used to talk about the present or the future. The purpose of this section is to consolidate the different structures which form the unreal past in English and to familiarise students with their many uses.

5 Students work individually or in pairs. Check that they understand they have to identify whether the sentence refers to the past, present or future.

Answers

1 were (present time)
2 had (present / future time), would be (present / future time)
3 didn't smoke (present / future)
4 wouldn't have been fined / hadn't dropped (third conditional – past hypothetical situation)
5 was going to be (past / future in the past)
6 were, would visit (present hypothetical situation)
7 did (present)
8 hadn't had (past)

→ Grammar reference 14, page 218

6 Students match the sentences in exercise 5 to the functions a–h. Allow them to refer to the Grammar reference section again if necessary.

Answers

| 1 c | 2 g | 3 f | 4 b | 5 a | 6 h | 7 e | 8 d |

7 Students complete the sentences with the correct form of the verb in brackets.

Answers

1 were	2 were	3 had not made
4 took	5 took	6 Were
7 had not bought	8 had not told	9 was / were
10 had seen		

8 Students should do the exercise individually. This will confirm whether any students are still having problems. Check the answers with the class, and elicit which other words determine the structures required. Students should underline these or make notes in their notebooks.

Answers

1 only	2 was / were	3 as	4 were
5 had	6 have	7 rather / sooner	8 than
9 wish	10 time	11 lived	12 if / though

TEACHING IN PRACTICE: ELICITING ANSWERS

When checking the answers to a class exercise it is obviously better if you can elicit the correct answers from students, rather than just 'telling' them what the correct answer is. In most cases at least one student in the class will know the correct answer (you hope!).

9 Ask students to complete the sentences independently, then elicit their answers.

Answers

1 high time you turned / switched off
2 would rather try to save / we tried to save
3 wish I had not / hadn't been
4 if you saw / should see
5 had not / hadn't been so polluted
6 like she knows everything, but / which / though

See *Ideal world* photocopiable activity, page 144.

Listening sentence completion

1 Discuss the question with the class and elicit various ideas. The aim here is to introduce the subject of the listening, which explains how different amounts of oxygen in Earth's history have both helped and hindered the survival of various species. If necessary, prompt students with questions, e.g. *Why can't I live on the moon?* (There's no oxygen.) *What covers over two thirds of the Earth's surface and makes it possible for all life to exist?* (Water!)

EXAM SPOTLIGHT

To emphasise once more the importance of reading the questions first, read through the information and the example sentences in the box with the class, and elicit suggestions for a word to complete the sentence. (Students will probably say: *disappearance* because this is what is most often talked about in relation to the dinosaurs.) Continue reading the information with your students and ask if anyone has changed their mind.

2 Ask students to answer the questions in relation to the example in the box. They should all now realise that the missing word is in fact *appearance*.

Answers

1 circumstances, leading up to, dinosaurs
2 are not often questioned = few people wonder
3 extinction

3 Explain that students will be given enough time in the exam to study the question and find the key words in the sentences. Let them spend about one minute doing this before you move on to the next exercise.

Answers

Underline:
1 years
2 oxygen / gases
3 animals / leave the water / the land
4 animals underwent / stage of
5 400 million years ago / species / oxygen levels fell
6 300 million years ago higher oxygen / enabled / to flourish
7 animals / died / not adapt quickly / low oxygen
8 Birds / fly at / shortage of oxygen

4 Do this as a class activity, thereby reinforcing the usefulness of this technique.

Answers

1 a number (of years)
2 a number (percentage)
3 verb meaning 'live in a place'
4 noun meaning 'change'
5 adjective showing the effect on a species of not enough oxygen
6 noun (species)
7 verb (connected to dying)
8 noun relating to how birds fly

---

5 ⊙ 46 Play the recording twice, giving time for students to complete or correct their answers.

Answers

1 600 million	2 21	3 colonise	4 evolution
5 extinct	6 reptiles	7 suffocated	8 altitudes

Audioscript ⊙ 46

We all take for granted the air we breathe and the oxygen essential for our survival. But the Earth's atmosphere didn't always contain oxygen! In fact, for most of its history there wasn't really any oxygen in the air at all! It's only been during the last 600 million years that there's been enough to support life, which, as it happens, is how long there has been life on land. The amount of oxygen in the atmosphere has swung wildly between tiny amounts – as little as 12% compared to today's 21% – to huge proportions – up to 30% during one particular period. This variation has of course had a massive impact on the animals living on Earth at any particular time. Animals have either taken advantage of the sudden increases in oxygen in order to evolve and colonise the land, or they have faced being made extinct during the periods when oxygen was scarce.

Palaeontologists have always had an interest in the occurrences that may have caused species to become extinct. The leading causes have been identified as meteors, ice ages, climate change, and so on, but fascinatingly enough, it's now clear that each mass extinction on Earth coincided with times of reduced oxygen. These periods have usually been followed by bursts of much higher oxygen levels, which again have coincided with a time of incredibly fast evolution in animal species. In most cases it appears that the most successful animals to inhabit the land during these times were those that developed more advanced respiratory systems. For example, invertebrates appeared on land for the first time around 420 million years ago – at a time when oxygen levels were higher than today's. Yet soon after that, approximately 400 million years ago, oxygen levels suddenly fell dramatically and most of these animals disappeared: either becoming extinct or returning to the ocean. Oxygen levels didn't increase again for another 50 million years or so, during which time only a small number of animals could survive on land. Then, 350 million years ago, oxygen levels started to rise, reaching their highest ever levels around 280 to 300 million years ago. This is when reptiles appeared, and they thrived in this rich atmosphere, but as oxygen levels started to fall once more over the next 50 million years, animals had to make some swift adjustments, or they suffocated for lack of air.

The animals that adjusted most efficiently were the dinosaurs. What they did was to add another pair of air sacs next to the lungs. This enabled them to extract even greater amounts of oxygen from the thinning air. Because of this evolutionary adaptation, it appears that they were the only animals that managed to do well during the mass extinction of 200 million years ago, the time with the lowest recorded oxygen levels. We can still see these air-sac adaptations in their descendants today – the birds – and it's actually this which then allows some birds to fly at altitudes with little oxygen.

Speaking evaluating

6 Discuss the question with the class. This will get your students' thoughts focused on the content of the listening section. Make a note of all useful vocabulary and new animal species on the board.

7 ⊙ 47 Play the recording, twice if necessary, and check students' answers. The point here is to highlight that not only is it perfectly OK to change your mind during this part of the Speaking Paper, it can actually help to give you more things to say.

Answers

Elisabeth: deforestation, pollution, weather, climate change, flooding
Giovanni: extinction of species

Audioscript ⊙ 47

Interlocutor	Now, I'd like you to talk about something together for about two minutes. Here are some of the ecological issues that need attention. First, you have some time to look at the task. Now, talk to each other about how serious each of these issues is.
Elisabeth	OK … well, at first glance I would say that deforestation is probably the most important ecological issue. What do you think?
Giovanni	Yes, I agree. It's terrible that they're cutting down the rainforests so fast. These forests are important because they're the home to so many species of animals and plants. If they're all cut down it'll cause lots of problems.
Elisabeth	Yes, and the forests also affect the weather and the Earth's temperature, I think, don't they? However, we shouldn't ignore the issue of pollution. That's another very serious issue.
Giovanni	Yes, you're quite right. Pollution is dangerous for our health and it's also dangerous to wildlife. Some species may disappear for ever because their habitats have been destroyed by pollution. On the other hand, the extinction of species is a very serious issue. I've read that if we don't do something now, over half the Earth's species could be extinct in the next hundred years.
Elisabeth	Yes, and that's a frightening idea!
Interlocutor	Thank you. Now you have about a minute to decide which is the most serious issue.
Elisabeth	I don't know about you, Giovanni, but taking everything into consideration, it seems to me that climate change is the most urgent issue.
Giovanni	Why do you think that?
Elisabeth	Well, if the world's temperature rises by even a couple of degrees, it'll almost certainly have a catastrophic effect on nearly everything. For example, if the Greenland ice cap melts, sea level will rise, causing flooding in lots of places around the world.
Giovanni	That's true, and of course that would destroy a lot of habitats, possibly resulting in the loss of species living there. Yes, I would agree with you.
Interlocutor	Thank you. Can I have the booklet, please?

8 Elicit answers to the question from the class.

> **Answer**
> climate change

9 Each pair or group of three should work simultaneously while you monitor from a distance. Afterwards select pairs or groups to demonstrate to the class what they have practised. Time them and make sure they speak for three minutes. If they end too soon, give them a signal to keep going. If they are still speaking when the three minutes are up, cut them off. This is what the interlocutor will do, so they need to get used to it!

Use of English word formation (2)

> **SUFFIXES**
>
> Read through the information in the box with the students. Brainstorm examples of suffixes and write them on the board.

10 Go through the exercise with the students and make sure they recognise the patterns.

> **Answers**
> a isation   b ise   c ly

11 Students work individually to add the suffixes to the word stems. Check the answers with the class.

> **Answers**
> 1 affectionate   2 evolution   3 activate
> 4 historic / historical 5 diversity / diversification 6 development
> 7 modernise   8 childish / childlike

12 Ask students to read the text all the way through first. Allow three to five minutes for this. Then ask questions to see if they have understood the gist of it, e.g. *How many species are on Earth? Why should we hurry up if we want to study biodiversity? Why is biodiversity important?* When you are satisfied that students have a good understanding of the text, ask them to fill the gaps.

> **Answers**
> 1 confidence   2 scientific   3 broaden
> 4 destruction   5 extinction   6 biological
> 7 madness   8 indefinitely

→ Vocabulary organiser 14, exercise 4, page 175

> **Vocabulary organiser answers**
> 1 ridiculousness   2 postage   3 courageous
> 4 affectionate   5 insecticide   6 refugees
> 7 diversification 8 ecological

Student's Book pages 140–141

Writing an essay (discussing issues that surround a topic)

Aim: This section shows students how to organise their ideas and plan their work efficiently, as well as developing their vocabulary skills.

→ Writing guide, page 222

1 Before you start, analyse the title of this section with your class and elicit what is meant by 'issues that surround a topic'. Students then read and discuss the sample question. Brainstorm possible ideas and write key words and points on the board.

2 Students work individually at first. Check answers with the class and for each issue ask students to provide at least one reason why they think it is serious.

> **Answers**
> population increase: poverty and famine / illness and disease
> international conflict: claims on territory / land
> pollution: species extinction / loss of biodiversity, depletion of Earth's resources

3 Students work individually, reading the essay and underlining reasons. Take feedback from the class.

> **Answer**
> The increase in human population is the most serious issue because it causes depletion of the Earth's resources, pollution, climate change, species extinction.

4 Elicit answers from the class and write them on the board.

> **Answers**
> It's too short, has no paragraph structure, and doesn't deal sufficiently well with the issues surrounding the question to provide a coherent, conclusive answer. Also the student does not provide reasons for his / her opinions. It's also repetitive in style and wording.

5 Students work individually or in pairs to find the meaning of the words. Allow a few minutes for this. Check answers with the class.

> **Answers**
> 1 make worse   2 very fast   3 use up   4 different species

6 Read the information in the Exam spotlight box with the class. The main purpose of exercise 6 is to help students brainstorm all the different issues surrounding a central issue. Allow them to work in pairs or individually, and check answers with the class.

> **Answers**
> 1 depletion / overuse of natural resources
> 2 climate change / global warming
> 3 loss of biodiversity / extinctions
> 4 poverty / famine / starvation
> 5 disease
> 6 international conflict

7 Ask students to do a brief paragraph plan, deciding which two points they would include, and writing an introduction and conclusion.

8 Ask students to read the task. Elicit the number of bullet points they must discuss and what they are asked to do, before they brainstorm ideas and draw a spidergram. They can work in pairs, or do the activity as a class.

9 Ask students to plan, write and check the essay in no more than 45 minutes (either in class or as homework).

Vocabulary organiser 14, page 175

> **Answers**
> **1**
> | 1 salinity | 2 metabolism | 3 phenomenon |
> | 4 entity | 5 biosphere | 6 diversity |
> | 7 void | 8 myriad | 9 equilibrium |
>
> **2**
> | 1 profound | 2 attain | 3 postulated |
> | 4 imprecise | 5 provoked | 6 optimum |
> | 7 sustain | 8 allotted | |
>
> **3**
> | 1 of | 2 about | 3 with | 4 at | 5 to |
> | 6 by | 7 for | 8 in | 9 from | 10 on |
>
> **4**
> | 1 ridiculousness | 2 postage | 3 courageous |
> | 4 affectionate | 5 insecticide | 6 refugees |
> | 7 diversification | 8 ecological | |
>
> **Bank of English**
> | 1 biosphere | 2 geography | 3 biology |
> | 4 geology | 5 biographer | 6 geometry |
> | 7 biodiversity | 8 biodegradable | 9 geophysicist |
> | 10 geopolitical | | |

Photocopiable activity instructions

Odd animal out! (page 143)

Aim: to help students learn the names of animals and some animal groups.

Instructions:

1 Give student pairs a copy of the animal grid which you have cut into strips. Tell them to place the strips face down on the desk between them.

2 Write the following animal groups on the board:
1 invertebrates	2 fish
3 amphibians	4 insects
5 reptiles	6 birds
7 mammals (excluding apes)	8 apes

3 Students take turns picking up one strip at a time. If they can name the animal group that three of the animals belong to and identify the odd one out, they can keep the strip. They should write the name of the animal group on the strip and put a cross through the odd one out. If they can't name the animal group they have to put the strip back on the table.

> **Answers**
> 1 Group: Reptiles. Odd one out: worm (a worm is an invertebrate. It doesn't have a backbone).
> 2 Group: Insects. Odd one out: spider (a spider is an arachnid and has two body segments and eight legs; insects have three body segments and six legs).
> 3 Group: Fish. Odd one out: snake (reptile).
> 4 Group: Mammals. Odd one out: goose (bird).
> 5 Group: Apes (mammals). Odd one out: spider monkey.
> 6 Group: Invertebrates. Odd one out: tuna (a tuna is a fish and therefore a vertebrate, it has a backbone).
> 7 Group: Birds. Odd one out: pterosaur (a pterosaur, now extinct, was in fact a dinosaur that could fly).
> 8 Group: Amphibians. Odd one out: platypus.

Ideal world (page 144)

Aim: to give students extra practice at using the unreal past.

Instructions:

1 Students form pairs or groups of three. Photocopy, cut out and give one eight box table to each group.

2 Students have to discuss the idea of an 'ideal world' and come up with some suggestions about what they believe would make an ideal world.

3 Each idea that they agree on should be written into the boxes using the cues provided.

4 When everyone has completed their box, they have to 'present' their ideal world to the rest of the class.

5 When everyone has presented their ideas, the students vote to decide which pair / group has the best ideas.

Odd animal out!

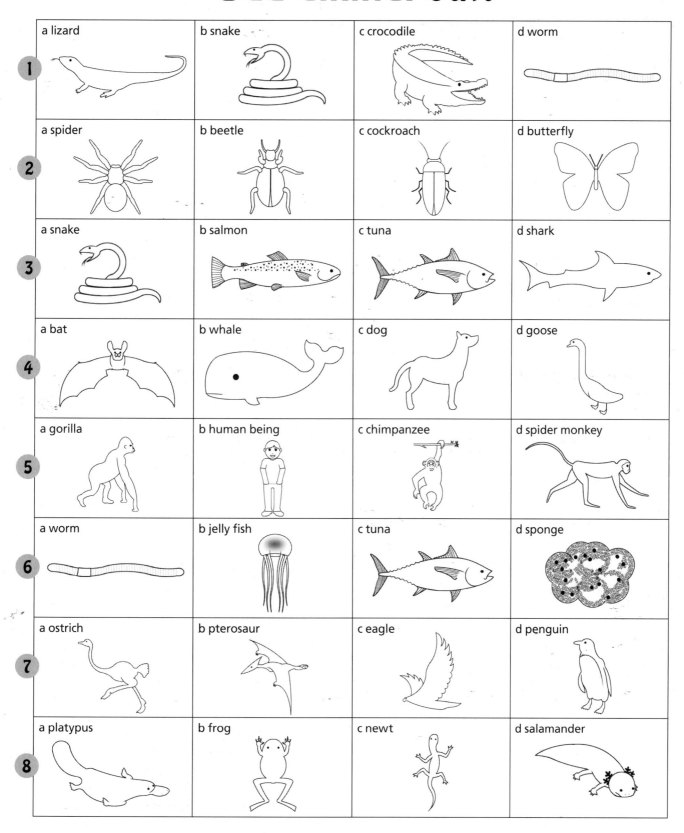

	a	b	c	d
1	a lizard	b snake	c crocodile	d worm
2	a spider	b beetle	c cockroach	d butterfly
3	a snake	b salmon	c tuna	d shark
4	a bat	b whale	c dog	d goose
5	a gorilla	b human being	c chimpanzee	d spider monkey
6	a worm	b jelly fish	c tuna	d sponge
7	a ostrich	b pterosaur	c eagle	d penguin
8	a platypus	b frog	c newt	d salamander

Ideal World

Write down your hopes for an ideal world …

If only …	I'd rather …	Were it possible …	Suppose …
I wish …	I'd prefer it …	It's time …	Imagine …

✂ -

Write down your hopes for an ideal world …

If only …	I'd rather …	Were it possible …	Suppose …
I wish …	I'd prefer it …	It's time …	Imagine …

✂ -

Write down your hopes for an ideal world …

If only …	I'd rather …	Were it possible …	Suppose …
I wish …	I'd prefer it …	It's time …	Imagine …

15 OUR GLOBAL VILLAGE

Unit introduction

The topic of the unit is cultures, customs and civilisations.

Nowadays we come face to face with other cultures, belief systems, traditions, languages and environments far more frequently than ever before. It is therefore necessary to learn more about other people, the places they come from, and the way that they do things there.

Warm-up activity

Ask students to prepare for the lesson by doing research into one unique culture or custom of their choice from another country. This can be anything they like, from how people in Denmark celebrate Christmas, to how the Yanomami Indians of the Amazon rainforest remember their dead. They can prepare by searching internet sites (in English) and make a short presentation at the beginning of the lesson. This can be done in pairs or small groups, to save time. There is the possibility of extending this task into a larger project to be submitted as a longer essay at the end of the unit.

TEACHING IN PRACTICE: MULTICULTURAL GROUPS

When teaching multicultural groups, it's important to watch out for anything that may cause offence. However, there is also the opportunity for you and your students to share information and find out so much more about different cultures. Another advantage of multicultural groups is that students are forced to communicate with each other in English, and it makes a good opportunity for pairwork, as students from different countries often have different issues with English and can help each other.

Getting started

BACKGROUND: THE GLOBAL VILLAGE

The term *global village* was first popularised in the 1960s, but today it's mostly used as a metaphor to describe the Internet and World Wide Web. On the Internet, where physical distance does not exist, social spheres are greatly expanded by the ease with which people can interact with others in online communities. This has fostered the idea of a unified global community.

1 Discuss the title of the unit with the class and elicit ideas about what they think it means. Then invite students to look at the picture and identify the country and tradition shown. Talk about any other issues that may come up connected to the subject and note down key vocabulary.

Answer

The photo shows the dragon dance, which is performed at different festivals in China, such as Chinese New Year or the Lantern Festival.

2 Students describe customs from their own culture. They can do this first in pairs, then discuss their different customs with the class.

Extension

A possible game here would be along the lines of Ten Questions, where a student does a short mime of a traditional custom and the other students take turns asking questions in order to guess what is. Questions should take the form of *yes / no* answers only. For each *yes* answer a student receives, he / she gets to ask another question. For each *no* answer, play moves on to the next student.

→ Vocabulary organiser 15, exercises 1 and 2, page 176

Vocabulary organiser answers
1
Students' own answers
2
1 catalyst
2 mundane
3 detrimental
4 enlightened
5 advancement (note that *change* can be positive or negative; *progress* and *advancement* are always positive)
6 perpetually

Reading cross-text multiple matching

CROSS-TEXT MULTIPLE MATCHING

Read the information in the box with the class and emphasise that the texts in this part of the exam are usually of an academic nature. This section aims to help students look at a selection of texts with a common theme and to quickly compare the opinions expressed in them.

3 Explain that this exercise will help them with the exam task in exercise 4. Ask students to work through the exercise in pairs. Then elicit their answers.

Answers

1 No. (The writer says that by having traditions for everyday practices we don't need to experiment with different ways of doing them. This gives us time to think about how we can improve other areas of life.)
2 Yes.
3 Yes.
4 Yes.
5 No. (The writer says that people and institutions adopt traditions because they have been proven to work.)
6 No. (The writer says that tradition can be adapted in order to help us move forwards.)
7 No. (The writer says that we shouldn't waste time trying to find new ways to do things that have been tried and tested. By unnecessarily looking for solutions to problems that have already been solved, we don't give ourselves time to explore new ideas.)
8 Yes.

4 Ask students to reread the texts to work out the answers individually. Be prepared for them to find this hard, but explain that making notes about the writers' opinions (as in exercise 3) will be a useful stage before answering the exam questions.

Answers

1 D   2 B   3 B   4 A

5 Ask how far students agree with each writer, and what their own opinions are.
→   Vocabulary organiser 15, exercise 3, page 176

Vocabulary organiser answers

1 something that gets in the way, so that physical or metaphorical movement or progress is difficult
2 likely problems
3 agreed with by most people
4 ignore
5 deep and very close
6 something that severely limits movement, in a damaging way
7 careless, doing things without considering the consequences
8 the state of being damaged or worse than before

Student's Book pages 144–145

Language development phrasal verbs and phrases with *pass*

1 Start the section by brainstorming any phrasal verbs or phrases with *pass* that students remember. Write them on the board, or elicit example sentences for each one. Students then complete the exercise.

Answers

1 over   2 on   3 up   4 off   5 away   6 as   7 out   8 by

2 Students choose the correct option to complete each phrase. They may be familiar with some of the idioms, but not all of them. Either allow them to use their dictionaries or let them try to guess the answers. Afterwards, check answers with the class by eliciting further examples.

Answers

1 b   2 c   3 a   4 c   5 a   6 c   7 b   8 a

Key word *pass*

3 Read the two sentences with your students and elicit what the mistake is. Explain that the word *passed* is the past participle or the past simple form, and would need to be used either as the main verb or with an auxiliary, e.g. *Julian had passed me in the street earlier* or *Julian passed me in the street*. Point out that this is quite a common mistake, even among native speakers.

Answer

b is incorrect: The correct answer would be *walked past me* because *past* is the spelling of the preposition.

4 Students work individually or in pairs to answer the question. Go through the definitions with the class and make sure they have correctly understood the different meanings.

Answer

definition 2

Extension

Write the following additional sentence on the board and ask students to decide which definition in exercise 4 matches it (answer: definition 3).
He passed a hand through his hair in exasperation as he realised they could not understand him.

5 Allow enough time for students to write their own five sentences. Tell them that the sentences need to be simple but clear enough to show the meaning. Afterwards students swap their sentences with their partners who try to match them. You can either go round the class checking answers or ask students to read their sentences and definitions after the activity.
→   Vocabulary organiser 15, exercise 4, page 176

Vocabulary organiser answers

1 pass away   2 pass (something) on
3 pass out   4 pass up
5 pass off (as)   6 pass with flying colours
7 let something pass   8 pass the buck

Listening (1) multiple speakers

6 ⊙ 48 Read the information in the box with the class. Point out that exercise 6 is not an exam task, but that it will help students focus on a useful skill: identifying who said what. Students read through the questions first. Tell them that for this task you will only play the recording once.

Answers
1 A   2 B   3 B   4 A   5 A   6 B   7 B

Audioscript ⊙ 48

Interviewer: Today we're here to discuss the subject of kissing and its origins. With me in the studio are two anthropologists: Professor Rosemary O'Bryan and Dr Andrew Peters. Professor O'Bryan, is kissing learnt or instinctive behaviour?

Rosemary: Affectionate kissing is a learnt behaviour that most probably originated from a mother gently touching or nibbling her child's body with her lips, to cement the bond between them, or it may have arisen from premasticating food to make it easier for her child to swallow. From there it developed into a way of showing affection towards family members, close friends or other members of society and as a sign of respect to older, senior group members.

Interviewer: And yet, according to some anthropologists, kissing is an echo of an ancient form of communication that was necessary for the healthy and successful continuation of the species. Dr Peters.

Andrew: Yes, kissing in humans is an instinctive behaviour which most likely evolved from grooming behaviour common in mammals. However, recent research has indicated that this kind of behaviour had a much more serious biological function than just social bonding. Kissing, or rubbing noses, actually allows prospective mates to smell or taste each other's pheromones …

Interviewer: You mean the chemicals which give off information about our biological make-up?

Andrew: Correct, and thus we get more information about our biological compatibility. Women are more attracted to men who are more genetically compatible to them, and a woman picks this up by breathing in his pheromones. Any resulting offspring will have better resistance to a greater number of diseases, and will consequently have a better chance of survival. That's why we still like to kiss – to maximise our chances of sampling each other's aroma.

Interviewer: So that's why couples are more likely to bond if they have the right 'chemistry'.

Andrew: Yes, and it's not just a mating tool. Chimpanzees, for instance, use it for reconciliation, by kissing and embracing after fights, providing good evidence that kissing in the higher primates has the function of repairing social relationships.

Interviewer: So when did the romantic act of kissing one's sweetheart on the mouth as a form of affection actually develop?

Rosemary: Well, not until comparatively late in the evolution of love in fact. In antiquity, kissing – especially on the eyes or cheek – was mainly a form of greeting, but there's no evidence of it being romantic. One of the earliest descriptions of kissing as a form of love and affection comes from the sixth century, in France. Around that time it seems to have become fashionable for a young man to give his betrothed a kiss on the lips as a seal of his affection.

Interviewer: But the rest of the world did not practise kissing as a sign of affection?

Rosemary: In the years before cinema the lovers' kiss was largely a western habit – unknown in other parts of the world. By the end of the second world war western motion pictures had carried the image of romantic couples engaged in a kiss to many other parts of the world. Until quite recently, it was only in North America and Europe that kissing was an important aspect of courtship, which puts paid to the notion that kissing must be instinctive in all people. For instance, the Chinese and the Japanese never kissed on the lips.

Andrew: Yes, but in other cultures affection was expressed in a number of ways – for instance, in Samoa, lovers would express affection by sniffing the air beside each other's cheek; in Polynesia affection was shown by rubbing noses together. The same goes for Eskimos and Laplanders, as with many animals who smell each other or rub noses to smell each other's pheromones. This indicates that it's still instinctive …

Rosemary: It's hardly the same thing …

Andrew: What about monkeys? Bonobos? They'll kiss each other on the lips for just about any excuse at all. They do it to make up after fights, to comfort each other, to develop social bonds, and sometimes for no clear reason at all – just like us …

7 ⊙ 48 This is an exam-style task. As students have heard the recording once already they may not need to listen to the recording twice for this task; decide according to the level of the group. You may want to pre-teach some of the words from the multiple-choice questions (see Vocabulary box). Allow enough time for students to read the questions. Afterwards check answers with the group and refer to the audioscript if necessary.

Answers
1 C   2 D   3 A   4 A   5 B   6 C

VOCABULARY

prospective mates: possible future partners
groom (v): to clean fur
offspring (n): young, child / children
primates (n pl): order of mammals which includes apes and monkeys
bestow (v): to give (formal)
constitute (v): to be something

Speaking talking about your country, culture and background

8 In multicultural teaching groups students will benefit from working with partners from different countries. In monocultural groups one student in each pair can pretend to be from another country, asking questions to find out more about their partner's countries.

9 Students continue to work in pairs or open pairs. Monitor them in the class.

Degree of difficulty

Decrease the level: To make it easier for younger or weaker students to answer these questions, have a brainstorming session before they begin the pairwork, and write general ideas and suggestions on the board. Most students, however, should be able to say some things about the customs and traditions in their countries.

Increase the level: More advanced students shouldn't need any further guidance with these topics, and should also have a few things to say about question 3.

Student's Book pages 146–147

Grammar adverbial clauses

1 Students should read the extract from the audioscript and explain what the purpose of each word in bold is. Prompt them if necessary, or guide them to the information box below, or the Grammar reference section. As a follow-up, ask students to read the audioscript and find further examples of adverbial clauses.

Answers

thus: tells us the result
by: tells us how they do it
consequently: tells us the result
That's why: explains the reason

CLAUSES OF TIME, PURPOSE, REASON, CONCESSION AND RESULT

Read the information in the box with the class. Write the following sentence on the board and ask students to identify the adverbial clause, say what type it is and explain its meaning:
I won't be able to meet you until I've finished my homework.
(The adverbial clause is *until I've finished my homework*, it is a clause of time, and the meaning is: I can't meet you before I've done my homework, but I will be able to meet you after I've done it.)

2 This exercise can be done as a class activity if you think some students need extra help, or it can be done in pairs or individually. You may have to explain the meaning of *concession*, which has already had an example supplied.

Answers

Time	I'll meet you when I've finished.
Place	She wanted to know where I'd been.
Manner	He asked me how I'd done it.
Comparison	It was as bad as I feared.
Cause / reason	I walked fast because it was late.
Purpose	She smiled so that I'd feel welcome.
Result	It got so hot that I couldn't concentrate.
Condition	If I'd known you'd be late I'd have started without you.
Concession	She won the game although she'd never played before.

→ Grammar reference 15, page 219

3 Students work individually to choose the best options. Afterwards, check the answers with the class. You could also elicit example sentences for the two options which are not used.

Answers

1 Due to	2 in order to	3 the minute
4 Nevertheless	5 No matter how	6 Seeing as

4 Students should do the task individually in class. Allow approximately ten minutes for this. Elicit answers and iron out any problems.

Answers

1 and consequently I got
2 in order to make
3 seeing as it is / it's such
4 being the only person
5 in spite of the fact that
6 reason why I took up

Extension

For extra practice with adverbials write the following sentences on the board, or dictate them. Students should complete them in their own words.

1 I haven't seen Bertie since …

2 I had so little money …

3 Be home by midnight or else …

4 In spite of the weather we …

5 Smart though Sara is …

6 He decided to take a taxi for fear of …

The following answers are examples only:

1 1975. (point in time)

2 that I couldn't afford a bus ticket.

3 you'll be in big trouble.

4 decided to go for a walk.

5 she'll fail her exams if she doesn't do some work.

6 being late again.

See *Home exchange holidays* photocopiable activity, pages 153–154.

Use of English open cloze text

5 The aim of this section is to give further practice of open cloze texts and to consolidate what students have learnt in the Grammar section. Many of the gaps are based on adverbial clauses. Students do exercise 5 individually. Allow approximately ten minutes. Check answers with the group.

Answers			
1 so	2 take	3 example / instance	4 in
5 to	6 because	7 of	8 other

6 This exercise gives more practice in using some common expressions and collocations. Students should note down any new meanings or expressions in their vocabulary notebooks. In feedback, explain that *party* can be used to describe any group of people doing something together, e.g. *a party of schoolchildren / climbers / tourists*. A *pack* is used for a group of dogs or other similar animals (e.g *wolves, hounds*).

Answers			
1 sight	2 leave	3 party	4 return
5 sight	6 leave	7 person	8 return
9 vision	10 pack		

→ Vocabulary organiser 15, exercise 5, page 176

Vocabulary organiser answers

1 ignorant

2 offensive, insulting

3 inferior

4 point (a foot), touch (the head), bow

Listening (2) short extracts

7 🔘 49 Students should read through the questions and identify key words, and think about what they expect to hear. Play the recording twice.

Answers									
1 F	2 E	3 H	4 A	5 G	6 C	7 A	8 D	9 F	10 G

Audioscript 🔘 49

Speaker 1: I was born in Britain, and my family came to Japan when my father was transferred here 15 years ago – he works for an engineering company that's a Japanese-British joint venture. I was only five at the time, and my memories of Britain have faded – it's almost as though I've never been there. Originally my father planned to stay here for three years, but the whole family liked living here so much, we stayed. There are people from lots of different countries in Tokyo, where we live, and that's great. I have plenty of friends, both Japanese and other foreigners, so I feel I fit in pretty well, even though I don't speak perfect Japanese.

Speaker 2: My parents are Greek Cypriots, and moved to Britain before I was born, so I grew up there. We used to go to Cyprus on holiday every year to see the relations, and I've always been just as comfortable here as in Britain – both places are special to me. For events like my grandmother's 80th birthday, all my 35 cousins were here – most had flown in from other countries for the celebrations. I can understand why not everyone would want to have so many cousins and aunts and uncles, but I love it! In fact, that's one reason I came to live in Cyprus after university. Now I spend my holidays in Britain, to see my friends there.

Speaker 3: I grew up in a tiny community in Britain where you had to behave in certain ways, and believe certain things, and if you didn't, there was no place for you. Well, I couldn't stand it, and by the age of 18, I was desperate to get away – the further the better. I didn't want to study or work anywhere in Britain. I spent a year travelling round the world, and ended up in Thailand. And at last I'm beginning to find out what sort of person is the real me, and to realise that I can be that person just as easily in Britain as in Thailand. So maybe one day I'll go back to Britain – but not yet.

Speaker 4: It's quite difficult to say how British I am, because although the language within my family is English, I've spent all my life in Germany: my parents settled here before I was born. So I'm bilingual. I've been to the UK on holiday, of course, with my parents. They intend to move back when they give up work, but I'll probably stay in Germany and just go over on holiday. I expect I'll settle down with a German wife, and if we have a family, this will be their home. Britain will be somewhere that we visit from time to time, because of my parents, but it won't be any more than that.

Speaker 5: When I finished my French and business degree in Britain, I wanted to do an MBA at a French business school. I applied, and was accepted, but at the last minute, both my parents fell ill, and I stayed at home to look after them. They eventually recovered, but by then I didn't feel like becoming a student again, though I still fancied using my French. So I came to France as a sales rep for a British food exporter. I thought my French was quite good, but living here soon showed me how wrong I was. I'm trying very hard to improve. After all, you can't really become part of the culture if it's a struggle to communicate.

Student's Book pages 148–149

Writing a report

Aim: To practise writing an article about a personal experience or something that involves a degree of description, narrative or anecdote.

1 Ensure students understand the meaning of *ceremony* and how it differs from *celebration*. Discuss the points with students and elicit a few personal descriptions of some of them. If necessary explain or give definitions for any unknown events.

BACKGROUND: SOME TRADITIONAL CEREMONIES

A *baby shower* is a party where parents or expectant parents receive gifts for their newborn or expected child. By convention, a baby shower is intended to help parents get items that they need for their baby, such as baby clothes. In some countries this party is not celebrated until the baby is born.

A *name day* is a tradition of celebrating on a particular day of the year associated with one's given name. It is common in many countries in Europe and Latin America. The custom originated with the Catholic and Orthodox Calendar of Saints, where believers, named after a particular saint, would celebrate that saint's feast day.

An *Anniversary* is not a person's birthday, but celebrates the day an event took place in a previous year, e.g. *wedding anniversary, company / corporate anniversary.*

2 Read the question with the students or get them to read it individually and underline key words. Elicit what is required in the task.

Answers

describe a traditional ceremony, discuss how popular it is now compared with in the past, and make recommendations (**not** predictions) regarding its future.

3 Students should decide in pairs which paragraph each idea should go into.

Possible answers

Paragraph 1: Which ceremony is my report about? What's the purpose of the ceremony?
Paragraph 2: What do people do? Who attends?
Paragraph 3: Do more or fewer people attend now? Are there more or fewer ceremonies now?
Paragraph 4: Do we need the ceremony? What should be changed?

4 Students should read the report, underline the main ideas and answer the questions individually. Allow a few minutes for this. Tell students not to worry about new vocabulary or Japanese words at this point. In feedback, if you have any Japanese students in the class, encourage them to speak about their own experiences of Seijin Shiki.

Answers

Paragraph 1: What does 'coming of age' mean? When is the ceremony held?
Paragraph 2: Where is the ceremony held? What do the participants wear?
Paragraph 3: Is the ceremony still celebrated in the same way? Do people still wear the same clothes?
Paragraph 4: Do we need the ceremony? What should be changed?
The writer doesn't discuss whether there are more or fewer ceremonies these days because Seijin Shiki is an annual event.

NOT KNOWING THE RIGHT WORDS

Read through the information with the class and make sure students understand the main point here. You could also elicit some examples of words relating to ceremonies in the students' own languages that probably cannot be translated directly into English and may need to be treated in this way.

5 Students work individually or in pairs. Check answers.

Answers

Seijun Shiki: coming of age ceremony in Japan
furisode: a kind of traditional dress (usually worn by young, unmarried women)
kimono: traditional formal dress in Japan (usually worn by women)
hakama: traditional formal dress (usually worn by men)
zori slippers: traditional Japanese footwear

6 Students can work individually – in which case encourage them to try and think up two or three ideas and choose the best one – or you can do a class brainstorming session and write a few ideas on the board. Allow some time for students to carefully plan their headings and organise their ideas.

TEACHING IN PRACTICE: WRITING IN PAIRS

Sometimes getting students to write in pairs can be very useful for them, as it enables them to see how other students express themselves in writing. It also forces students to explain what they want to say out loud and to justify their ideas. A combined writing effort means students have to decide together what sounds good and what doesn't, what should stay and what should go. There are also advantages to having two people suggesting vocabulary and checking grammar instead of one.

7 Students either write individually, or in pairs. As they have already planned their report, they should spend no more than 30 minutes on writing and improving it.

Student's Book pages 150–151

Video the Hadzabe tribe

Aim: The main aim of the video is to introduce us to the unusual everyday life of the Hadzabe tribe of Tanzania. The Ideas generator suggests how we can explain customs and behaviour that are familiar to us, but not to the listener, and how to structure our explanation.

Synopsis: This video is about the Hadzabe tribe of north central Tanzania, and explains the significance of the tribe for the human race as a whole. According to anthropologist Dr Spencer Wells, the Hadzabe are mankind's common ancestor. Around 50,000 years ago there was an ice age in the northern hemisphere, while Tanzania was turned into desert. In order to survive, the Hadzabe had to develop new techniques, such as making fire, and fashioning tools. Some research indicates that there were as few as 2,000 human beings left. Those members of the tribe who decided to leave the region went on to eventually populate the rest of the world. Today, descendants of the original Hadazbe remaining in Tanzana are still hunter gatherers. The video shows us how today the tribe understands and exploits its environment for food and medicine.

1 Use the photo to generate interest about the Hadzabe tribe. Ask students to speculate about where the photo was taken. Ask students to ask and answer the questions, then ask follow-up questions. They can circulate round the class, or just ask students sitting near them. They can then share any interesting information with the rest of the class.

2 Students work in pairs to discuss the questions. Take feedback and have a whole-class discussion.

3 Read the words in the glossary with the class, then play the video. Students tick the activities from exercise 1 that they see in the video.

Answers

use a bow and arrow
collect berries to eat
make a fire from sticks
use wild plants as medicine
track wild animals
make their own tools
eat honey from a honeycomb

Videoscript

Narrator: *Homo sapiens* have been around for about 200,000 years and our various languages and cultures have been evolving for just as long. But our links to the past are becoming more and more fragile. Anthropologists estimate that 50% of human languages will disappear by the end of this century. And our ancient traditions are increasingly kept alive mainly for the sake of tourists.

However, in North Central Tanzania, in the Serengeti plateau, one tribe is resisting the pressure: the Hadzabe. A small group of them continue to live as hunter-gatherers, much as their ancestors have for 60,000 years.

Spencer Wells: They are one of the last groups of hunter-gatherers on Earth, essentially using fairly primitive technology to survive. And that's the way we lived for most of our history.

Narrator: In fact, as you will see, our collective history is tightly linked to the Hadzabe. Geneticist Spencer Wells is working with Chief Julius Endiyo to record and preserve their ancient traditions.

Julius: You take branches, the leaf, you are crush and then you are going there for three times per day and then two days, coughing is gone.

Wells: Julius can read the forest, the savannah that we're walking through as though it's a book. It's like walking through a library with him and he'll pull a volume from the shelf and he'll fan it to page 45 and read some passage to you.

Julius: This here is poison, very poisonous. But is, the roots is very nice medicine for stomach.

Narrator: It is precisely these skills, accumulated knowledge, advanced tools and language that helped human beings survive the bleakest period in their history. About 130,000 years ago, an ice age froze most of the northern hemisphere but turned the lush African lands into desert. There was no rain, and people were forced to move in search of food and water. Such harsh conditions lasted thousands of years. It was truly survival of the fittest. And scientists believe that human population numbered as few as 2,000 members.

Wells: If you take that at face value, our species is hanging on by its fingernails. We were on the verge of extinction. It wasn't until we went through that climate crunch that you really needed those skills in order to survive.

Scientist: Really this climatic variability is what's driven us. It's forced us to be inventive and made one particular population so inventive that they've managed to cope with all this, and with a bit of luck, here we are.

Narrator: With a bit of luck, here we all are. Because one choice made by the ancient ancestors of the Hadzabe affects us all. They decided to leave Africa. Little did they know that their descendants would come to populate the whole planet. So, whether you are European, American, Asian or Australian, we are all related to those ancient ancestors of the Hadzabe.

4 Students discuss which aspects the video focuses on.

Answers

1 and 2

5 Give students a minute to read the notes so they know what they need to listen out for. They may already be able to complete some of the notes. Play the video all the way through again.

Answers

1 of human languages	2 tourists
3 hunter-gatherers	4 the forest / savannah
5 poisonous	6 froze
7 desert	8 food
9 water	10 extinction
11 Africa	

6 Students discuss which activities from the list only exist for tourists. Lead a discussion about the balance between genuine tradition and tourism.

Read through the Ideas generator box. Ask the students to put themselves into the shoes of a member of the Hadzabe tribe who is trying to explain their traditions and behaviour to an outsider. Elicit possible *Wh-* questions they might use, e.g. *who, what, why, when, where?*

> **Answers**
>
> Any of the words in the list could be used, except for *expensive* (hunter gatherers are not likely to use any sort of currency, or to buy or sell goods, so the concept of price and how cheap or expensive things are is irrelevant).

7 This exercise gets students to focus on common topic areas that could come up in the first part of the Speaking paper. It is essential that students have sufficient topic vocabulary on each of these topics so they do not stumble or find themselves lost for words should these topics be discussed.

8 Students work in pairs, taking it in turns to ask and answer the questions using the notes they have compiled.

9 Students reflect on their performance and reformulate one of their answers, working with a new partner.

Vocabulary organiser 15, page 176

Answers

2
1 catalyst　　2 mundane　　3 detrimental　　4 enlightened
5 advancement (note that *change* can be positive or negative; *progress* and *advancement* are always positive)
6 perpetually

3
1 something that gets in the way, so that physical or metaphorical movement or progress is difficult
2 likely problems
3 agreed with by most people
4 ignore
5 deep and very close
6 something that severely limits movement, in a damaging way
7 careless, doing things without considering the consequences
8 the state of being damaged or worse than before

4
1 pass away　　　　2 pass (something) on　3 pass out
4 pass up　　　　　5 pass off (as)　　　　6 pass with flying colours
7 let something pass　8 pass the buck

5
1 ignorant　　　　2 offensive, insulting　　3 inferior
4 point (the foot), touch (the head), bow

Photocopiable activity instructions

Home exchange holidays (pages 153–154)

Aim: to justify choices, explain reasons, debate pros and cons. This is also an opportunity for students to use adverbial clauses and can be used in conjunction with the grammar section.

Instructions:

1 Divide the class into two equal groups: 'home-seekers' and 'property owners'.

2 Photocopy one copy of both sheets for every 12 students and cut out the 'home-seekers' (page 153) and 'properties' on offer (page 154). Give each student either a home-seeker card or a property card. All the cards must be used at least once, so in groups smaller than 12, some students may have to have two identities! If a second set of cards is used you do not need to use the whole set, as some students can have two matches.

3 Each home-seeker should write a short description of the kind of property they think would suit them. Each property owner should write a short description of the kind of family / individuals they think their property would best be suited to.

4 When everyone has finished the teacher calls on students at random to talk about who they are and what they are looking for (home-seekers) or to describe their properties and the people they think their home would be suitable for (property owners).

5 As soon as someone from either group thinks they have identified a close enough match, they should raise their hands and explain why they think the home exchange would work.

6 The aim is to match up all the pairs if possible. If someone doesn't think a particular property or home-seeker is suitable, they should identify the one they do think is most suitable and explain their reasons.

Alternative

Students could carry this out as a mingle, and write the names of any students that match their details.

Home exchange holidays

Ms Camelia Rhodes from New York, USA

Single professional businesswoman, 40s, seeks to travel in Europe, for shopping and entertainment.

The Dirkin family from Canada

We are a family of two adults and two young children, one boy aged six and one girl aged eight. We would like to explore and see new things. A child-friendly house would be nice.

Pete and Sue, Jim and Emily from Australia

We are two married couples in our 30s, no children, looking for an exciting break somewhere warm. We all love sports, relaxation, history and culture.

The Wilkinson family from Chicago, USA

We are a family of five: two adults, two boys aged 15 and 17 and one 13-year-old girl. We would consider an exchange anywhere either Europe or further afield. Something comfortable and pleasant.

Mr and Mrs Roberts from Ireland

Retired couple in their 70s who want to travel – nothing too adventurous though. We like arts and culture and going somewhere new.

The Joneses from Devon, UK

Adventurous family of four (children 14 and 11), we love outdoor sports, summer or winter activities, exploration and leisure activities. Open to all offers.

Phuket, Thailand

Treat yourself and your family to a unique getaway at Phuket's loveliest beach. This unique, private home is built in traditional Thai style and features a central pool, silent air conditioning, ceiling fans, a state-of-the-art entertainment centre. There are over 1,000 square metres of tropical landscape and adjacent 5,000 square-metre park. Maid service and pool cleaning three times per week. Hear the surf from the pool deck! NOTE: With its deep pool and high waterfall, this villa is not suitable for children under 12 or for those who cannot swim.

Alberta, Canada

Our home is surrounded by huge fir trees and there is hiking and cross-country skiing. There is also a very good golf course nearby. Our home has approximately 3,500 square feet of living space, two fireplaces, large recreation rooms and a hot tub. It's a half-hour drive to the beautiful National Parks and the Rocky Mountain Range. Excellent ski hills in the area in winter as well as fabulous camping facilities and hiking trails in summer. Also, the Dinosaur National Park and the Royal Tyrell Museum (a World Heritage Site) are a 90-minute drive from our home.

Nairobi, Kenya

Small three-bedroomed bungalow set in a lovely, well-kept half-acre garden with lots of shade. Located to the west of central Nairobi with easy access to shops and the city. The exchange potentially comes with a four-wheel-drive car that enables self-drive safari travels for up to four people to nearby national parks (day trips and weekend trips). Child seats available. The house is well equipped for small children, has satellite TV and internet connection, and a home help to do cleaning, washing and cooking.

Red Sea, Egypt

One minute from the beach we have newly furnished apartments fully equipped for comfortable self-catering holidays. The area is a fascinating holiday destination with plenty of bohemian charm, world-class scuba diving and windsurfing. It is also popular for yoga breaks, relaxation and safaris. The apartments have two bedrooms with sea views, and a spacious open-plan living area with a fitted kitchen. The comfortable lounge area opens onto the balcony with views over the rooftops and minarets of the Bedouin village to the Sinai mountains beyond.

London, England

Stylish, contemporary modern apartment in one of the best squares in London. The flat has one bedroom and overlooks a picturesque, quiet residential square. Large studio room with full-height windows, separate double bedroom and modern contemporary bathroom and fully equipped kitchen with all mod cons. The beautifully maintained apartment is situated in an 1820s Georgian house within easy walking access to the museums, Harrods, Knightsbridge shops, the West End and the royal parks. The flat also has a high-speed internet connection.

Sydney, Australia

Our two-bedroomed house is three minutes', walk to the bus stop and there are many shops and restaurants nearby. Our street is a quiet cul-de-sac but is still within walking distance of the Aquatic Centre, Rowing Club and the Bay Walk. Sydney Opera House, Harbour Bridge, The Rocks Precinct and the Olympic site are all within easy reach. The Blue Mountains and the wine-growing Hunter Valley are both within two hours' drive. Our house is low-maintenance and there are no lawns to mow as the garden is small. A home help will clean twice a week.

16 ENDINGS – AND NEW BEGINNINGS

Unit introduction

The topic of the unit is endings and saying goodbye.

To show that the book has come full circle, and that every ending opens the door to new beginnings, this unit touches upon a variety of subjects that do just that, including making changes and coping with changes, and looking to the future. The writing section looks at writing letters of reference, and includes a final reminder checklist for students to check their work.

Warm-up activity

Ask students to look at the unit title and photo, and elicit what feelings the people in the photo are showing (e.g. a sense of achievement, pride, satisfaction, joy, but also, in some cases, disappointment). Ask the students what their plans are for when they have finished the course. Consider handing out *Just a minute!* photocopiable activity, page 161 to your class. Instructions can be found on page 160.

Getting started

1 Students work in pairs to form the collocations. Go through the answers together, but do not expect them to know all of the combinations. Elicit (or, if necessary, explain) the difference between *ceasefire* and *extinguish a fire*, *finalise a business deal / contract* and *terminate a deal / contract*, *complete a rescue operation* and *abort a rescue operation*.

Answers
abort: a plan, a pregnancy, a rescue operation
cease: fire, production, trading
complete: a course, a form, a questionnaire, a plan, a race, a rescue operation, operations, production, school
conclude: an argument, a business deal, an essay, a meeting, a speech
discontinue: manufacturing a product, production
end: a contract, a course, a meeting, a race, a speech, an argument, an essay
extinguish: a fire, hope
finalise: a business deal, a contract, a plan
finish: a course, a race, school
settle: a dispute, a lawsuit, an argument, differences
terminate: a business deal, a contract, a pregnancy

Reading multiple matching texts

2 Tell students to read through the extracts quickly, to find the information they need for each question.

Answers
1 C	2 D	3 A	4 A, C

3 Ask students to underline the key information in each extract.

Answers
1 *Saying goodbye to the place that had been our home for 35 years was a huge wrench; Heartbreaking though it was; It was a very emotional time, and we didn't always see eye to eye.*
2 *not allowing the glaring ethical dilemma to cloud my conscience; a documentary about the horrors of battery farming and the slaughterhouse shocked me out of my ignorance.*
3 *Friends accused us of going too far, the kids blamed us for cutting them off from the rest of the world, but this was countered by the fact that my son lost ten pounds within a month.*
4 *The last straw, however, came when my son was diagnosed as obese; Then my wife fell and broke her hip, and that clinched it.*

4 Students do this individually. It is a good idea to time them in preparation for the actual exam. Check answers and give feedback, if needed.

Answers
1 B	2 D	3 E	4 C	5 A
6 A	7 C	8 E	9 B	10 D

→ Vocabulary organiser 16, exercise 1, page 177

Vocabulary organiser answers
1 skinny	2 promote	3 useless
4 trial	5 confuse	6 teach
7 provide	8 be in pain	9 involve

Extension

At this late stage in the course, there probably won't be time for a follow-on discussion of the topic, but students may wish to comment on one or more of the moral questions raised in these extracts. The question of banning the TV, for instance, is potentially controversial! Also, vegetarianism and home-schooling could raise some interest. If so, then transform it into practice of a Speaking test, Part 4, by placing students in pairs, and asking each pair a specific exam-style question, allowing them only two or three minutes to answer it.

Student's Book pages 154–155

Language development word partners

1 Tell your students that one of the options in each item 1–8 forms a phrase which appears in the reading extracts on page 153 of the Student's Book. Check answers, and clarify any points which may cause disagreement.

Answers

1 knowledge	2 talk	3 man
4 mind	5 temper	6 freedom
7 the road	8 place	9 baby

→ Vocabulary organiser 16, exercise 2, page 177

Vocabulary organiser answers

1 drastic changes	2 emotional time
3 dispel rumours	4 confirmed bachelor
5 shocked me out of my complacency	6 staple ingredient
7 cut off from the rest of the world	8 cloud my conscience

See *Advanced particle dominoes* photocopiable activity, page 162.

Key word *end*

2 Students work in pairs, or individually. Do not expect them to know all of these items, but encourage them to work out the meaning from the context. Elicit answers.

Answers

1 b	2 a	3 a	4 a	5 a	6 b	7 a

VOCABULARY: KEY WORD *END*

it's the end of the road / line: used when you've tried everything and you can't continue

I'm at my wits' end / at the end of my tether: I don't know what to do and can't cope any more

thrown in at the deep end: put in a new situation and left to manage on your own

on the receiving end of something: affected by someone else's behaviour (usually negative)

for hours on end: for hours and hours

no end of: a large amount of something

it's not the end of the world: things aren't as bad as they seem

be at a loose end: have nothing to do

come to a sticky end: to die in a violent way (usually because of involvement in crime)

at the tail end of: at the very end

get the wrong end of the stick: misunderstand a situation

→ Vocabulary organiser 16, exercise 3, page 177

Vocabulary organiser answers

1 d	2 c	3 e	4 a	5 b

3 Students work in pairs. Elicit answers and ensure students understand the meaning of each sentence.

Answers

1 disposed	2 draw	3 close
4 disposed	5 end	6 draw

4 Ask students to do this individually as a timed exam practice task. Check answers with the whole class.

Answers

1 shocked me out of my	2 wrong end of
3 a confirmed bachelor	4 down the law
5 cloud my conscience	6 to dispel rumours of

Grammar making and intensifying comparisons

5 Students work individually. Check answers, and clarify any problem areas.

Answers

a far more enjoyable than (ever before)
b Nothing compares to
c significantly more expensive than
d wasn't as spectacular as
e The more ... the healthier
f isn't nearly as tasty as

6 Ask students to read the information in the box. Suggest that they could use the Grammar reference on page 221 to help them complete this exercise. There is more than one possible answer for most of the sentences. Elicit suggestions and give feedback.

Possible answers

1 ... is not nearly as happy ...
2 This is by far the best holiday ...
3 ... is nowhere near as calm as ...
4 ... was far more interesting than ...
5 ... works a lot harder than ...
6 ... considerably more time for ...
7 ... a lot earlier, so he's got significantly more energy ...
8 ... considerably longer to ... than ...

7 Students should be able to do this without referring back to the text. You could ask them to refer to the text to check their answers once they have finished.

Answers

1 much, a lot   2 By far   3 both, than

8 Do this as a class exercise. Elicit comparisons from the class. If they haven't discussed the question of living without a TV, you could ask students what they think of the idea now.

Possible answers

The family have a lot more time to talk to each other than they did before. They are far more active than they were before. The children were not nearly as interested in talking about what they had been doing when they had the TV. The son is considerably healthier than he was before. The children are significantly more interested in their daily lives than before. They have found more interesting hobbies.

9 🔘 50 Ask students to read the rubric and the gapped text. Play the recording. Elicit answers. If necessary, play the recording again.

Answers

1 not as	2 by far
3 best book	4 compared to
5 a lot more	6 the most exciting
7 more	8 nowhere near as

Audioscript 🔘 50

James: Here you are, Sally. I've finished it.

Sally: Hmm? Oh, *The Last Will*! Thanks, James. What did you think of it? Great, wasn't it?

James: Actually, I found it rather disappointing in comparison with his other books. Not so believable, if you know what I mean.

Sally: Really? I find that hard to believe. I thought it was by far his best ever! Far superior to *Waiting to Die* and *A Just Cause*, for instance.

James: I feel just the opposite. Compared to his first novel, the plot in this one is far-fetched and unrealistic, to say the least.

Sally: You're joking! For a start, we see a lot more courtroom drama in this book, which is lacking from his others. They tend to focus purely on lawyers playing detective, which is not always very convincing.

James: It keeps things interesting, though, wouldn't you say?

Sally: Perhaps. But you have to admit that the courtroom drama in this novel lends weight to it, makes it even more believable.

James: Well, admittedly, the courtroom scenes are the most exciting in the book, quite gripping in places in fact, but the rest of the book is often slow and boring. I mean, all that description during the search in South Africa – I practically fell asleep!

Sally: But the protagonist is significantly more rounded and better developed here, wouldn't you say? The way we are led through his drug-induced self-pity to his struggle to redeem himself is cleverly created.

James: It was exactly this that I found just too good to be true! Our hero goes from being a total waster to becoming a knight in shining armour, against a background of support characters who are singularly wooden in their weakness and selfishness. They're nowhere near as realistic as the cast in *A Just Cause*, where good and bad qualities are more evenly shared out.

Sally: Funny! I didn't feel that way at all when I read it, and I thought you'd like it more than that. A pity ...

10 Elicit some ideas from the students, and allow some discussion.

Student's Book pages 156–157

Use of English multiple-choice cloze

1 Ask students to read the gapped text. Then elicit their views on the subject.

2 Explain some of the vocabulary in the text before your students do the task. Do not set a strict time limit unless you are confident that your class can cope with this by now. Check answers and clarify any problem areas.

Answers

1 C   2 C   3 A   4 B   5 C   6 B   7 C   8 A

EXAM SPOTLIGHT

Ask students to read through the information in the Exam spotlight box. Elicit examples, and give feedback.

→ Vocabulary organiser 16, exercise 4, page 177

Vocabulary organiser answers

1 stationary	2 solitary	3 compulsive	4 evolved
5 pull out	6 flowed	7 delighted	8 slight

Listening three short extracts

3 🔘 51 Ask students to read the information in the box, then look at exercise 3. They should listen to the extract once only. Check answers.

Answers	
1 F	2 T

Audioscript 🔘 51

Extract 1

Man	For a while, it felt like we were on a second honeymoon. But then the quiet started getting to us.
Woman	Well, I won't say I don't miss Mike, but frankly I was glad when he went to university. It was as if the house was no longer big enough for the two of us. We both like our independence, and I think the pressure was getting us both down.
Man	But don't you feel lonely in the house?
Woman	Well, that's just it. I like having the house to myself, but I can see Mike when we both feel like it. And it's good for him to know that I'm not waiting by the phone for his every call. That puts a lot of pressure on any child.
Man	Too right! Jan gets frantic if more than three days go by without a phone call from one of the boys, and I know that bugs Davy, in particular! I try to tell her to relax about it, that 'no news is good news', and all that.
Woman	Mmm, at their age, it can be restrictive to have to account for their movements all the time. They don't want to be thinking about us right now, but about enjoying themselves as much as possible.

4 🔘 52 Ask students to read the rubric. Play the recording twice. Check answers, and, if necessary, clarify any problem areas.

Answers					
1 B	2 C	3 C	4 A	5 A	6 B

Audioscript 🔘 52

Extract 1 (See audioscript 51)

Extract 2

Woman	So, how did you feel when you first retired?
Man	Guilty, basically.
Woman	Guilty? About what?
Man	The fact that I wasn't going to work. As the weeks went by, I became bored and irritable. The change was hard on my wife as well, because I started making demands on her time. I'd expected to do more things together, while she thought that she would go on as before, meeting up with her friends for coffee, going on shopping sprees, all without me. That was difficult for both of us. I had to find my own interests, and she had to make some room for me.
Woman	So how do you feel now?
Man	Well, I wonder how I ever had the time to go to work! I find I'm busy nearly all the time now. I think the secret to enjoying your retirement is firstly, health, and then having enough

money to do the things you really want to do. Those two elements prevent you from being a burden on your children. Having a good circle of friends has helped. We see the kids when we can, of course, but we're not under their feet, and they're not under ours, either! So, life's fairly good now.

Extract 3

Woman	My decision to start my own business was all about money. I was stuck in a poorly paid job, with virtually no prospects. I saw an opportunity and grabbed it. However, I knew I'd need some kind of routine to my working day, and that there'd be too many distractions at home! Difficult to ignore the pile of washing up in the sink, and the ironing waiting by the ironing board! So, I opened an office, and I think that was the key to making it work – keeping work and home separate.
Man	Yes, I can see that. Working at home just didn't work for me. I also found it stressful having to rely on myself for all the decision-making. Sometimes, I wanted to share ideas with someone, to get some feedback before putting things into operation, and there was no one. That began to get to me. Now, I'm back in an office, with other people around me, and I feel part of the team again.
Woman	That's it, though I've never really been a team player, so as I said, that isn't my reason for the way I work. I like the independence of making my own decisions. I won't say it always works, though!

LISTENING PAPER SUMMARY

To round off this section, you may like to give your students a quick general reminder of the task format for each part of the Listening paper, by outlining the content and task type:

PART 1   Task type: multiple choice

Focus: feeling, attitude, opinion, purpose, function, agreement, course of action, gist, detail, etc.

Format: three short extracts from exchanges between interacting speakers with two multiple-choice questions on each extract.

Number of questions: six

PART 2   Task type: sentence completion

Focus: specific information, stated opinion

Format: a monologue (which may be introduced by a presenter) lasting approximately three minutes. Candidates are required to complete the sentences with information heard on the recording.

Number of questions: eight

PART 3   Task type: multiple choice

Focus: attitude and opinion

Format: a conversation between two or more speakers of approximately four minutes; multiple-choice questions, each with four options.

Number of questions: six

PART 4   Task type: multiple matching

Focus: gist, attitude, main points, interpreting context

Format: five short themed monologues, approximately 30 seconds each; each multiple-matching task requires selection of the correct options from a list of eight.

Number of questions: ten

Speaking individual long turn

5 Elicit ideas from the class. Students then work in pairs for the rest of this section.

6 Direct students to the 'Comparing pictures' box. The following exercises aim to get students thinking about different ways of making comparisons, and to encourage them to vary their language when they do this task. Suggest they refer to the Grammar reference section on page 221 for help. Elicit answers.

> **Possible answers**
> The second room is not as spacious as the first one.
> The first room is (far) more spacious / not as cramped as the second.
> The first room is (significantly) lighter / nowhere near as dark as the second.
> The second room is not as light as / (much) darker than the first one.

7 Do this as timed exam practice. Remind students that they must each talk for about a minute without interruption. Allocate parts A and B and ask students to follow the instructions and speak to their partner. Time the speakers, and monitor the pairs.

At the end of the Speaking section, give general feedback to the class. Highlight positive aspects of their performance where possible.

See *Just a minute!* photocopiable activity, page 161.

Student's Book pages 158–159

Writing letter of reference

Aim: This final writing section aims to look at writing letters of reference, and also focuses on encouraging students to check all aspects of their work thoroughly.

1 Elicit what students know about letters of reference. Brainstorm ideas about what information you should include in such a letter. Ask students to read the exam question. Discuss the key points, and make sure students cover all of them.

> **Answers**
> student of yours, nanny, English family, good at dealing with small children, knowledge of first aid, your student's character and personal qualities and skills, previous relevant experience, reasons why they should be considered

A LETTER OF REFERENCE

Ask students to read the information, and elicit any queries they may have.

2 Students work in pairs. Elicit who the writer is, what the writer's relationship is to the person they are recommending, and who the target reader is. Students complete the plan. Check answers.

> **Answers**
> Paragraph 2: Talk about their qualities and relevant skills, previous experience with children, and whether they know first aid.
> Paragraph 3: Emphasise the reasons why you think they are suitable for this job.

TEACHING IN PRACTICE: ELICITING STUDENTS' IDEAS

By now, your students will have a good idea of what is required in this paper, so many of these exercises are designed to consolidate what they know. For this reason, throughout the section, elicit information from your students instead of giving it yourself.

EXAM SPOTLIGHT

Ask students to read the final reminder checklist, and then look at exercise 3.

3 Students work in pairs, or individually. Tell them to use the checklist and go through the sample answer carefully.

> **Answers**
> **Relevance:** yes, the letter does answer the question satisfactorily
> **Register:** on the whole, it is fairly formal, but unfortunately, it ends informally with *Yours*
> **Use of language:** there are some careless mistakes in tenses at the beginning
> **Range of vocabulary:** fairly good, although some words are inappropriately used
> **Spelling and punctuation:** these are both very good, with only a few mistakes
> **Organisation:** yes, the answer is well organised
> **Length:** 221 words, just within the lower limit
> Students should underline the following mistakes: was asked (have been asked), I know since (have known since), teach Maria for (have taught), had (has), relates us (relates), skilful (talented), took up (took on), entertained (established), serene (calm), administrated (took care of / ministered to), Yours (Yours faithfully).
> Suitable mark: band 3 or 4

4 Ask students to read the question and rubric. Brainstorm ideas about the key points to include in the answer. Students do this task individually.

TEACHING IN PRACTICE: REVISING VOCABULARY

You may wish to discuss vocabulary revision with your students. Recap the different ways in which they can organise this by eliciting ideas from the students themselves. Invite questions on how they may capitalise on their revision time, and draw their attention to items you have found effective during the course, such as grouping words of similar meaning together, words centred upon a theme, synonyms / antonyms, word webs and spidergrams, etc.

Student's Book pages 160–161

Review 4

1
1 terminated   2 ruthless   3 contagious
4 conclusion   5 compulsive   6 compatible
7 peace   8 returned   9 conclude
10 annual

2
1 has been discontinued   2 came
3 have disposed   4 was drawn
5 is completing   6 clarify
7 had been published   8 were exchanging

3
1 set sail   2 bogged down
3 got wind of   4 hot / deep water
5 end of my tether   6 authority on
7 are at a loose end   8 let it pass

4
1 would / 'd rather cook something fresh than
2 would not / wouldn't have learnt so much
3 would be better if I found
4 in spite of / despite the fact that
5 had the lightning struck when
6 is not / isn't nearly as tasty as

5 and 6
1 shock – d   2 drastic – g   3 emotional – a
4 confirmed – b   5 staple – h   6 cloud – c
7 dispel – e   8 (be) cut off – f

7
1 B   2 C   3 B   4 D   5 C   6 A

8
1 theirs   2 it   3 that / when   4 with
5 instead   6 why   7 but   8 until

9
1 obsessed with   2 immune to   3 deficient in
4 derived from   5 eligible for   6 ashamed of

Vocabulary organiser 16, page 177

Answers

1
1 skinny   2 promote   3 useless
4 trial   5 confuse   6 teach
7 provide   8 be in pain   9 involve

2
1 drastic changes   2 emotional time
3 dispel rumours   4 confirmed bachelor
5 shocked me out of my complacency   6 staple ingredient
7 cut off from the rest of the world   8 cloud my conscience

3
1 d   2 c   3 e   4 a   5 b

4
1 stationary   2 solitary   3 compulsive   4 evolved
5 pull out   6 flowed   7 delighted   8 slight

Bank of English
rebuild (V), reconsider (V), reform (V / N), reformist (N / A), regain (V), regenerated (V / A), reintroduction (N), rejuvenate (V), relapse (V / N), remake (V / N), remix (V / N), renewal (N), reorganise (V), repeatable (A), replay (V / N)

Photocopiable activity instructions

Just a minute! (page 161)

Aim: students practise sustaining a monologue describing their feelings about a subject for one minute, in preparation for Part 2 of the Speaking test.

Instructions:

1 Photocopy the *Just a minute!* sheet and cut out the questions in the boxes.

2 Make sure you have a watch or clock with a hand that counts the seconds.

3 Hand out a question to each student. Tell them they must answer their question, describing their feelings and why they would feel that way, and keep talking for one minute.

4 Time each student, and interrupt them as soon as the minute is up.

Advanced particle dominoes (page 162)

Aim: to revise phrases and collocations learnt throughout the 16 units of the Student's Book.

Instructions:

1 Photocopy the *Advanced particle dominoes* activity page, and cut out the square cards.

2 Students play in two teams. Deal each team 25 cards.

3 Toss a coin to see which team places a card on the table first.

4 The other team must match one of their cards to it to make a phrasal verb, noun, verb or adjectival phrase.

5 The winners are the first team to use up all their cards.

Possible answers

pass off, blame on, ashamed of, bring back, accuse of, turn into, serious about, eligible for, authority over, search out, pull through, confide in, derived from, witness to, contact with, admit to, take away, look out of, alternative to, pick up, deficient in, keen on, obsessed with, distressed by, convinced of

Just a minute!

How would you feel when you came to the end of a difficult exam?

How would you feel at the end of a race, if you won?

How would you feel when you reached the end of a particularly enjoyable book?

How would you feel at the end of the last episode in a moving TV serial?

How did you feel when you finished primary school?

How would you feel at the end of a long journey?

How do you feel now you've reached the end of this course?

How do you feel at the end of a boring lesson?

How would you feel at the end of a race, if you came last?

How would you feel when you finished a demanding piece of work, or an assignment?

How would you feel at the end of an enjoyable holiday?

How would you feel as you completed making or painting something successfully?

Advanced particle dominoes

pass	of	blame	to	ashamed
with	in	bring	to	over
accuse	about	turn	serious	eligible
away	authority	search	out	of
up	pull	of	back	confide
derived	in	witness	by	contact
admit	through	take	to	for
look	off	alternative	on	pick
from	deficient	of	keen	out of
obsessed	make	distressed	into	convinced

EXAM BOOSTER ANSWER KEY

Unit 1

Getting started

1
Across		Down	
1 inaugurate		1	initiate
5 prompts		2	embark
6 trigger		3	provoke
8 kick off		4	establish
10 produce		7	generate
11 launch		9	found
12 stimulate			

Reading

1
1 T	2 T	3 T	4 T	5 T	6 T
7 T	8 F	9 F	10 F	11 T	12 T
13 T	14 F				

2   1 A, B, D   2 B, D   3 A, B   4 A, B, C

3   1 C   2 D   3 B   4 D

Language development

1   1   start from scratch, go back to the drawing board, start from square one
    2   make a fresh start, turn over a new leaf, wipe the slate clean

2   1 f   2 g   3 i   4 a   5 e   6 b
    7 h   8 j   9 c   10 d

3
1	made off	4	made up
2	make it up to you	5	made off with
3	make out	6	make up for

Grammar

1
1	had ever seen	5	didn't call
2	had been walking	6	takes
3	was listening	7	is going / is going to go
4	have never been	8	have been sitting

2
1	have eaten	5	chopped
2	was walking	6	haven't read
3	has been working	7	is having
4	broke	8	have you been doing

4
1	haven't forgotten	11	marched
2	had expected	12	tossed
3	had been training	13	blew
4	woke	14	passed
5	was shining	15	cheered
6	put	16	were putting
7	waited	17	was beginning
8	arrived	18	saw
9	were already doing	19	kicked
10	have been training	20	was

Listening

1   1 B   2 C   3 B   4 A   5 B   6 A

Use of English

1   1   I had had enough pie
    2   has been under construction for
    3   to make the most of

4   was three years before I heard
5   not as easy to get
6   make ends meet

Unit 2

Getting started

1
1	march	5	clamber
2	bound	6	wrestle
3	heave	7	wander
4	wade	8	tiptoe

The word 'movement' is spelt out.

Reading

1   1   Three people are mentioned.
    2   Two people speak.
    3   Joseph Hooper and his son, Edmund.

2   **After gap 2:** 'But I came through ... He felt exonerated.'
    After gap 5: 'Though he remembered ... the high windows.'
    Paragraph A: 'Looking up now ... his own son was pale.'
    Paragraph B: 'Mr Hooper coughed ... his own father.'
    'Hooper' refers to the son.
    Edmund Hooper is preoccupied with the book he is reading, and a boy called Kingshaw, who bothers him.

3   1 D   2 B   3 G   4 F   5 E   6 A

Language development

1   1   down in the mouth
    2   (just) gave me the cold shoulder
    3   was all fingers and thumbs
    4   is a pain in the neck
    5   have never seen eye to eye
    6   had a (brilliant) brainwave

2
1	take your pick	5	pick you up
2	pick your brains	6	pick up the pieces
3	picked it up	7	picked holes in
4	picked her way	8	picked up on

3
1	office	4	counter
2	risk	5	engine
3	story		

Grammar

1   1 b   2 a   3 a   4 b   5 b

2   1   a   ... nine-year-old James Edwards is very talented.
        b   ... very talented.
    2   a   ... is / has been rumoured that Mrs Reed is leaving the school.
        b   ... is rumoured to be leaving the school.
    3   a   ... was thought / felt / believed that the new sports programme had benefited the school.
        b   ... was believed to have benefited from the new sports programme.
    4   a   ... has been suggested that graphic novels could encourage children to read.
        b   ... have been made that graphic novels could encourage children to read.

5 a   ... is often assumed that an only child will be selfish.
  b   ... are often made that an only child will be selfish.

3   (Possible answers):
1   had her camera
2   is having / getting his washing machine
3   get / have her hair
4   had / got our sitting room window
5   his hand

Listening

1
1   visually stimulating   5   stepping stone
2   novels   6   three
3   Tokyo / Japan   7   mixed abilities
4   poetry   8   practical

Use of English

1
1   perception   5   method
2   unconscious   6   entrusting
3   imbued   7   findings
4   instincts   8   incentive
2   1 D   2 C   3 A   4 B   5 C   6 B
    7 B   8 D

Writing

1   Underline: 'describing the services it provides'; 'stating whether all the added services are really useful'; and 'saying who you would recommend your choice of mobile phone to and why'.
2   Example b is the best. (Example a threatens to be irrelevant by becoming a report and examining 'different types of mobile phone' when the question asks for one; Example c is too informal and vague in style.)
3   The sample conclusion is unsuitable because it fails to follow the instructions in the question rubric.

Unit 3

Getting started

1
1   white water rafting   4   triathlon
2   yacht racing   5   mountain climbing
3   snowboarding

Reading

1   1 B   2 D   3 C   4 D   5 D   6 C

Language development

1
1   down   5   up
2   up   6   up
3   down   7   down
4   up   8   up
2
1   takes after   5   taken [you] for
2   take over   6   take apart
3   take back   7   took to
4   take on   8   taken up
3
1   lying down
2   it or leave it
3   the bull by the horns
4   hat off to her
5   the wind out of my / his / her sails
6   with a pinch of salt
7   it out of you
8   it from me

Grammar

1   1 B   2 C   3 D   4 A

2   1 e   2 f   3 a   4 b   5 h   6 i
    7 j   8 d   9 g   10 c
3   a   1   d   6, 7, 10
    b   2, 4, 5   e   8, 9
    c   3
4   1 a   2 b

Listening

1   **certainty:** definite, confident, secure, unambiguous
  uncertainty: doubtful, unconvinced, hesitant, cynical
  positive feelings: exuberant, delighted, elated, thrilled
  negative feelings: frustrated, annoyed, irked, exasperated
2   1 A   2 C   3 B
3   1 A   2 B   3 D

Use of English

1
1   which   5   another
2   from   6   whoever
3   each   7   to
4   or   8   something

Unit 4

Getting started

1   A   Cretaceous, evolution, erosion, fossils, geology, Jurassic, Tyrannosaurus rex
  B   artificial intelligence, artificial life, cells, DNA, genetics, laboratory, microchip, nanotechnology, $E = MC^2$, forensic
  C   sci-fi, androids, robotic implants, virtual reality
  D   cortex, grey matter, neurology
  E   black hole, dark matter, extraterrestrial, supernova
2
1   palaeontology   6   psychology
2   android   7   cortex
3   nanotechnology   8   dark matter
4   extra terrestrial   9   artificial intelligence
5   DNA   10   grey matter

Reading

1   1 C   2 A   3 B   4 C   5 D   6 B
    7 A   8 B   9 D   10 A

Language development

1
1   target   6   conducive
2   cognitive   7   hamper
3   suppressing   8   testimonial
4   accomplice   9   calibrated
5   communal
2
1   began to tell   5   I told you so
2   tell them apart   6   only time will tell
3   tell on   7   never can tell
4   as far as I can tell   8   telltale
3
1   blue   7   red   13   blue
2   red   8   red   14   black
3   green   9   black   15   red
4   red   10   green   16   blue
5   blue   11   blue
6   black   12   greener
4   **red:** in the red; see red; be caught red-handed; red tape; red herring
  blue: out of the blue; (talk) till you're blue in the face; feel blue; once in a blue moon; like a bolt from the blue
  black: black mark; black humour; be on a black list;
  green: green fingers; green with envy; the grass looks greener on the other side

Grammar

1. 1 a 2 b 3 a 4 b 5 b 6 b 7 a
2. 1 in ten minutes   4 as soon as
   2 in three weeks' time   5 until then
   3 by then
3. 1 is bound to pass
   2 what the future will hold
   3 will have been doing / in business
   4 'll / will be waiting (for you) outside
   5 are on the point of discovering
   6 is / will be coming to help us

Listening

1. 1 E   2 F   3 H   4 B   5 A   6 H
   7 C   8 A   9 F   10 G

Use of English

1. gaps 2 and 4
2. 1 inevitably   5 exposure
   2 unhealthy   6 findings
   3 Epidemiologists   7 typically
   4 unexpected   8 implications

Writing

1. Underline the three bullet points (convenience, cost, enjoyment). The answer must deal with any two of those.
2. (Possible answers):
   Paragraph 1: Introduction, referring to the interviews.
   Paragraph 2: discuss one of the three areas that the presenter focused on
   Paragraph 3: discuss the other area that you have chosen to write about
   Paragraph 4: Conclusion, including saying which area you think most influences how people shop, with your reasons

Unit 5

Getting started

1. 1 fraud   9 virus
   2 arson   10 convict
   3 crimeware   11 implicate
   4 sentence   12 murder
   5 hacking   13 kidnapping
   6 confess   14 victim
   7 incriminate   15 charge
   8 acquit
   The phrase in the central column is 'forensic science'.

Reading

1. 1 F   2 C   3 A   4 E   5 B   6 G

Language development

1. 1 b   2 a   3 a   4 b   5 b   6 b
   7 d   8 c   9 a   10 d
2. 1 T   2 F   3 T   4 T   5 F   6 T
   7 F   8 T
3. 1 enforce   2 obey   3 break   4 lay down
4. 1 b   2 a   3 c

Grammar

1. 1 racing   9 to kill
   2 to drop   10 seeing
   3 to do   11 to find
   4 to ram   12 to steal
   5 to board   13 chasing
   6 to knock   14 to head
   7 to tie   15 to continue
   8 to defend

Listening

1. 1 d   2 b   3 f   4 e   5 a   6 c
2. 1 the risk   5 dignity
   2 website   6 (unfair) criticism
   3 probation officers   7 small
   4 regular contact   8 the unexpected

Use of English

1. 1 any   5 above
   2 out   6 low
   3 by   7 forward
   4 down

Speaking

1. (Possible answers): The facilities: attractive shops, cafeterias, bars, restaurants, and also cinemas, and a theatre, without the chaos of a big city.
   The atmosphere: constant buzz of conversation and laughter, without the intrusive noise of the traffic!
   Access to other places: it is easy to escape the town to the country.

Writing

1. (Possible answers): The notes are irrelevant for this question and too knowledge specific, and there is no organisation of ideas. The student has misunderstood part of the input material, has failed to use it effectively, and has not created headings for each paragraph.
2. (Possible answers):
   Paragraph 1: Introduction (purpose of the report).
   Paragraph 2: Use of mobile phones (approximately 75% of students have a mobile phone; They must switch them off in the classroom).
   Paragraph 3: Potential dangers (unknown, but possible brain damage, and increased risk of disease from long-term exposure).
   Paragraph 4: Recommendations (teachers give talks advising students on the dangers of using phones too much; students switch off phones as soon as they arrive at school, and only switch them on again when the final bell rings).

Unit 6

Getting started

1. a acupuncture   d homeopathy
   b aromatherapy   e reflexology
   c herbalism   f meditation
2. 1 herbalism   4 homeopathy
   2 acupuncture   5 reflexology
   3 aromatherapy   6 meditation
3. 1 aromatherapy 2 homeopathy   3 acupuncture

Reading

1 1 D   2 C   3 A   4 B
2 1 strive   9 feed
   2 overindulge   10 opt for
   3 excuse   11 resist
   4 transform   12 bombard
   5 drive home   13 deny
   6 turn up   14 ward off
   7 cut out   15 constitute
   8 boil down to
3 1 bombarded   6 opt for
   2 ward off   7 boils down to
   3 transformed   8 (have / 've) overindulged
   4 strive   9 drove home
   5 feeding   10 cut out

Language development

1 1 b   2 b   3 a   4 a   5 b   6 b
2 1 lifelong friends
   2 lay down their lives
   3 life-threatening illness
   4 fact of life
   5 have the time of their lives
   6 the life and soul of the party
   7 a lifetime's ambition
   8 a matter of life and death
   9 life-jackets
  10 a new lease of life

Grammar

1 1 If you were to go to America …
   2 Should you see Garry in town …
   3 As long as you eat all your green vegetables …
   4 If you happen to find …
   5 But for Julian's intervention …
   6 Even if you had been on time / hadn't been late …
2 1 had remembered / wouldn't have run out
   2 had / would be able to
   3 walks / will be
   4 hadn't driven / could have got
   5 had taken / would be
   6 comes / will have
   7 was / didn't he
   8 runs out / stops

Listening

1 1 C   2 B   3 C   4 D   5 A   6 B

Speaking

1 These pictures both show … ; … while the other picture … ; The main similarity / difference between the two pictures is that …

Use of English

1 1 B   2 B   3 D   4 A   5 B   6 C
   7 D   8 A

Unit 7

Getting started

1 1 trip   6 package holiday
   2 safari   7 voyage
   3 excursion   8 flight
   4 ride   9 travel
   5 cruise   10 journey

2 a 2   b 5   c 4   d 8

Reading

1 1 C   2 A   3 B   4 A   5 D   6 B
   7 C   8 D   9 A 10 C

Language development

1 1 C   2 B   3 C   4 A
2 1 like the look of it
   2 much to look at
   3 get a look-in
   4 look the other way
   5 looked him in the eye
   6 overlook
   7 look ahead
   8 by the looks of it
3 1 roadhouse   6 road map
   2 road rage   7 road works
   3 road test   8 road block
   4 roadside   9 road sign
   5 road hog   10 road show

Grammar

1 1 the rope would never
   2 was she aware
   3 than
   4 should you leave
   5 he had left
   6 have we seen
   7 failed
   8 had they arrived
   9 am I to be
  10 had finished
2 1 Only later were the details of the scandal made known …
   2 No sooner had we arrived than …
   3 Barely had the concert started …
   4 Seldom do you see …
   5 On no account must you …
   6 Never have I seen …
   7 Scarcely had Gina walked …
3 1 had just come out when
   2 have checked your passport will you
   3 had the plane taken off when
   4 time did Tom apologise
   5 the bus driver stopped did he
   6 are customers allowed

Listening

1 1 H   2 C   3 B   4 E   5 G   6 D
   7 B   8 E   9 C 10 F

Use of English

1 1 the   5 how
   2 not   6 despite
   3 by   7 with
   4 before   8 very

Writing

1 Underline: 'tourist agency', 'adventure holidays', 'website', 'unappealing, hard to navigate and unclear', 'proposal', 'best ways to update the website',
2 (Possible answers): Proposal to update website
   1 Making the site more appealing: testimonials from customers, video clips of customers engaged in adventure activity

2 Navigation: consistent features on each page; clearly defined categories/titles; clickable links to pages showing different types of adventure holiday

3 Types of holiday: Family Adventure, Extreme Adventure, Expeditions

Unit 8

Getting started

1 1 The Great Sphinx of Giza
   2 Stonehenge
   3 The Parthenon
   4 The Eiffel Tower
   5 The Statue of Liberty
2 A 4   B 3   C 1   D 5   E 2

Reading

1 1 C   2 B   3 C   4 B   5 A   6 B

Language development

1 1 brought home to me
   2 brought him to his knees
   3 bring your characters to life
   4 brought back to me
   5 bring me to eat
   6 has brought triplets into the world
2 1 bring down [the government]
   2 correct
   3 bring in [enough money]
   4 bring off [running a business]
   5 bring out [the best]
3 11 times
   1 2   2 5   3 2   4 0   5 2
4 7 times

Grammar

1 1 by which time
   2 whose cat
   3 correct
   4 neither of whom
   5 who / that you were ...
   6 correct
   7 where I was born / in which / that I was born in
   8 correct
2 1 ND   2 ND   3 D   4 ND   5 D
3 1 point   5 neither
   2 case   6 both
   3 time   7 which
   4 result   8 whom

Listening

1 a Speaker 3
   b Speaker 2
   c Speaker 1
2 1 B   2 C   3 A   4 C   5 C   6 A

Use of English

1 1 seemingly   5 colony
   2 ventilation   6 survival
   3 organism   7 diligence
   4 inhabitants   8 inconceivable

Writing

1 1 one of the historical monuments in your country
   2 its past; its present condition; why it may be interesting to visit
   3 neutral / formal
   4 by using the key information as paragraph topics
2 1 amphitheatre   7 mythology
   2 architecture   8 entertainment
   3 construction   9 earthquakes
   4 spectators   10 symbol
   5 spectacles   11 attractions
   6 contests   12 procession
3 elliptical, largest, greatest, ruined, iconic, popular, incredible, vast
4 Paragraph 1: what the Colosseum is + a description of the shape of the Colosseum and why it is famous
   Paragraph 2: the history of the Colosseum + when it was built and what it was used for
   Paragraph 3: the present condition + why it has been ruined and what you can see there

Unit 9

Getting started

1 a 2   e 6
   b 1   f 4
   c 5   g not used
   d not used   h 3

Reading

1 1 A   2 D   3 D   4 B

Language development

1 1 c   2 f   3 h   4 b   5 d   6 a
   7 g   8 e
2 1 d   2 a   3 j   4 b   5 h   6 i
   7 f   8 c   9 g   10 e
3 a pay me a compliment
   b paid through the nose
   c pay [you] back
   d pay my respects
   e paid tribute to
4 1 pay you back
   2 pay out
   3 pay this cheque into
   4 paying out on
   5 paid him off

Listening

1 (Possible answers):
   1 pages with simple, clear titles and headings
   2 long texts
   3 information in bullet-pointed lists and use sub-headings etc
   4 using PDFs for general product information
   5 photos of produce / prices of product
2 1 D   2 B   3 C   4 A   5 B   6 B

Grammar

1 (Possible answer): 'When we are obliged to read, because of computers, we expect the words to be arranged in helpful modules, with plenty of graphics.'
2 1 a 2   b 1
   2 a 1   b 2
   3 a 1   b 2

3 1 How he manages to run six miles after a full day's work
   2 Easy though the job may seem
   3 What you should do is buy
   4 (It's quite simple.) All you need to do is (to)
   5 Where he gets his bad temper from
4 1 What did Sarah do?
   2 What did Sarah steal (from the boutique on the corner)?
   3 Where did Sarah steal a dress from?
   4 Who stole a dress from the boutique on the corner?
   5 Who saw Sarah steal a dress?
   6 Where did Sarah hide the dress?

Use of English
1 1 all you do is tell him
   2 Mandy, it was Peter, not
   3 though she may be
   4 what / the sweets / the ones I like most of
   5 but for Mr Smith's
   6 has not / hasn't spoken to her grandfather

Speaking
1 1 B   2 A   3 C

Writing
1 The main reason for this is; for example; Take the Highway
   Code, for example; This is because; For all the above reasons

Unit 10

Getting started
1 1 material wealth   4 A good job or career
   2 Good health   5 A happy family
   3 Social standing   6 Personal success

Reading
1 1 F   2 C   3 B   4 G   5 E   6 A

Language development
1 1 strains   4 line
   2 alarm   5 toll
   3 up
2 1 to pull out (of)   6 to pull away / out
   2 to pull on / at   7 to pull (something)
   3 to pull off   8 to pull through
   4 to pull down   9 to pull back together
   5 to pull over   10 to pull (something) apart

Listening
1 1 E   2 C   3 H   4 A   5 F   6 F
   7 D   8 E   9 C   10 B

Grammar
1 1 Jenny told Ed that she wished they could go on holiday
       the following week.
   2 Michael asked if / whether he could have a salad for lunch.
   3 Mum wanted to know if / whether I / we had any
       homework to do.
   4 Philip said it was the best meal he had eaten this / that
       year.
2 1 [It] wasn't me who broke the porcelain vase!
   2 I'm paying for lunch. [Anyway,] it's my birthday.
   3 [You] spoiled the surprise party we had planned for Dad!
3 1 begged Sara not to leave
   2 threatened to tell Mum

3 advised Jim to get his arm seen (to)
4 admitted to having [had] / that he had had
5 mother encouraged her to take
6 blamed Tony for the fact that
7 complained that his beer was warm
4 1 decided to wear / put on
   2 dismay that he was
   3 Feeling slightly hurt
   4 he liked
   5 couldn't see what
   6 that she had already decided to wear
   7 that they couldn't go
   8 annoyed
   9 she had a number of dresses
  10 him he was being ridiculous
  11 that if he was going to wear
  12 wouldn't go

Speaking
   1 describing   5 speculating
   2 comparing   6 contrasting
   3 speculating   7 speculating
   4 describing   8 comparing

Use of English
1 (Possible answers): She decided to play the songs in
   alphabetical order; Martin received an order from his Captain;
   Jesse ordered chicken but was served veal.
   The students were presented with the award for Best Dressed
   Class; I presented my ticket to the guard but he wouldn't let
   me onto the platform; May I present Lady Smythe, my Lord.
2 1 luck   6 luck
   2 range   7 range
   3 mental   8 mental
   4 luck   9 shook
   5 shook   10 range

Writing
1 1 outline and suggest
   2 the newspaper editor
   3 formal / neutral
4 a There should be one adult member of the family at home
      to look after the dog's needs.
   b Elderly people or people who are ill should not have large
      dogs that need more exercise than they can give them.
   c Any dog used for protection should have regular exercise
      and training.
   d The organisations that deal with homing dogs should have
      strict rules regarding ownership so that potential owners
      make good choices.

Unit 11

Getting started
1 1 workaholic   6 transaction
   2 consumer   7 accountant
   3 debt   8 credit card fraud
   4 identity theft   9 finance
   5 expenditure   10 invest

Reading
1 1 C   2 B   3 B   4 B   5 C   6 C

2
1	sequence	7	random
2	spin	8	implication
3	fortune	9	adept
4	inane	10	incredulous
5	mechanically	11	composure
6	ostensibly		

Language development

1
1	your mind	4	the blue
2	place	5	luck
3	money		

2
1	put out	4	hand out
2	find out	5	sort out
3	work out		

3
a Nouns: outback, outbuilding, outboard, outburst, outcome, outcry, outfall, outfit, outfitters, outflow, outgrowth, outgoings, outhouse, outing, outlay, outlet, outline, outlook etc.

b Verbs: outclass, outflank, outfox, outgrow, outguess, outgun, outlast, outlaw, outline, outlive, outmanoeuvre, outnumber, outpace, outshine, outwit etc.

c Adjectives: outgoing, outlandish, outmoded, outnumbered, out of touch, out of date, outlying, outrageous, outright, outstanding, outstretched, outspoken etc.

4 (Possible answers): The school has a large outdoor swimming pool in its grounds; It's such a lovely day that you should be outdoors playing football, not sitting in front of the computer.

5
1 raise money
2 not made of money
3 pumped money into
4 save money
5 money is no object
6 put your money where your mouth is
7 have money to burn
8 Money talks
9 got our money's worth
10 throw money

Listening

1
1	means	5	income
2	unforeseen emergencies	6	periodic
3	five	7	habits
4	chart	8	budget

Grammar

1
1	resignation	6	criticism
2	prediction	7	resignation
3	criticism	8	annoyance
4	annoyance	9	plan
5	plan	10	prediction

2
1 might have / could have
2 wouldn't be
3 would
4 could
5 will

3
1 will be / is going to be
2 will buy / get
3 will (all) have
4 might have killed / run over / hit
5 will keep
6 may / might as well

Use of English

1
1	D	2	B	3	C	4	B	5	D	6	C
7	B	8	C								

Speaking

1 (Possible answers):
a 'I agree with you to a certain extent, but ...'; 'I think you've got a point, but ...'; 'Up to a point, you're right, but I have to say ...';
b 'I'm afraid I can't agree with you there'; 'Personally, I don't feel that way'; 'I think there's another way of looking at it'; 'Perhaps, but I think there's another way of looking at it'; 'I don't think that's true for everyone ...'

Writing

2 (Possible answer):

Introduction

The aim of this report is to examine the issues surrounding the workers' complaints, and to make some recommendations for improving the current situation.

Exposure to chemicals in a poorly ventilated environment

It was discovered that due to production demands and recent cutbacks in the workforce, workers are now working for more than three hours at a time without a break, and are constantly exposed to fumes from the paint chemicals. As the ventilation filters are damaged, air is not circulating effectively on the factory floor. We need to ensure that workers have a 15-minute break every one and a half hours, during which they should leave the factory floor. The air filters should be replaced, and checked more regularly.

Protective clothing

Furthermore, the clothing currently provided to the workers for their protection is sadly inadequate. The overalls are faded and worn, and the facial masks fail to give workers sufficient protection from the hazardous fumes. Providing workers with new overalls, and masks with air filters would ensure they are not affected by chemical fumes while working.

Conclusion

As can be seen from the points raised above, there are several problems facing workers at present. However, with the implementation of the improvements suggested, the situation will soon improve, to the satisfaction of workforce and management alike.

Unit 12

Getting started

1
1	blockbuster	8	plot
2	musical	9	photography
3	screenplay	10	director
4	setting	11	trailer
5	documentary	12	script
6	cast	13	thriller
7	actor	14	lyrics

The word 'cinematography' is spelt out.

Reading

1
a irony (n); ironic (adj); ironically (adv)
b sarcasm (n); sarcastic (adj); sarcastically (adv)

2
1	B	2	D	3	C	4	B	5	A	6	C
7	B	8	D	9	A	10	C				

3 1 take the reins
   2 pin (something) down
   3 a means to an end
   4 to bridge the gap (between)
   5 to climb through the ranks
4 1 period-piece
   2 dot-com
   3 digital
   4 genre
   5 apprentice

Language development

1 (Possible answers):
   1 painful   4 dull / boring
   2 beautiful   5 devoted
   3 slow   6 natural
2 1 d   2 e   3 a   4 c   5 b
3 1 perplexingly named
   2 especially underpowered
   3 coolly ruthless agent
   4 coldly suppressed rage
   5 crash-bang Bond
   6 deafening episodes
   7 similarly powerful vehicle
   8 baffling decision
   9 thrilling music
   10 short, sharp, bone-cracking bursts
   11 cool, cruel presence
   12 perpetually semi-pursed
   13 some new nastiness
   14 smart elegance
   15 conventional action
   16 indefinably difficult task

Listening

1 1 C   2 B   3 B   4 A   5 C   6 B

Speaking

2 Roberta could have interrupted after 'replaced by something even better' and 'in 2050'.
   Marcel could have invited Roberta to speak after 'a universal theme – love.' and 'when you watch the documentary.'
   Inviting partner to speak: <u>'What do you think about the cartoon idea?' 'Oh, why do you say that?' 'don't you?'</u>

Grammar

1 1 e   2 f   3 a   4 c   5 g   6 h
   7 d   8 b
2 1 b   2 c   3 a   4 b   5 a   6 d
   7 c   8 b   9 a   10 c   11 d   12 c
   13 b   14 a
3 1 Cynthia and I, both being fans of ...
   2 The film, directed by Woody Allen had received ... / Directed by Woody Allen, the film had received ...
   3 Having been given ...
   4 Crossing the road ...
   5 Dick and Isabella, who, being good friends of Cynthia's, we invited
   6 Arriving at the cinema
   7 Not wanting to go ...
   8 Having already seen the film she
   9 Not wanting to see
   10 nearby restaurant run by an Italian couple

Use of English

1 They admire it as an icon.
2 1 after   5 own
   2 such   6 of
   3 without   7 is
   4 deal   8 whatever

Writing

3 Points mentioned: an outline of the story, a description of the characters, what you liked about it, background information, the writer, director or actors, how successful it was
4 1 d   2 e   3 c   4 a   5 b
5 1 e   2 a   3 c   4 f   5 d   6 b

Unit 13

Getting started

2 publicise

Reading

1 1 D   2 B   3 G   4 A   5 E   6 C

Language development

1 1 to   2 of   3 of   4 into
2 1 of   5 of
   2 to   6 with
   3 to   7 of
   4 to   8 over
3 1 be settled in certain habits and find it difficult to change
   2 don't approve of
   3 is due to
   4 a fixed choice of food
   5 is determined to
4 1 f   2 b   3 j   4 d   5 a   6 e
   7 g   8 c   9 h   10 i
5 1 set in   4 set back
   2 set off   5 set down
   3 setting aside

Listening

1 1 C   2 D   3 F   4 E   5 A   6 H
   7 E   8 F   9 C   10 B

Grammar

1 1 playing football, cycling and picking blackberries
   2 the fact that he told the class
   3 the difficulty people have (in expressing their feelings)
   4 the various ways
   5 writing a letter and phoning
2 1 It   2 There   3 there   4 It   5 It

Use of English

1 1 by   7 across
   2 over   8 into
   3 at   9 off
   4 back   10 on
   5 down   11 out
   6 to   12 round
2 1 all   5 such
   2 of   6 each
   3 by   7 do
   4 It   8 which

Writing

1   1   b   2   c
2   a: b is too chatty and informal, and c does not address the task
3   b, d, e, f
4   (Possible answers):
    teenagers: b are no longer children, but neither are they completely adults; c have interests that their parents don't share
    parents: may need to encourage their children to make decisions and choices for themselves; could participate more in their children's activities
5   (Possible answers):
    Paragraph 1: introduction / no longer children
    Paragraph 2: problems communicating
    Paragraph 3: practical solutions / solutions that work
    Paragraph 4: conclusion / a final word

Unit 14

Getting started

1   **Down**   **Across**
    1 primate   2 ape
    2 amphibian   5 insect
    3 mammal   6 invertebrate
    4 reptile   8 fish
    7 bird
2   Planet Earth
3   1   f tuna   5   a worm
    2   c snake   6   g pterosaur
    3   h platypus   7   d goose
    4   b spider   8   e spider monkey

Reading

1   1   D   2   C   3   B   4   C   5   A   6   B
2   1   paradoxically
    2   testaments
    3   waned
    4   erratic
    5   omens

Language development

1   1   out of the woods   4   in deep water
    2   get wind of   5   bogged down in
    3   clear the air   6   the tip of the iceberg
2   1   of   6   about
    2   with   7   with
    3   for   8   about
    4   with   9   to
    5   to   10   of
3   1   c   2   g   3   e   4   h   5   i   6   f
    7   b   8   j   9   a   10   d

Grammar

1   1   h   2   j   3   b   4   f   5   g   6   a
    7   i   8   c   9   d   10   e
2   1   I didn't have much money, so I didn't travel around the world.
    2   I did watch a lot of TV, so I didn't read very much.
    3   I studied French instead of Spanish so I went to France / didn't go to Spain.
    4   He didn't work hard enough so he didn't pass his course.

3   1   hadn't gone
    2   could have been
    3   might / would never have met
    4   had never seen
    5   would probably never have got
    6   stayed
    7   might have got
    8   could save
    9   had
   10   got
4   1   is / 's (high / about) time you stopped wasting
    2   wish you had / you'd come
    3   had / 'd better take (some)
    4   wish I knew how Sara is / 's
    5   only I had gone sky-diving
    6   would / 'd rather you helped

Listening

1   1   ecosystems
    2   wiped out / extinct
    3   viruses, parasites (in either order)
    4   five planets
    5   seven billion
    6   90 million
    7   policies
    8   side-effects

Use of English

1   1   compassionate
    2   remarkably
    3   climatic
    4   prioritise
    5   installation
    6   joyful / joyless
    7   considerably / consideration
    8   remorseless / remorseful
    9   hesitation / hesitant
   10   conservation / conservationist
2   1   seasonal   5   fragility
    2   rapidly   6   extensive
    3   migration   7   endangered
    4   primarily   8   predatory

Writing

2   (Answers are clockwise from top centre): earthquakes / tsunamis; species extinctions; desertification / dying forests / threatened ecosystems; rising global temperatures; cities destroyed / millions displaced / famine / disease / conflict; melting ice caps = rising sea levels; polar bears face drowning / starving; hurricanes / storms / forest fires; human deaths / injuries
3   Paragraph 2: how the weather will change
    Paragraph 3: the impact of the weather on nature
    Paragraph 4: how human civilisation will suffer

Unit 15

Getting started

1   1   E   2   G   3   C   4   B   5   H   6   C
    7   G   8   H   9   A   10   B

Reading

1 1 B 2 C 3 D 4 C
2 1 a false b true c true
   2 a true b false c false
   3 a false b true c false
   4 a true b false c true
3 Text A: 'Its previous incarnation was perfectly suited to students new to cultural studies, simultaneously providing an accessible overview for those already familiar with the theoretical concepts it covered.'
4 Text A: 'However, Smythe redeems himself with the clarity of his explanations and inclusion of excellent references to further reading on each of the book's central themes.'
   Text C: 'What the author does, however, is provide a wealth of examples demonstrating how the theories outlned in the book are applied in the real world, which students new to the subject will no doubt find invaluable.' And: 'He also refers readers to other works in the field, and this is one aspect of the book which ought particularly to be applauded.'
   Text D: 'J Smythe provides an extensive examination of the theories of popular culture, which will undoubtedly hold wide appeal for those studying or having a general interest in the field.'
5 Who the book is aimed at; how useful the content of the book is; the written style of the article; the author's assumptions about readers' viewpoints.
6 1 – 2 + 3 + 4 + 5 – 6 –
   7 + 8 +

Language development

1 1 c 2 d 3 h 4 f 5 g 6 i
   7 b 8 a 9 e
2 1 let it pass
   2 flying colours
   3 pass my lips
   4 came to pass
   5 pass the buck
3 (Possible answers):
   1 a long illness.
   2 a drop of blood.
   3 post office.
   4 travel around the world.
   5 employee etc.
   6 message that dinner will be at 8.
   7 it was clearly her brother's work.
   8 mother to child.
4 a pass off as e pass up
   b pass down f pass on
   c pass by g pass away
   d pass out h pass over

Listening

1 1 C 2 B 3 D 4 A 5 A 6 B

Grammar

1 1 in case
   2 Hardly / Barely
   3 so that
   4 where
   5 Consequently / As a result / Therefore
   6 In spite of / Despite / Notwithstanding
   7 While / When
   8 For fear of

2 1 no sooner … than (time)
   2 as … as (comparison)
   3 so … that (result)
   4 if (condition)
   5 Nevertheless (concession)
3 1 to her house to talk …
   2 Despite being / In spite of being
   3 For fear of forgetting …
   4 No matter how tough it was …
   5 with a view to going …
   6 Seeing as you've …
   7 Such is the extent of the damage that …
   8 do as you're told or else / otherwise …
4 1 For this reason 6 with a view to
   2 otherwise 7 Consequently
   3 In order to 8 due to the fact that
   4 This is why 9 so as
   5 When 10 although

Use of English

1 1 back 5 so
   2 for 6 them
   3 which 7 with
   4 addition 8 order
2 1 B 2 A 3 A 4 C 5 B

Writing

1 (Possible answers): an incredible experience, not least because … ; During the course of … ; However, the real celebrations start … ; The most memorable part of the wedding for many is … ; A word of warning though … ; You can imagine how embarrassing that proved to be
2 Paragraph 1: Where I went (introduction to the experience)
   Paragraph 2: General summary of the experience
   Paragraph 3: Details of what made it special / memorable
   Paragraph 4: What happened at the end

Unit 16

Getting started

1 1 discontinued 6 instigated
   2 founded 7 incited
   3 finalise 8 abort
   4 settle 9 generated
   5 launching 10 completed

Reading

1 1 C 2 D 3 A 4 B 5 C 6 D
   7 A 8 D 9 A 10 C
2 1 successor 6 obsolete
   2 nostalgia 7 outweigh
   3 instantaneous 8 eliminated
   4 ritualised 9 wince (at)
   5 cutting-edge 10 console (myself)

Language development

1 1 drastic 5 complacency
   2 dispel 6 cloud
   3 staple 7 cut
   4 confirmed 8 expound
2 1 start 4 end
   2 cut 5 take
   3 means

3   1 f   2 j   3 a   4 h   5 c   6 i
     7 g   8 d   9 e   10 b

Listening

1   1 C   2 B   3 C   4 A   5 B   6 B

Grammar

1   (Possible answers):
    1 as good as
    2 (much) faster than
    3 less exciting than
    4 just as tasty as
    5 far more interesting than
    6 not as friendly as
    7 doesn't suit you as much as
    8 more attractive than
    9 is much easier to do / use than
   10 a lot less expensive than
2   1 She works a lot harder at school than she used to.
      She works much harder at school than she used to.
    2 This book isn't nearly as good as the last one he wrote.
      The last book he wrote was considerably better than this one.
    3 Dale is fitter by far than his brother, Simon.
      Dale is a lot fitter than his brother, Simon.
    4 They are much happier now that they've moved to the country.
      They are happier by far now that they've moved to the country.
    5 He's considerably more irritable than he used to be.
      He's much more irritable than he used to be.
    6 I've never tasted such an awful curry!
      This is by far the worst curry I've ever tasted!
3   a much   b a lot   c by far   d not nearly as   e far

Reading and Use of English

1   1 A   2 A   3 D   4 A   5 C   6 B
     7 D   8 C

Writing

1   Underline: reference for a friend of yours who has applied for a job as a tourist guide for your local town; will speak English well, be good at dealing with different people and will display knowledge of the local area; include information about your friend's character and personal qualities and skills, their previous relevant experience and reasons why they should be considered for this job.
2   Opening paragraph: my relationship with the person, and how long I have known them.
    Second paragraph: the person's qualities that make her suitable, and her fluency in English.
    Third paragraph: knowledge of and interest in local history, and her reasons for wanting this job.
    Conclusion: summary of why she is suitable for the position.

Practice Test

READING AND USE OF ENGLISH

Part 1

   1 A   2 D   3 B   4 C   5 B   6 B
   7 A   8 A

Part 2

   9   according   13 whose
  10 What   14 being / getting
  11 despite   15 some
  12 not   16 to

Part 3

  17 profitable
  18 consumption
  19 invaluable
  20 regeneration / regenerating
  21 sleeplessness
  22 irritability
  23 increasingly
  24 outlive

Part 4

  25 had no / hadn't any hesitation in accepting
  26 without doubt the group's best performance
  27 on / at the point of leaving
  28 from being the terrifying
  29 has been made in / with regard to
  30 we took umbrellas in case it

Part 5

  31 C   32 A   33 B   34 B   35 D   36 B

Part 6

  37 D   38 A   39 C   40 D

Part 7

  41 G   42 F   43 B   44 E   45 C   46 A

Part 8

  47 C   48 A   49 D   50 B   51 C   52 B
  53 D   54 A   55 B   56 C

LISTENING

Part 1

   1 B   2 B   3 A   4 A   5 C   6 A

Part 2

   7   Exotic Earth   11 soil
   8   creativity   12 (the) climate
   9   drawing skills   13 practical purpose
  10 urban gardens   14 headaches

Part 3

  15 A   16 B   17 D   18 D   19 C   20 B

Part 4

  21 C   22 H   23 A   24 F   25 E   26 A
  27 C   28 E   29 H   30 B

Reading and Use of English

Part 1

1 A   2 B   3 C   4 B   5 D   6 A   7 C   8 D

Part 2

9 Instead   10 in   11 who
12 which   13 more / better   14 had
15 Although / Though / While / Whilst   16 as

Part 3

17 dreadful   18 enthusiasts   19 comparable
20 excessively / exceedingly   21 disagree   22 length
23 enables   24 broaden

Part 4

25 is said to have been built
26 he would / he'd + like me to help
27 nobody / no one + would have any interest
28 impressed by / with / at + how fluent she was / is
29 as though everyone / everybody + apart
30 has been an increase of

Part 5

31 B   32 A   33 C   34 D   35 A   36 D

Part 6

37 B   38 C   39 D   40 C

Part 7

41 C   42 F   43 E   44 A   45 D   46 G

Part 8

47 D   48 F   49 A   50 C   51 A
52 B   53 F   54 D   55 B   56 E

Listening

Part 1

1 B   2 B   3 A   4 C   5 A   6 C

Part 2

7 lifeblood   8 food security   9 cod   10 dolphins
11 dynamite   12 agriculture   13 coastal development   14 diving

Part 3

15 D   16 A   17 A   18 C   19 D   20 B

Part 4

21 A   22 D   23 H   24 B   25 E
26 H   27 E   28 A   29 D   30 B

Writing (sample answers)

1

For millions of people, work is hard and a matter of survival; any pleasure in the job would seem a luxury. However, for some, generally the more affluent, the possibility of enjoying work has become a reality, and may even be regarded as a right. People gain job satisfaction from various sources. Surveys consistently show that social interaction with colleagues is rated very high in importance, above the size of one's salary and the physical working environment.

Another potential source of job satisfaction is the sense of knowing what one is doing. This may come from a job description – a written formulation of what the job involves – or from a verbal equivalent. Without it, the employee may feel they are outside their comfort zone. However, it is rare for this situation to continue for more than a few days.

Of greater significance, in my opinion, is the individual's future career path. A 'dead-end' job, with no scope for change or improvement, is demoralising; most people need to develop skills that they can use in future posts. These might be technical skills, such as using spreadsheets, or so-called 'soft skills' relating to interpersonal interaction.

It is up to the employer to encourage staff to build up their skill set, both in relation to their current job and as preparation for possible future positions. Not only will the individual gain from it, but so will the employer, as they will have more highly skilled staff. In fact, providing such opportunities creates a win-win situation.

2

Falling customer numbers at Bluebell Restaurant

Background

The Bluebell used to be very successful, with many new customers coming because of word-of-mouth recommendations from friends. The twin keys to its success were the high quality of the food and the fact that every customer, of whatever age, was treated as a VIP.

Since the recent change in management, however, the number of customers has fallen by around a fifth, and reviews on social media websites have become much less positive.

Possible cause

As a part-time employee, I have observed that the management's attitude towards staff has become far less supportive. Employees are treated as though they can easily be replaced, and morale is much lower than it used to be. Customer service has got worse as a result.

Proposal for improvement

Plenty of research shows that when employees are well-treated, they in turn treat customers well. To achieve that, I propose the following:

- that a neutral consultant is paid to hold discussions with all the employees in small groups, and to interview the management team individually, in order to discover everyone's opinion of the situation
- following on from that, it will probably be necessary for the consultant to recommend changes in the behaviour of managers
- customer service training should be organised for everyone, including the managers.

I am sure that staff morale and customer service would improve, and this in turn would lead to an increase in customer numbers.

3

Hi Sarah

Here I am at last, but the first few days have been quite a challenge!

I've been allocated a shared room in a university hall of residence which has seen better days. The roof leaks whenever it rains, and the desk is supported on books. There's a kitchen on each floor, designed for a dozen people but used by 20, so you can imagine the chaos!

The university grounds are very attractive, and the view from my window is of trees, grass and a small lake, with swans and ducks. I love it! The rest of the town is very different from what we're used to, though. There are factories everywhere, even near the centre, so the air is quite polluted. I'm looking forward to getting out into the countryside, which I've been told is really worth exploring.

I suspect that studying here is going to be much more difficult than at home. The library has very few desks, so it's almost impossible to work there. The seminars I've attended so far have been excellent – they've really made me think. And I'm relieved that I can understand the language well enough to cope with the lectures. I have to say, though, that I miss the efficiency I took for granted at university – here, it's hit and miss whether I find out about a class before it takes place.

Once I get used to everything, I'm sure it'll be much easier. And if I hate it, at least I'm only here for a year!

All the best

Darren

4

Maurice Carter live

To me, American blues singer Maurice Carter has always been someone from the past. When I was growing up, my father was a big fan, and always going on about him. That was enough to put me off him for life!

So when I saw an advert for a live appearance by Carter in a small local venue, it didn't make me drop everything and buy tickets. However, the next day was my birthday, and my parents gave me – you've guessed it! – two tickets for the gig. I did my best to sound grateful, but it wasn't easy. And I only persuaded a friend to come with me by bribing him with a meal out first.

I was convinced it would be one of the most boring evenings of my life, but how wrong I was! Carter, now in his seventies, has a vitality that many younger performers lack, and a sense of humour that endeared him to the audience.

My impression of blues singers was always that they sang for themselves only, and ignored the audience. Carter turned that perception on its head, making me feel he was singing just for me.

The big difference from my father's old records was, of course, that it was Carter in the flesh, sitting just across the room from me. I don't expect I'll enjoy his records any more now than I did as a child, but certainly the evening with him was an evening very well spent.

Practice test audioscript

To reproduce exam conditions, play all four parts of the test all the way through. All the repeats are included on the recordings, as in the exam.

Please note, however, that longer pauses are not included on the recording.

Where this instruction is given: [PAUSE RECORDING FOR …]

you will need to stop the recording for the length of time specified.

Part 1 ⊙ 53

Cambridge Certificate in Advanced English: Listening

Practice Test

I am going to give you the instructions for this test.

I shall introduce each part of the test and give you time to look at the questions.

At the start of each piece you will hear this sound:

[beep]

You will hear each piece twice.

Remember, while you are listening, write your answers on the question paper. You will have five minutes at the end of the test to copy your answers onto the separate answer sheet.

There will now be a pause. Please ask any questions now, because you must not speak during the test.

Now open your question paper and look at Part 1.

You will hear three different extracts. For questions 1–6 choose the answer (A, B or C) which fits best according to what you hear. There are two questions for each extract.

Extract One

You hear two friends talking about a workshop that the woman wanted to attend.

Now look at questions one and two.

Man: Hello, Carol. You went to that painting workshop at the college, didn't you? How was it?

Woman: Believe it or not, they put it off at the last moment, but I didn't know, so I still turned up.

Man: But you'd registered for it. Didn't the college get in touch with you?

Woman: My friend Andrew booked for us both, and just gave his own contact details. So they sent him a text, and he forwarded it to me, but I didn't have a chance to read it until I arrived at the college! We'd planned to meet there, so it was only when he didn't turn up that I realised something was up, and had a look at my phone for messages.

Man: That's a shame. So did you go straight back home, or make the most of your unexpected free time?

Woman: Well, I was just leaving the college to drop in on some friends who live near there, when another woman turned up for the workshop. We struck up a conversation, and in the end we went into town for a cup of coffee, which was really enjoyable. And then I went home and started a new painting.

Man: So at least you had a good time.

Woman: Oh yes. It was fun.

[RECORDING REPEATS]

Extract Two

You hear two students discussing the possibility of studying in France.

Now look at questions three and four.

Woman: Are you applying to study in France, Peter? Lots of our year are.

Man: I can't decide. I could probably get by in French, but I wouldn't be able to go on treading the boards – acting in French is beyond me!

Woman: But you could still sing in a choir and play tennis. And you're always saying you're rushed off your feet with everything you do.

Man: That's true. I suppose that'd be an advantage of going. But there are so many people I'd miss – you, for instance.

Woman: It's easy to keep in touch with people these days, Peter!

Man: I know, but I'd miss doing things together. Phone calls and texts just aren't the same.

Woman: I know what you mean about deciding. When I was a teenager, some Spanish friends of my parents invited me to stay with them. It was six weeks before I said yes. And even then it was only because my mother sat me down and issued an ultimatum – she said I had to decide there and then. There are lots of things you could consider, like language, weather, and so on, and I think you're getting bogged down in detail. Why not just go with your gut feeling – it's as likely to be the best decision as any.

[RECORDING REPEATS]

Extract Three

You hear two friends discussing the business that the man intends to set up.

Now look at questions five and six.

Woman: Has your tea and coffee business got off the ground yet, Mark?

Man: No, I'm still on the lookout for reliable suppliers.

Woman: That's essential, because you'll be pretty dependent on them. I hope you're investigating competitors, too.

Man: Absolutely. And I'm thinking up ways to outdo them.

Woman: When will you start selling?

Man: When I'm in a position to offer everything I might be asked for, including cakes and biscuits, and even crockery.

Woman: Surely you can go on building the range once you're in business? If you're not careful, you'll *never* get started.

Man: I think it's really important to have everything in place first.

Woman: OK. So how will you advertise?

Man: I thought I'd join a local business club, to meet café owners.

Woman: But that'd be very limited, geographically. Don't you want to sell nationwide?

Man: Well, yes. But my website will show what I sell, and I hope people who find it will email me to say what they want to buy.

Woman: You'll end up forever chasing payments. I'd do online sales, so they have to pay *before* you send the goods.

Man: That's an idea. And if I advertise in trade magazines, it'll help to raise my profile.

Woman: I'm not so sure; it'll be worth asking customers how they found out about you.

[RECORDING REPEATS]

That's the end of Part 1.

Part 2 ⊙ 54

You will hear part of a talk about dangers threatening the oceans. For questions 7–14, complete the sentences with a word or short phrase.

You now have 45 seconds to look at Part 2.

Good morning, and thank you for coming to hear this talk, which as you know will be about the challenges that the oceans face. We tend to think of them as a vast, unknown wilderness, because we know far less about them than we do about land areas. But without the oceans the planet couldn't support life, so to me it's more accurate to say they're its lifeblood, because they're essential for survival – and not just our own.

One thing we *do* know about the oceans is that they've been damaged. The evidence of the impact of human beings on oceans and the life within them is immediately obvious to scientists, and many species that live there are at risk of extinction. But the damage to our oceans isn't just an issue in terms of lost biodiversity. It also has implications for food security, reducing the proportion of the world's population who have enough to eat and are able to live healthily, without having to worry about their next meal. Potentially, the damage might also bring about changes to key planetary processes.

Fishing is, of course, one of the main ways in which we affect the oceans. Overfishing is placing cod and other species at risk, although some, like mackerel, aren't under threat.

Fish are not the only species affected by fishing; dolphins are among a number of ocean-dwelling species that are in danger because they get caught in fishing nets accidentally. Even birds aren't safe, with albatrosses, for example, also frequently being trapped.

Marine habitats are also being destroyed, sometimes because of fisheries ploughing up the sea bed. Then there's dynamite fishing, which is intended to kill or stun schools of fish, making them easier to catch, but which all too easily destroys the habitats where they breed.

Fishing practices aren't the only threats to wildlife, of course – marine species and habitats are being destroyed by a whole range of human activities. Pollution is a highly significant factor – we're surely all aware of dramatic incidents like oil spills, both from the sea floor and from tankers. And agriculture can cause pollution through the run-off of chemicals, causing algae to build up offshore. Incidentally, the same industry uses over a third of all fish that are caught, for conversion into fishmeal, most of which is used to feed poultry and pigs.

Coral reefs, which are the habitats of vast numbers of fish, face a variety of dangers, including poorly planned coastal development. The construction of piers and airstrips, for example, and industrial discharge, can all destroy the reefs. This in turn directly affects fisheries, as many fish species depend on reefs. It also affects the economies of those countries that rely on tourist income from activities such as diving. Without the reefs, this would be far less attractive and the tourist industry of that area would certainly be adversely affected.

Now I'd like to go on to …

Now you'll hear Part 2 again.

[RECORDING REPEATS]

That's the end of Part 2.

Part 3 ⊙ 55

Now turn to Part 3.

You will hear two friends, Johnny and Lindsey, talking about a school reunion. For questions 15–20, choose the answer (A, B, C or D) which fits best according to what you hear.

You now have 70 seconds to look at Part 3.

Woman: How was the school reunion you went to, Johnny? It was last weekend, wasn't it?

Man: That's right. Well, it was interesting. But let me go back to the beginning. When I left school, I turned my back on it, I swore I'd never go back, or have anything to do with it again. There's only one person from school, David, who I've been in touch with from time to time.

Woman: Uhuh.

Man: So when I received an email from him saying the school was inviting all the students from my year to a reunion, my immediate reaction was to delete it. There was no way I wanted to see those people again, and have all the emotions I had then brought back. It's ten years since I left, and as far as I'm concerned, that's not nearly long enough.

Woman: OK. So what happened?

Man: The next morning, when I woke up, I saw it in a different light, I suddenly thought, it was my chance to show I wasn't really the failure I'd seemed at school. I suppose it was more for myself than for them – I didn't imagine any of them would care. And to be honest, I was also a bit curious about how I'd feel when I saw them all.

Woman: You mean, whether you'd still loathe them, or would find you've mellowed a bit.

Man: Something like that, yes. So I contacted the organiser and asked her to add me to the list of attendees. When I arrived, the first person I set eyes on was the English teacher who'd given me a really hard time. She didn't recognise me until she asked me my name, and then I saw her jaw drop as she remembered. At school, whenever she asked me a question in class, and I gave the wrong answer, she was always really sarcastic – not to anyone else, just me. That made me so nervous that even when I knew the answer, I either couldn't get it out or somehow made a dog's dinner of it. But her sarcasm made everyone laugh – except me, of course.

Woman: Gosh.

Man: Mm. But I didn't know what to do about it. Anyway, I got my own back at the reunion. You know my surname is pretty rare – there are probably only a handful in the country, and one of them, no relation, won an award for a novel a couple of months ago. So the English teacher asked me if that was me.

Woman: Uhuh.

Man: And I smiled sweetly and replied, 'Oh, but you know I was always bad at English at school.' Which of course wasn't stretching the truth too far – it was her opinion, at least. But she jumped to the conclusion that I was just being modest, and later on I heard her telling one of the other teachers I'd won that prize, and boasting of the part she'd played!

Woman: Wow! That's quite a coup! What else happened?

Man: Nothing much, really. My old classmates were perfectly polite, as though it'd gone right out of their heads how they used to make my life a misery. It was a bit of an anticlimax. I exchanged a few words with three or four of them, and a couple of teachers who were still at the school, then left. Apart from the thing with the English teacher, it was hardly worth going.

Woman: I have to say, I had some really close friends at school, and we've seen each other regularly ever since. I know it sounds daft, but that's one thing I'm really grateful to my school for – giving me the opportunity to make friendships that last for years, hopefully for the rest of my life.

Man: But don't you think you made friends because you were in the same boat – having the same lessons, meeting the same people, day in, day out?

Woman: You mean, if we'd met in different circumstances, we might not have become friends? I suppose so. Still, whatever the reason, I think they're generally stronger than friendships with people you meet as an adult. Those often seem pretty superficial.

Man: What a cynic you are, Lindsey! Ah well, we all …

Now you'll hear Part 3 again.

[RECORDING REPEATS]

That's the end of Part 3.

Part 4 ⊙ 56

Now turn to Part 4.

Part 4 consists of two tasks. You will hear five short extracts in which people are talking about going to university. Look at Task 1. For questions 21–25, choose from the list (A–H) the reason each speaker gives for choosing their course. Now look at Task 2. For questions 26–30, choose from the list (A–H) how each speaker feels about their studies. While you listen you must complete both tasks.

You now have 45 seconds to look at Part 4.

Speaker 1

I suppose I've always been more on the creative side – as a child I spent hours painting, or making models. But gradually school work took over, and art had to take a back seat. When I considered applying to university, I was at a loss as to what to study. Then a friend said art's a route to self-knowledge, and it suddenly seemed the right thing to do. I doubt whether I can make a living from it, though. The course certainly hasn't been a piece of cake, but I've enjoyed it. I wish it was longer, to be honest – there's so much more I want to get out of it, but all that's left is to hand in my last assignment.

Speaker 2

One of my weaknesses is that I'm easily influenced. I didn't plan to go to university until my parents encouraged me to apply, and even then I didn't know what to study. A couple of my closest friends applied to our local university to do a sociology degree, and when they suggested I followed suit, I said yes straightaway. After all, it'd be much easier than going somewhere where I didn't know anyone. Well, it's been a lot more interesting than I'd expected, and now I've set my sights on doing a master's in sociology. My tutor thinks I'll be accepted and I can work part-time to get enough money to live on, so it's looking very promising.

Speaker 3

History just wasn't my thing till I saw a TV programme with a really inspirational presenter. She knew so much, but her approach was to encourage viewers to think for themselves, rather than tell them everything. When I saw she was a university lecturer, I thought I could learn a lot from her. So I applied to study history at that university. I didn't expect it to be a walk in the park, and it certainly hasn't been. To be honest, I don't think I'd have coped if it'd been any more demanding, though it's certainly taught me a lot. Anyway, the three years are practically over, and now I'm ready for the next phase in my life.

Speaker 4

Right from the age of six, I've loved visiting different towns, and was determined that eventually I'd do something related to town planning for a living. It became a family joke – my parents would tell people that's what I was going to be, though they never put any pressure on me; they just wanted me to study something I would enjoy. Anyway, I never wavered, and that's why I'm doing a degree in town planning. I've been very lucky, because we've had a programme of visiting lecturers coming to talk about different aspects of the subject, and best of all, after the lectures we get a chance to talk to them, and find out more. That's been a real bonus.

Speaker 5

At school, I was generally near the bottom of the class. OK, I know I wasn't a genius, but I was convinced I could do better. By going to university I'd show people what I was capable of. I picked a course virtually at random, and applied to a university that none of my classmates were applying to. I wanted to start with a clean slate, with none of the other students having preconceived ideas about me. I think the subjects I opted for worked very well together. In fact, it's odd that people seem to shy away from that particular combination. In some ways it's harder than just taking one subject, but the variety keeps you on your toes.

Now you'll hear Part 4 again.

[RECORDING REPEATS]

That's the end of Part 4.

There will now be a pause of five minutes for you to copy your answers onto the separate answer sheet. Be sure to follow the numbering of all the questions. I shall remind you when there is one minute left, so that you are sure to finish in time.

[PAUSE RECORDING FOR 4 MINUTES]

You have one more minute left.

[PAUSE RECORDING FOR 1 MINUTE]

That is the end of the test. Please stop now. Your supervisor will now collect all the question papers and answer sheets.

SPEAKING TEST VIDEO

Teacher's notes

The worksheets on pages 178–181 of the Student's Book accompany the video of an *Advanced* Speaking test which is on the DVD. They provide an orientation to the exam and familiarise students with the format of the test. The interlocutor in the video is a trained *Cambridge English: Advanced* examiner and the two students were preparing to take their *Advanced* Speaking test a month after filming.

1 If students have already completed the 16 units of the Student's Book, they will now be familiar with the four parts of the Speaking test. This exercise checks their knowledge of the exam format and revises some phrases that interlocutors and candidates might say in each part of the test. Students match each sentence to the exam part from which it was taken, then decide if it was said by the interlocutor or the candidate.

Answers

3 Part 4, I	4 Part 1, C	5 Part 3, C
6 Part 4, I	7 Part 2, I	8 Part 1, I
9 Part 3, I	10 Part 2, C	11 Part 1, C
12 Part 3, C	13 Part 2, C	14 Part 4, C
15 Part 3, I	16 Part 3, C	

2 Students watch the video while referring to the information on pages 178–180 of the Student's Book, which includes the exam material used in the video. The idea is that they follow what happens on screen and understand the format of the questions and the materials used. The video follows the exam in real time, so playing it without stopping will give students a real experience of how the test will feel on the day.

After watching, you could provide some time for students to ask any questions they have about what they saw. At this point you could play sections of the video again to look at them in more detail.

Point out that in Part 1, the interlocutor doesn't have to ask any extra questions if the two-minute time limit has already run out.

3 In this exercise students will try to gauge how well they think the students did. Play the video and ask the students to score the two candidates using the table. Emphasise that students are not being asked to judge the standard of the candidates' language, but whether they have covered the key tasks required. To make it easier, you could put students in pairs, with Student A

concentrating on scoring the performance of Marine and Student B scoring Fenja. Afterwards they discuss the reasons for their scores.

There is not one correct answer to this task. Both candidates perform very well and will score 3 in most, if not all, categories. They would achieve a clear passing grade in the *Advanced* Speaking test.

After taking feedback from students, read the information in the Exam spotlight box. This explains (in brief) the marking criteria used by the examiners to assess the candidates' linguistic performance. Candidates will also be given a mark for *Global achievement*, according to how well they communicate and express their ideas.

ASSESSMENT OF THE TWO CANDIDATES IN THE VIDEO

The following summaries of the two candidates gives an overview of what these candidates might achieve in the *Advanced* Speaking test based on their performance in the video.

Marine would achieve a clear passing grade in the *Advanced* Speaking test. Her interactive communication is very good as she easily interacts with both the examiner and Fenja. She makes some errors but overall she uses a range of grammatical items and vocabulary. She could improve her fluency (especially in long turns). This could be done by learning a wider range of discourse strategies and vocabulary. She organises most of her responses well, though she often needs to work extra to make her message clearer. Her pronunciation is good and her accent has no effect on intelligibility. She could improve her use of intonation to convey mood or meaning.

Fenja would also clearly pass the *Advanced* Speaking test. She answers all the questions and achieves the tasks with ease. Her interactive communication is good. She shows that she is listening to the other candidate, and interacts confidently. Her pronunciation is very clear, and almost native-like, although she could improve her use of intonation, which often seems flat. Her long turn is performed well. She speculates clearly, and she makes good use of appropriate discourse markers. She could improve her extended turns by justifying her opinions more.

4 Put students into groups of three and ask them to practise the Speaking test using the worksheet materials. If you need (or want) to create groups of four, then the fourth student can mark the two candidates using the criteria in exercise 3.

There are an additional two worksheets on pages 181 and 182, which students can use to analyse the language used by the two candidates in more detail.

Video transcript

This is a word-for-word transcript of a real Speaking test. It is supplied for reference only, not as a model.

Part 1   00.01

Interlocutor: Good afternoon.

Marine: Good afternoon.

Interlocutor: Come in.

Fenja: Good afternoon.

Interlocutor: So, good afternoon. My name is Jenny, and this is my colleague, Claire. And your names are?

Marine: Marine.

Fenja: Fenja.

Interlocutor: Thank you. Can I have your mark sheets? Thank you … First of all, we'd like to know something about you. Marine, where are you from?

Marine: I'm from Belgium, from the capital city, Brussels. But not from the city centre, just next to Brussels, from the outskirts.

Interlocutor: And … what do you do here?

Marine: Err, I'm studying English for four months in King's College, just near from here, yeah.

Interlocutor: And Fenja. Where are you from?

Fenja: I'm from Germany. To be exact, from the north part, next to Hamburg, but it's just a small village with about 5,000 inhabitants.

Interlocutor: And what do you do here?

Fenja: I'm also studying English at King's College in Oxford. And I'm here until 1st December.

Interlocutor: How long have you been studying English?

Fenja: I started studying English when I was in primary school. Hmm … I think it was the fourth, yeah class four and hmm … I continued studying English in my high school and also in my leisure time. I went to England twice for a hmm … language course for two weeks and yeah ….

Interlocutor: Thank you. And … Marine, how long have you been studying English?

Marine: Err… I started six years ago, when I began high school and I went out … I went on studying English until last year.

Interlocutor: And what do you enjoy most about learning English?

Marine: Hmm … well, I like the fact that it's a language that … it's a very international language and everybody in every country knows it … and yeah, I really like it when I travel and things like that.

Interlocutor: And you, what do you like most about learning English?

Fenja: Hmm … I agree with Marine. It's a good possibility to speak to other people and to be able to communicate with them, even though they don't speak your language. Hmm … and yeah, most of the time hmm … you have to speak another language when you go to another country and most of the people hmm … can hmm …, are able to speak English.

Part 2   2.57

Interlocutor: OK, thank you. In this part of the test I'm going to give each of you three pictures. I'd like you to talk about two of them on your own for about a minute, and also, to answer a question briefly about your partner's photographs. Marine, it's your turn first. Here are your pictures. They show different types of meals. I'd like you to compare two of the pictures, and say what is good and bad about each choice of meal and what kind of person do you think would typically choose each type of meal. All right?

Marine: Yeah. OK, so I'm going to choose those two pictures. Err … in the picture on the left we see a big hamburger and French fries and I must say it's not a very healthy meal. Hmm … so I don't think there's something good about this meal because yeah, there's maybe just a tomato and a little piece of salad but it's not very healthy. And what is bad … bad about this meal is that it's junk food and very bad food. And what kind of person would choose this meal? I think maybe a person who is in a hurry and maybe it's during her break, err … his or her break at work. She just goes to a fast food and grab it, while in the second picture we see quite a healthy meal with salad, tomato, olives, eggs, mozzarella. And yeah, I think it's a healthy meal and what's good about it is that you have vegetables, you have cheese, you have, yeah … eggs, so it's … yeah.

Interlocutor: Thank you. Fenja, which of these meals would you prefer to eat?

Fenja: Hmm … well, I personally would prefer the salad because I don't like eating that much meat. Hmm … I prefer vegetables and salad and hmm … yeah. I just don't like the taste of meat that much.

Interlocutor: Thank you. Now, Fenja. Here are your pictures. They show different holiday locations. I'd like you to compare two of the pictures and say why people might choose to spend their holidays in places like these, and which one do you think is the best holiday location. All right?

Fenja: Yeah, I'm going to compare the first picture on the left side and this one, the big one on the right. So, hmm … yeah. In the first picture you can see New York City, it's in the United States of America, a very big city. Hmm … and on the right there is a beach far from any city or traffic or noise. So, I guess people would … yeah some people would like to go to the city because there a lot of entertaining things to do, they can visit some famous places or buildings, and hmm … yeah you know, New York is very famous city. And on the other hand, some other people would like to go to the beach because they enjoy the silence, and just enjoy relaxing in the sun doing nothing. And hmm … yeah, I think for me in personal … for me personally, hmm … the beach. I would prefer the beach, hmm … because hmm …

Interlocutor: Thank you. Err, Marine. Which of these places would you most like to go to on holiday?

Marine: Well, probably the first one because of course, I like going on the beach and enjoying the sun, but I would really … I've never been to the USA, and I would really like to go to New York because it's a very big city and there are a lot of things to visit, and yeah, I'd really like to go there.

Part 3   07.00

Interlocutor: Thank you. Now I'd like you to talk about something together for about two minutes. Here are some ways people use to stay in touch with family and friends, and a question for you to discuss. First you have some time to look at the task … Now talk to each other about how effective each of these ways are for keeping in touch.

Fenja: OK. Do you want to start?

Marine: Yeah. Err … maybe we can begin with this one. Text messaging, err … yeah, I think it's a very effective way to keep in touch with friends and family because, err … most of the people have a mobile phone and you just have to take your phone and send a message, so … what do you think about text messaging?

Fenja: Exactly, hmm … I think hmm … yeah, for me it's the same. Hmm … most of the people have a mobile phone and hmm …. It's very effective and fast way to communicate with friends and family.

Marine: And what about sending emails? I think …

Fenja: Yeah, what do you think?

Marine: I think it's quite effective, too because some people don't have a mobile phone for example, my grandparents and they have just a computer and hmm … and hmm … an email address and it's easier … it's easy to just send them an email when I want to have news from them. What do you think?

Fenja: Yeah, well … I get your point, but my grandparents, they even don't have a computer, so … and I think, hmm … some people don't use their email accounts that often, or don't check their email, so I think it's not hmm … so effective.

Marine: Yeah, I guess it depends on the people.

Fenja: Yeah.

Marine: Hmm … communicating on networking sites … what do you think?

Fenja: Err … I think this is a very effective way, hmm, yeah … especially for keeping in touch with your friends who don't live close to you, who live in another country or abroad. So, it's very effective to stay in contact with them.

Marine: Yeah, I completely agree with you because you can keep in touch with your friends, you can post pictures and, etc. What about making telephone calls?

Fenja: What do you think?

Marine: Yeah, I think it's quite … it's very effective, too because you can … it's even more effective than social networking sites or text messaging because you can just take your phone and call. You just have to have a … yeah, you just have to be somewhere where you can call people and yeah, I think …

Interlocutor: Thank you. Now you have about a minute to decide which two ways are the most effective for keeping in touch.

Fenja: OK, hmm … I think hmm … yeah, text messaging is …

Marine: Definitely, I agree with you.

Fenja: It's one of the most effective ways. Like we said, you just have to have a mobile phone and most of the people have one, and …

Marine: Yeah …

Fenja: And it's very quick and effective …

Marine: Yeah, I think it's the most effective and for the second one maybe I would choose social networking sites because it's not just about writing to friends, it's also about like I said, post pictures and you can even have a video call with friends with Facebook or things like that and …

Fenja: Yeah, yeah. I see what you mean, Hmm … but I think it's a nice way to keep in touch with friends, but not so effective because some people don't have Facebook or something like that at all, or other social networking sites. Hmm … I know a lot of people who don't and so I would say making telephone call is more effective than networking sites because you don't need to have a mobile phone, you can only have a telephone at home.

Part 4   11

Interlocutor: Thank you. Do you think social networking sites are important in modern life?

Marine: Yeah, of course. I think it's very important because nowadays, more and more people use social networking sites and err … yeah, like I said it's a way of sharing ideas and err … writing to friends who live maybe abroad and far from you and it's free so it's very, very important. What do you think?

Fenja: Yeah, I totally agree. You don't have to pay anything, hmm … yeah, so it's a very, very easy way to keep in touch with other people and, yeah, and to keep in touch with people who don't live close to you and in another country and when telephone calls for example, are very expensive. Yeah, telephone call to another country is very expensive, for example, so this is a good, hmm … way.

Interlocutor: Many people using social networking sites are not careful about what they post online. Why might this be a problem?

Fenja: Hmm … for example, if you get invitation for a party or something like that, but you don't want to go there, you would prefer to spend some time with another friend, and you say, 'no, sorry, I can't I have to learn' for example, or study or anything and then you go out with the other friends and post a photo on the social networking site and the other person sees this photo, hmm you can be …

Marine: It can be very bad …

Fenja: Yeah, and you can get into a lot of trouble.

Marine: Yeah and there are other problems and other dangers like sometimes bad people use these social networks to … to meet people, so for example if you're not careful you can just accept an adding of a friend you don't know and sometimes that can be very dangerous, I think.

Interlocutor: How do you think parents and teachers can help younger people to understand the dangers of the Internet?

Marine: Well, yeah, I think it's the role of parents and teachers to make their children aware of these dangers and how, maybe just by discussing of that … discussing of this problem with them and telling them the dangers of those websites. What do you think?

Fenja: Yeah, hmm … exactly. I think this is hmm … this is …

Marine: The best way …

Fenja: Yeah, the best way and the parents should just give their children some examples of where something went wrong or, yeah, some examples about the dangers, and also the school could have like an information day for such dangers, yeah …

Interlocutor: What kinds of subjects do you think are important for young people to learn at school nowadays?

Fenja: Hmm … I think for sure, the basics, like maths, reading, writing, this is sure, but also like, current affairs, hmm … are important for me, hmm … personally. I think people should be aware of things hmm … yeah of things which happen in their country or all over the world.

Marine: Yeah, and like you said current affairs and more politics and things that are happening in the world, like climate change. It's very important to make children aware of the climate change, I think.

Interlocutor: Is education or experience, more important in a job?

Fenja: I believe hmm … both is important for sure, but I, hmm … I would say that experience is more important because you really need to know what you do and people who don't have the best education for example, can still be very good in their job when they hmm … yeah earned a lot of experience.

Marine: Yeah, I think I agree with you because if you have a lot of experience you're more likely to be … to be taken in a job, err … while, if you don't have a good education you can just go to university and study and it'll be OK. It's not because you don't have a good education that you won't find a job, I think.

Interlocutor: Some people think that earning money is more important than job satisfaction. What do you think?

Marine: Err … I don't agree at all, because I think job satisfaction is very important in your life to be … to … to be happy in your life because if you do something you don't like it's terrible to go every day to your job if you don't like it at all. So, I think of course, earning money is important, too because if you don't have money you can't live, but I think both are as important.

Fenja: Yeah, of course it depends on the person, some people just want to earn some money but others, instead, they just do what they love and hmm … there are also hmm … jobs which are really hmm … badly paid, but they still do the jobs because they love what they are doing and maybe they help some people and they don't get a lot of money and they think, hmm … this is more important, yeah … loving what you do … to love what you do.

Marine: Yeah.

Interlocutor: Thank you. That's the end of the test.

Marine: Thank you.

Answers to photocopiable worksheets

Worksheet 1

1 a	2 a, b	3 c	4 b, d
5 c	6 a	7 e	8 a, b
9 b, c	10 c	11 d	12 a
13 b	14 e	15 e	16 c

Worksheet 2

1 someone	2 it	3 it	4 it
5 one	6 do this	7 them	8 there
9 one	10 they	11 this / that	12 it

Photocopiable worksheet 1

In Part 2 of the Speaking test, you have to talk for one minute about two pictures. You need to describe the pictures, but you also need to speculate, express opinions and justify them. You also need to organise your language so the listener can follow you easily. Match the sentences (1–16) with the functions (a–e). Sometimes there is more than one possible answer.

a	Helping the listener follow your talk
b	Describing
c	Giving an opinion
d	Justifying an opinion
e	Speculating

1   OK, so I'm going to choose these two pictures. _____

2   In the picture on the left, we can see a big hamburger and French fries. _____

3   I must say, it's not a very healthy meal. _____

4   There's just a tomato and a little piece of salad. _____

5   What is bad about this meal is that it's junk food. _____

6   And what kind of person would choose this meal? _____

7   Maybe a person who is in a hurry, and maybe it's during her break at work. _____

8   In the second picture, we can see a healthier meal with salad, tomato, olives … _____

9   What's good about it is that you have vegetables, cheese, eggs … _____

10 I personally would prefer the salad. _____

11 … because I don't like eating that much meat. _____

12 I'm going to compare the first picture on the left, and this one. _____

13 You can see New York City – a very big city. _____

14 I guess some people would prefer to visit a city … _____

15 On the other hand, some other people might prefer to go to the beach … _____

16 For me, personally, I would prefer the beach. _____

To prepare for the *Advanced* Speaking test, make sure you are aware of functions a–e.

Try to record yourself speaking when you prepare for the test. Then listen to yourself and make a note of what you do and what you don't do. Try to organise your talk better next time.

Photocopiable worksheet 2

In the video of the Speaking test, Marine and Fenja sometimes repeat the same words close together. Unfortunately, this means they might get a lower score for Discourse management. They would score higher if they used a range of reference words.

Use the words in the box to improve these sentences by replacing the underlined words. Sometimes more than one answer is possible.

someone	one	they	do this	there	them	it	this

1 What kind of person would choose this meal? I think maybe a <u>person</u> who is in a hurry. *someone*

2 I don't like eating that much meat. I just don't like the taste of <u>meat that much</u>. _____

3 Most people have a mobile phone and they just have to take <u>their phone</u> and send a message. _____

4 I must say it's not a very healthy meal. I don't think there's anything good about <u>this meal</u>. _____

5 I'm going to choose these two pictures. In the <u>picture</u> on the left we see a big hamburger and French fries. _____

6 It's a very, very easy way to keep in touch with other people and to <u>keep in touch</u> with people who don't live close to you. _____

7 Using English is a good possibility to speak to other people and to be able to communicate with <u>other people</u> even though they don't speak your language. _____

8 I would really like to go to New York because it's a very big city and there are a lot of things to visit, and yeah, I'd really like to go <u>to New York</u>. _____

9 You just have to have a mobile phone and most of the people have <u>a mobile phone</u>. _____

10 More and more people are use social networking sites and <u>social networking sites</u> are a good way of sharing ideas. _____

11 If you're not careful, you can just accept an invitation from someone you don't know and sometimes, <u>an invitation</u> can be very dangerous. _____

12 It's terrible to go every day to your job if you don't like <u>your job</u> at all. _____

To prepare for the *Advanced* Speaking test, make sure you are aware of small, but important words like *it, this, one*, etc. These often refer back to earlier ideas, and stop you from repeating yourself. Try to record yourself speaking when you prepare for the test. Then listen and notice how you use these words. Make sure that it is clear what you are referring to when you speak.

WRITING GUIDE ANSWER KEY

A Building a coherent answer (page 228)

1

Paragraph 1: *A few weeks ago, I was invited to …*
Paragraph 2: *All you need to take part in a game of Octopush …*
Paragraph 3: *From where I was sitting with my friends, …*
Paragraph 4: *Clearly, this isn't a game that …*

2

Paragraph 1: *introduction: the writer's preconceptions about the game, and what it is in fact*
Paragraph 2: *what you need to play, and the object of the game*
Paragraph 3: *the writer's personal experience*
Paragraph 4: *conclusion and recommendation*

3

b, d, a, e, c

5

1 this	2 one	3 others	4 it	5 his
6 That	7 their	8 which	9 such

B Structuring an essay (page 229)

1

1 *I believe that some of these could be renovated or rebuilt, with significant benefits to the community.*
2 *In fact, if developers renovated these buildings instead and turned them into characteristic apartments or cafés, local citizens would have a much more attractive environment to live in.*
A place where traditional styles have been not only preserved but improved upon can boost tourism and bring money into the local community.

2

our obsession with updating cities (paragraph 2) refers back to *our desire to modernise* (paragraph 1)
maintaining a city's architectural history (paragraph 3) refers back to *not see important cultural elements being destroyed.* (paragraph 2)
despite the demands of a growing population (paragraph 4) refers back to *the need to create homes, restaurants and shops for increasing numbers of residents.* (paragraph 1)

3

1 refers back to *many buildings*
2 introduces a result of *the need to create homes, restaurants and shops*
3 introduces a counter argument to the previous sentence
4 refers back to *city*
5 introduces a contrast to the previous two sentences
6 refers back to *preservation*

C Levels of formality

1 (Possible answers)

I would propose that; young people; enjoy themselves; There is no point in; their parents; ideal; I would suggest; fund

2 (Possible answers)

check→enquire; do mostly→specialise in; seeing→observing; It's all been→I have found it all; love to work→be very interested in working; let me know→inform me

D Spelling (page 230)

1

Verbs	Noun form(s)	Adjective form(s)
affect	effect	effective
appeal	appeal	appealing
correspond	correspondent / correspondence	corresponding
enquire	enquiry / inquiry	enquiring / inquisitive
prefer	preference	preferable
specify	specification	specific
vary	variety	variable / varied / varying / various

2

1 research	2 contemporary	3 techniques
4 occurred	5 controversial	6 harmonious
7 whether	8 stationary	

E Punctuation

Possible answers

Many young people enjoy playing video games because they allow you to take part in a <u>story, give</u> you some control over events and let you interact with other characters. Video games stretch your imagination so that you can exist for a while in a fantasy <u>world – a</u> world that is more immediate than a good allegorical novel, such as <u>Orwell</u>'s *Animal Farm*. Tests have shown that playing video games from an early age actually strengthens <u>hand-eye</u> co-ordination and stimulates brain development. Many video games require the player to make logical <u>decisions, which</u> help to develop brain function in a way that watching television never <u>can; this</u> can only be a good thing.

2

1 A recent survey has shown that video games are very popular, especially with young people.
2 The best video game I have ever played is 'Rachet and Clank'; it's fast paced, exciting, colourful and hugely imaginative.
3 With the exception of extreme cases, is there any evidence to support the criticism of video games?
4 However, not all video games are good for everyone, and not everyone enjoys them.
5 Parents, most of whom have concerns about the length of time their children spend using technology, often limit their children's exposure to video games.
6 If the game is good, what's the problem?
7 Psychologists have reached the following conclusions: video games have educational value, utilise various skills simultaneously, and help some children perform better at school.
8 There is increasing evidence that the elderly are enjoying games on tablet devices these days too, which is a recent development.

Cloze test: a type of gap-filling task in which whole words have been removed from a text. Candidates must replace the missing word.

Coherence: language which is coherent is clear and planned well. All the parts and ideas should form a unified whole.

Cross-text multiple matching: a task that involves comparing and contrasting opinions and attitudes across four short texts.

Discourse: written or spoken communication.

Essay: a structured piece of writing on a specific topic. An essay is often written for a teacher, or perhaps as a follow-up to a class activity. It should be clearly structured: with an introduction, organised development and a fitting conclusion. The main purpose of the task is to develop an argument and / or to discuss issues surrounding a certain topic. You're expected to give reasons for your opinions.

Gap-filling item: any type of item requiring the candidate to insert some written material into the spaces in the text. This material may include letters, numbers, single words, phrases, sentences or paragraphs. The response may be selected from a set of options, or supplied by the candidate.

Gist: the central theme / meaning of the text.

Interlocutor: the examiner in the Speaking test who conducts the test and makes an assessment of each candidate's performance.

Key word: the word which must be used in an answer to an item in the Reading and Use of English paper, Part 4.

Letter: written in reply to the situation outlined in the exam question. Letters in the *Cambridge English: Advanced* Writing paper need a response which is reliably suitable for the particular target reader. Exam candidates can expect to be asked to write letters to, for example, the editor of a magazine or newspaper, to the director of an international business, to a principal of a school, or to a friend.

Long turn: the section in the Speaking test allowing a candidate to talk without being interrupted for a period of time, and produce an extended piece of discourse.

Multiple choice: a task where candidates are given several possible answers, with only one being correct.

Multiple matching: in Parts 6 and 8 of the Reading and Use of English paper, a task in which a number of questions or sentence completion items must be matched with one text chosen from several; in Part 4 of the Listening paper, a task in which each recording must be matched with one option from a choice of eight.

Options: the set of possible answers for a multiple choice item.

Paraphrase: to use different words to convey the meaning of something.

Phrasal verb: a verb which takes on a new meaning when followed by a certain adverb or preposition.

Proposal: written for a superior work colleague or members of a committee, for example. You're expected to make at least one suggestion, and to support this with some factual information, in order to persuade the reader of a course of action. A proposal should be clearly organised and may include headings.

Register: the tone of a piece of writing. It should be appropriate for the task and target reader, usually in terms of being sufficiently formal or informal.

Report: usually written for someone higher than you at work, such as a boss or a college principal. Sometimes it's also written for a peer group, like fellow members of a club. You're expected to give some factual information and possibly make a suggestion or recommendation. A report should be clearly organised and may include headings.

Review: generally written for an English-language magazine, newspaper or website. The main objective is to describe and articulate a personal opinion about something which you have experienced. It may, for example, be about a film, a holiday, or a product. The review needs to give the reader a clear idea about the item discussed. Description and explanation are key areas for this task. A review will often include a recommendation to the reader as well.

Rubrics: the instructions to an examination question which tell you what to do when answering the question.

Stem word: the word at the end of each line in the Reading and Use of English paper, Part 3. This word should form the basis for the word that has to be formed.